European Commission
Directorate-General for Enterprise and Industry

E·S·R·C
ECONOMIC
& SOCIAL
RESEARCH
COUNCIL

Mergers and Merger Remedies in the EU

Mergers and Merger Remedies in the EU

Assessing the Consequences for Competition

Stephen Davies

Professor of Economics and member of the ESRC Centre for Competition Policy (CCP) at the University of East Anglia, Norwich, UK

Bruce Lyons

Professor of Economics and Deputy Director of the ESRC Centre for Competition Policy (CCP) at the University of East Anglia, Norwich, UK

Edward Elgar

Cheltenham, UK • Northampton, MA, USA

Published by
Edward Elgar Publishing Limited
Glensanda House
Montpellier Parade
Cheltenham
Glos GL50 1UA
UK

Edward Elgar Publishing, Inc.
William Pratt House
9 Dewey Court
Northampton
Massachusetts 01060
USA

A catalogue record for this book
is available from the British Library

Library of Congress Cataloging in Publication Data

Davies, Stephen, 1948–
Mergers and merger remedies in the EU : assessing the consequences for competition / by Stephen Davies and Bruce Lyons.
p. cm.
Includes bibliographical references and index.
1. Consolidation and merger of corporations—European Union countries. 2. Remedies (Law)—European Union countries. I. Lyons, Bruce. II. Title.
HD2746.55.E8D38 2007
338.8′3094—dc22 2007039448

ISBN 978 1 84720 741 8

Publications Office
Publications.europa.eu

EU ISBN 978–92–79–05565–2

Printed and bound in Great Britain by MPG Books Ltd, Bodmin, Cornwall

Contents

Tables

Figures and boxes

FIGURES

BOXES

Acknowledgements

The authors have benefited from two sources of funding for this book. An original study into how merger remedies might be improved was commissioned by DG Enterprise and Industry of the European Commission. Economic and Social Research Council (ESRC) funding for the Centre for Competition Policy (CCP) at the University of East Anglia enabled us to expand the work greatly. We are grateful to both institutions. Stephen Davies is also Academic Adviser to the UK Office of Fair Trading; and Bruce Lyons is also a member of the Economic Advisory Group for Competition Policy (EAGCP) to the European Commission and a part-time member of the UK Competition Commission. The views expressed in this book are their own as independent academics and should not be attributed to any of these institutions.

We would like to acknowledge the helpful comments and assistance from various people, notably: Alexander Kopke and Miguel de la Mano of DG Competition, Stefano Vannini, Juergen Foecking, Thomas Heynisch, Joan Salmurri, and especially Damien Levie of DG Enterprise and Industry. Within the CCP, Peter Ormosi and Matthew Olczak provided valuable research assistance and Laurence Mathieu translated one of the case studies. We would also like to thank our former colleague Andrew Scott for comments on the first full draft, and Cheryl Whittaker for editorial comment, proofreading and indexing of the text.

Preface

WHY THIS BOOK?

Decisions prohibiting mergers always make the headlines. In practice, they are rare. The European Commission, for example, imposes remedies about ten times more often. Merger remedies are not only much more frequent; they are also more complex: predicting with reasonable certainty which elements will restore competition after completion of a merger and its related remedies is often a challenge. The concerns and the toolkits used when devising and monitoring remedies are close to those used in the regulatory field, for example when a public authority privatizes a state-owned (monopoly) business or auctions licences for new activities. Merger remedies can therefore blur the distinction between competition policy, regulatory policy and industrial policy. They can influence to different degrees the structure and performance, and hence competitiveness, of the industries concerned.

Until recently, however, merger remedies have remained a neglected area. Inside the European Commission, we were encouraged to investigate the subject, following up on a seminar co-organized in 2002 by the French Ecole des Mines and the University of California Law School on the differences between US and EC approaches to merger remedies. One of the audience's key messages was that the European Commission had to perform an *ex post* study comparable to the one performed by the US Federal Trade Commission (FTC) in 1996–99. After this conference, two departments of the European Commission took a particular interest in the topic. DG Enterprise tendered a study which Stephen Davies and Bruce Lyons won in the summer of 2002. Their proposal was interesting because they wanted to apply simulation techniques to merger remedies. At the same time, DG Competition started preparing its first *ex post* merger remedies study, which was published in late 2005. It looked at a sample of about 100 remedies decided in the years 1996–2000. I was seconded on a part-time basis from DG Enterprise to join the team and keep open a two-way channel between the projects: Davies and Lyons provided academic advice for that study and benefited from input of the study team.

This book is the result of intensive collaboration between industry experts and competition experts within the European Commission and in the firms concerned. This collaboration has ensured access to market participants and key information, with due respect for their confidentiality concerns.

WHAT'S IN THE BOOK?

Beyond a concise and critical review of the relevant literature, the 'main course' is Davies and Lyons's proposed practical methodology for a competition authority to assess merger remedies. The authors recommend using what they call the 'basic' simulation methodology. They explain it clearly and apply it to merger remedies in seven merger cases which they assess critically. This assessment is put into perspective by a useful competitiveness analysis of the two industry sectors in which these mergers took place, that is, the pharmaceuticals and paper industries.

The authors recommend using a simplified simulation methodology. The focus is not so much on using one or another mathematical model, but on asking a few fundamental questions about the relevant market, the nature of competition among the firms in this market, demand elasticities, and claimed efficiency savings: what would have happened post-merger, had the remedy not been imposed; and what can be expected to happen post-remedy. These questions are not new but should be answered anyway.

Davies and Lyons are not 'extremists' of simulation techniques: their methodology enables them to ask the right questions and collect the right data from the start of the investigation. For them, the output of the simulations is almost secondary to this task and the data collection process. They also acknowledge that simulation techniques may appear too sophisticated, ill adapted to the tight deadlines of merger appraisal and useful only for certain 'structural' remedies (with a clean break) in horizontal mergers taking place in rather stable or mature markets. This leaves outside vertical and conglomerate mergers and the often related 'behavioural' remedies, as well as sectors with strong buyer power or strong regulator influence. Nevertheless, it remains applicable in a majority of the cases.

The authors also recognize the 'price to pay', in terms of (legal) certainty. If less weight were attached to market shares, firms would be far less able to 'read' in advance the Commission's likely response to any particular merger. Their view is that this is a price worth paying in return for an effective, effects-based analysis, and hence a more efficient merger policy. Readers will judge for themselves.

Davies and Lyons conclude with a set of policy recommendations for the European Commission as competition authority in designing remedies.

For example, they challenge the preference for structural remedies where remedies are limited to national markets but the merger is worldwide. Behavioural remedies might be better in these national markets, especially if a national authority or a trustee can monitor the parties' compliance with their commitments, such as price commitments.

APPRAISAL OF THE BOOK

Most studies commissioned by the European Commission are not turned into a book. The fact that it has happened in this case is a tribute to the quality of the authors' work, and to their perseverance. Both are outstanding economists who combine sound academic knowledge, real-life experience and an excellent written style, all typical of their Centre for Competition Policy at the University of East Anglia.

Several colleagues in the Commission, like the authors, spent more time on this project than originally expected. Indeed, one of our tasks as 'reviewers' was to ensure that it would also be understandable by readers who do not have a PhD in economics or econometrics. Quite a few colleagues in the Commission took part in 'steering' the study: Geneviève Pons-Deladrière, Geert Dancet, Carles Esteva Mosso, Alexander Kopke, Stefano Vannini, Miguel de la Mano, Juergen Foecking, Thomas Heynisch and Joan Salmurri Trinxet. This collective effort certainly contributed to its quality, in my – somewhat biased – view.

This book provides a useful guide to applying simulation techniques in merger appraisal, recognizing fairly the limitations of that approach: basic simulation is not a well-developed science; it involves much judgement and uncertainty. Also, merger simulation needs to be designed in careful consideration of what it is *possible* to perform (from data gathering to material performance of the exercise) within the tight timescale of the proceedings, and in this respect the book takes a reasonable approach.

If I may add a critical note, the authors identify the limitations of the effectiveness criteria used by both the FTC in its 1999 study (is the buyer still in business 12 months after divestiture?) and by DG Competition in its 2005 study (a qualitative multi-factor assessment), but they themselves do not provide a better, systematic benchmark to evaluate the outcome of merger remedies. This is of course not an easy matter.

Lastly, their methodology provides a useful integrated approach to analyse the intricate trade-offs between claimed merger efficiencies and remedies. This may help to preserve welfare-enhancing mergers.

THE BOOK'S AUDIENCE

The book is meant for practitioners and academicians interested in antitrust remedies, merger control policy in general, merger simulation techniques, merger analysis in the pharmaceuticals and paper industries and, last but not least, merger remedies.

THE BOOK'S TIMING

The book is being published at a time when the Commission has adopted a new merger remedies' notice and modified its implementing rules of the Merger Regulation. These revisions draw extensively on the results of the merger remedies study of DG Competition and the Commission's practice. This book appears at a time when a new merger wave is ongoing and is also affecting the two selected industrial sectors: pharmaceuticals and paper (pulp, paper and board) industries. The lessons that it draws from the seven cases studied remain valid. There is, for obvious reasons, very little case-specific information in the public domain; this is another advantage of the book.

Furthermore, Davies and Lyons have developed and updated most parts of the manuscript, which was submitted in 2005 as a study report to the European Commission, especially the methodological and analytical parts.

Whenever the current merger wave declines, I can only hope that the Commission will find the resources to look again *ex post* at the way imposed remedies have worked in practice, perhaps with a similar approach to the one adopted in this case: combining an in-house stocktaking exercise and practical experience with independent academic input.

Damien Levie

1. Mergers and remedies in the EU: an overview

1.0 INTRODUCTION

Mergers constitute a major potential means of restructuring, allowing a more efficient allocation of resources as market conditions and firm-specific capabilities change over time. This can enhance the competitiveness of the merging firms, leading to increased competition within the industry concerned and improved competitiveness of the industry on the world stage. Potentially, both consumers and producers can ultimately gain from that restructuring.

However, mergers may also dampen the competitive process, by reducing the number of effective competitors, by softening competition, by impeding entry, and by reducing the incentives to innovate. This can harm both domestic consumers and international competitiveness.

The focus of this research is on the remedies that the European Commission sometimes requires before clearing prospective mergers. First note that 90 per cent of merger proposals falling within the Commission's scrutiny are allowed without any conditions. Headlines are made when a merger is prohibited, but this has happened only 19 times in 17 years, during which time over 3000 mergers have been appraised. Clearances subject to conditions (that is, remedies) happen over ten times more often, yet they have received far less attention both in the popular press and in the academic literature.

In broad terms, a remedy is an intervention designed to avoid the anticompetitive consequences, while not impeding the hoped-for efficiency gains from the merger. Unlike prohibitions, remedies are far more complex than a simple yes/no decision by the Commission. They require considerable judgement by the Commission – for example, alternative divestment packages can potentially lead to quite different post-merger market structure configurations and subsequent firm behaviour. Furthermore, the process of imposing remedies involves detailed negotiations with the parties, and, particularly in the case of behavioural remedies, ongoing monitoring will be required. Ultimately, the effectiveness of a remedy depends on whether or not it achieves the same level of competition in the market as pre-merger, in particular in eliminating any harm the merger might otherwise have imposed on consumers.

1.1 OBJECTIVES OF OUR RESEARCH

The original objective of this research was *to develop a practical methodology for assessing the effectiveness of remedies agreed by an antitrust authority as a condition for allowing a merger to proceed.* Our belief was that simple simulation models could be selected and modified according to the case at hand, then calibrated using readily available data and employed to improve decision making by a competition agency. While such an approach would have significant limitations, the benchmark for comparison should be with existing practice, and not with some ideal assessment. We needed to test our ideas using data that are realistically available to such an authority at the time of a merger decision. This project would not have been possible without the strong cooperation and part-funding of the Commission, which allowed us unusual access to detailed data from original merger files, and administered a follow-up questionnaire that allowed us to fill in some crucial gaps (for example, on industry estimates of cross-price elasticities).

In order to provide a benchmark for the competitive effect of a remedy, it was necessary also to apply our methodology to the original merger appraisal to identify the source of a significant impediment to effective competition created by the merger.[1] This ensures a desirable consistency between the appraisal of the merger and the remedy. However, given that the Commission's original appraisal will have relied more on market share analysis than does our simulation methodology, this presents an important by-product for this study: *the predictions from our simulation models provide a critique of simple market share analysis in merger appraisal.*

As the project developed, we were able to extend our objectives in a further direction. For all but one of our merger case studies, we were given the opportunity to review interview evidence gathered by DG Competition as part of a major internal study on the success and problems of past remedies. Together with our detailed knowledge of the competitive effects of the original mergers, these provided the foundation for our *ex post assessment of remedies and recommendations on remedy implementation.*

Finally, we have taken the opportunity to introduce these case studies with a broad *review of the newly emerging academic literature on the topic of merger remedies.*

1.2 MERGERS AND REMEDIES IN THE EU, 1990–2006

Since the European Merger Regulation (ECMR) came into effect in 1990, the Commission has made judgements on over 3000 mergers.[2] In only 19

(0.6 per cent) of these did the Commission prohibit the merger entirely. However, in a further 219 cases (7 per cent), it required commitments from the merger parties to remove specific competition concerns raised by the Commission. Put another way, mergers agreed subject to conditions and commitments are an order of magnitude more frequent than prohibitions. It is these commitments that translate into the merger remedies with which this book is concerned.

The Commission's merger appraisal may involve one or two phases. In Phase I, it undertakes an initial investigation taking five weeks, with a further two weeks if remedies are being negotiated. In 88 per cent of all merger proposals, the Commission judged in Phase I that no competition concerns were raised, and the mergers were allowed to proceed without modification. In 4.5 per cent of cases, remedies were agreed in Phase I, and on that basis, the merger was allowed to proceed. Just over 5 per cent of cases were referred to Phase II for a more extensive investigation of up to 18 weeks or 21 weeks if remedies are being negotiated. The remaining 2.5 per cent of cases were withdrawn by the parties, and it is possible that some of these anticipated an adverse decision.

Exactly half of all Phase II cases end up with agreed remedies (that is, 2.5 per cent of all mergers). A further one in five were cleared unconditionally in this phase, one in eight were prohibited and one in seven withdrawn by the merging parties. It seems likely that a significant proportion of Phase II withdrawals were in anticipation of an adverse decision (for example, an expectation that approval would require remedies that would make the merger no longer attractive to the merging firms).

Figure 1.1 shows the evolution over the 17 years concerned. As can be seen, there was an almost unbroken upward trend in total mergers considered in the 1990s, followed by a marked downturn between 2001 and 2004, and recovery of such strength that 2006 was a record year. The trend in remedy agreements appears to be broadly similar, but this figure masks some interesting detail. Table 1.1 groups merger decisions into three periods. The first, 1990–96, can be thought of as a period of settling in to the new regulation. The next five years, 1997–2001, was a period of accelerating mergers combined with growing confidence of the Merger Task Force (MTF). The final five years includes major internal reorganization within DG Competition, not least the dispersal of the MTF across sectoral divisions, and major challenges to their decisions in the European Court (see Lyons, 2004). The latter affected both procedure and substance.

Starting at the bottom of Table 1.1, we can see that the 'intervention rate' (that is, remedies plus prohibitions in either phase) increased between the first and second periods, but has fallen substantially from 9 per cent to just over 6 per cent more recently. Within this, there has been a striking decline

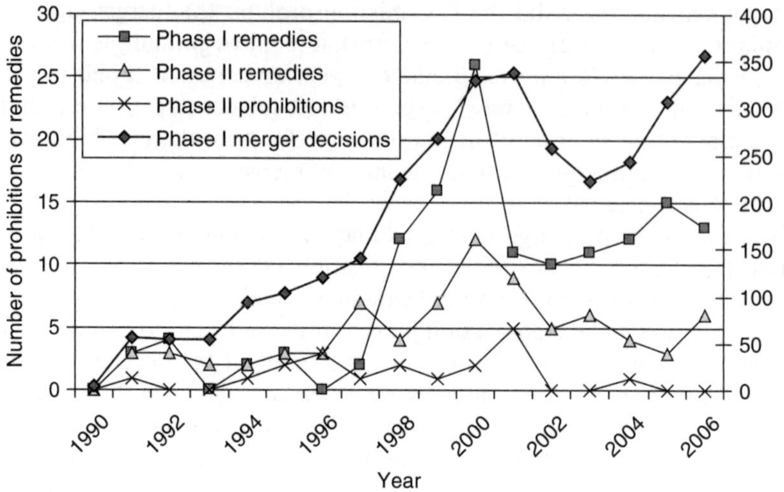

Source: Derived from DG Competition web pages; excludes referrals to national authorities.

Figure 1.1 EC mergers and remedies (1990–2006)

Table 1.1 Trends in merger remedies

	1990–96	1997–2001	2001–6	Total
Phase I merger decisions	485	1161	1387	**3173**
of which %				
Phase I unqualified clearance	86.8	86.0	90.8	***88.2***
Phase I remedies	2.5	5.6	4.4	***4.4***
Phase II initiated	6.8	6.0	3.4	***5.1***
Withdrawn by parties	3.9	2.4	1.4	***2.4***
Phase II merger decisions	33	71	45	**158**
of which %				
Phase II unqualified clearance	24.2	15.5	26.7	***20.3***
Phase II remedies	48.5	45.1	53.3	***50.0***
Phase II prohibitions	21.2	14.1	2.2	***12.0***
Withdrawn by parties	6.1	25.4	17.8	***17.7***
Final decisions (that is excluding referral to Phase II)	485	1300	1385	**3170**
of which %				
Phase I+II clearances	88.5	86.8	91.8	***89.2***
Phase I+II remedies and prohibitions	7.2	9.0	6.2	***7.5***
Phase I+II withdrawals	4.3	4.2	1.9	***3.2***

Source: Derived from DG Competition web pages; excludes referrals to national authorities.

in the prohibition rate, particularly in the last period. There were five prohibitions in 2001 (that is, a quarter of all prohibitions in just one year), three of which were subject to major appeals in the Court,[3] since when there has been just one prohibition.[4] Over the same period, the Phase I remedy and referral rates have drifted down, only partly compensated by a slightly higher Phase II remedy rate. Finally, it is worth noting that the withdrawal rate has fallen in both phases, suggesting that firms and their advisers are increasingly understanding and working with the merger control system.

1.3 SELECTION OF CASE STUDY INDUSTRIES

Table 1.2(a) shows the breakdown of EC mergers and the incidence of remedies by industrial sector. At the fairly aggregate level shown, it could be misleading to draw any definitive conclusions. Clearly, the incidence of both mergers and remedies varies significantly across broad sectors of the economy, but for present purposes a deeper (that is, more disaggregated) analysis is unnecessary, except in one respect. At the outset of this research project, we needed to select two sectors for the case studies that follow.

The idea of focusing on several mergers in each sector was that we could develop the necessary industry-specific knowledge in order to model a number of mergers appropriately. With this in mind, this book contains two substantial chapters providing background understanding of each sector. Furthermore, in order to facilitate comparisons between and within sectors, it was necessary that they should both be fairly merger- and remedy-intensive. For comparative purposes, and in order to examine our methodology under very different circumstances, it was decided that one sector should be broadly traditional (that is, with a well-defined and relatively mature and stable technology), while the other should be more innovation-intensive, with a higher incidence of new products. As such, the competitive process in the former would tend to revolve around capacity/output/price, while R&D and innovation would be more prominent in the latter. We also needed to select mergers from the timeframe 1996–2000, which was a period sufficiently recent for the issues to be remembered by interviewees for the *ex post* study, yet sufficiently long ago for the impact of remedies to have become apparent. These various constraints led us to consider the broad sectors of chemicals and paper, and printing and publishing. Then, within these, we selected pharmaceuticals and pulp, paper and board from which to sample our merger remedy case studies. As shown in Table 1.2(b), both industries displayed relatively large numbers of mergers and a higher than average incidence of remedies.

Table 1.2 Distribution of mergers and remedies across broad sectors

	Mergers*	Remedies				Remedies as % of mergers
		Total	Phase I	Phase II	Prohibition	
Transport, storage and communication	479	45	30	9	6	9
Wholesale and retail trade	392	14	10	3	1	4
Financial intermediation	361	11	11	0	0	3
Chemicals	**276**	**54**	**33**	**19**	**2**	**20**
Electrical and optical equipment	243	19	8	7	4	8
Transport equipment	208	14	5	6	3	7
Real estate, renting and business activities	196	2	1	0	1	1
Electricity, gas and water	187	19	9	8	2	10
Machinery and equipment n.e.c.	171	12	8	2	2	7
Food products; beverages and tobacco	158	20	13	7	0	13
Basic metals and fabricated metal products	147	10	5	4	1	7
Pulp, paper, publishing and printing	**109**	**14**	**8**	**5**	**1**	**13**
Other community, social and personal services	109	12	5	3	4	11
Other non-metallic mineral products	89	8	3	3	2	9
Mining and quarrying of energy-producing materials	58	6	2	4	0	10
Rubber and plastic products	53	2	1	1	0	4
Construction	52	0	0	0	0	0
Others	246	36	18	18	0	15

Note: * Some mergers straddle more than one sector, so these totals exceed the total numbers of mergers and remedies.

Source: Derived from DG Competition web pages, October 2006.

Table 1.2(a) The case study industries

	Mergers	Remedies				Remedies as % of mergers
		Total	Phase I	Phase II	Prohibition	
Pharmaceuticals	53	15	13	2	0	28
Pulp, paper and board	70	9	4	4	1	13

Source: As for Table 1.2(a).

1.4 OUTLINE OF THIS BOOK

Following this introductory chapter, Chapter 2 provides a survey of the literature on merger remedies. It draws on various sub-literatures including academic work by economists and lawyers, as well as work carried out by major competition authorities. One theme emerging from this literature is the distinction between structural and behavioural remedies. Chapter 3 develops some of these ideas on how to classify remedies in a useful way, either in terms of the competitive harm they are intended to address or the nature of their implementation. In doing this, we suggest a 'clean break' principle.

Chapter 4 contains our proposed methodology for assessing the efficacy of remedies – basic simulation. There are two central ideas. First, in order to identify the potential harm of a merger and so to be able to appraise the effect of a proposed remedy, the market should be modelled in terms of oligopoly theory. Second, this model should be calibrated so that the merger and remedy effects can be simulated to give an idea of the extent of harm (or benefit) to competition that should be expected. Of course, such modelling must be accompanied by the standard range of reality checks and an understanding of the institutional constraints of the case in hand. However, the force of our proposal is that a simplified simulation methodology directs the Commission to ask the right questions and to collect the right data from the start of the investigation. The output of the simulations is almost secondary to this thought and data collection process.

Notice that we are not suggesting 'full-blown' econometric simulations. This is for two reasons. First, they have enormous data and resource requirements that make them practically impossible to conduct in the context of a Phase I inquiry, and extremely difficult even in Phase II. Second, if large resources are expended on a full-blown simulation, it may gain a disproportionate claim to be 'right' at the expense of other traditional sources of information on competitive harm. Thus, apart from very substantial benefits in terms of time saving and resources that our simplified models have over more complex modelling, they fit neatly alongside the other less quantitative work that goes on in any merger appraisal.

Chapters 5–8 introduce the case study sectors and illustrate how our methodology can be applied in practice. Paper was chosen as representative of 'traditional' industries which supply more or less homogeneous products, based on a mature technology, and in which competition is effected largely on the basis of price and quantity/capacity. Pharmaceuticals was selected to represent more 'dynamic' industries, in which innovation, marketing and product design are the main drivers of the competitive process. In each case, we provide an opening survey of the sector and the nature of competition therein. Specific mergers and, for each merger, specific product and geographic markets are earmarked to apply a range of basic simulation techniques. Following our *ex ante* case studies, which use only data that were available at the time of the merger and the Commission's decision, we provide an *ex post* review in the light of information collected for their follow-up study by DG Competition.

Chapter 9 presents our substantive conclusions on the practicability and value of the proposed methodology. It also compares basic simulation with the current market share analysis used by the Commission. Finally, it summarizes the lessons from the *ex post* studies, and puts them together with our *ex ante* analysis and the broader literature to make some constructive suggestions for how the Commission should reform its remedy procedures.

NOTES

1. Under the EC Merger Regulation that was current at the time of the mergers reviewed in this book, the European Commission must prohibit mergers 'which create or strengthen a dominant position as a result of which effective competition would be significantly impeded in the common market'. The 2004 Revision now emphasizes that a merger should not result in a 'significant impediment to effective competition'.
2. All figures are as at 31 December 2006.
3. Tetra Laval/Sidel, Schneider/Legrand and GE/Honeywell.
4. ENI/EDP/GDP, which would have brought together the very dominant gas and electricity suppliers in Portugal.

2. The literature on merger remedies

2.0 INTRODUCTION

There is a small but growing literature on merger remedies, which is summarized in this chapter. The literature is quite new, with little published before 2001. This review also incorporates some elements of the wider literature on mergers, but only to the extent necessary to place the remedies literature in its appropriate context. Section 2.1 reviews some principles of what makes for a good remedy, and Section 2.2 reviews some remedy classifications. Our own taxonomy is set out in Chapter 3. The economic theory and some econometrics of merger remedies are reviewed in Section 2.3, and some special issues relating to high-technology mergers are set out in Section 2.4. Empirical work on the efficacy of remedies has been conducted mainly in house by the major competition authorities, and these studies are reviewed in Section 2.5. Particular attention is paid to the DG Competition study. Our review of newer approaches to remedy appraisal using simulation methods is reserved until Chapter 3. The perspective of transaction cost economics is introduced in Section 2.6, and in Section 2.7 we briefly consider the long-term limitations on merger remedies due to the wider economic forces that tend to determine long-run industrial structure. We close the chapter in Section 2.8 by outlining the ongoing debate about what are the regulatory objectives implicit in any policy of merger control.

2.1 PRINCIPLES OF A GOOD REMEDY

The economics literature on principles is not large (for example, Lévêque and Shelanski, 2003; papers in *The George Washington Law Review* Special Issue on Merger Remedies, 2001).

It is convenient to start with Lévêque (2001), who sets out four criteria:

- Effectiveness of restoring pre-merger competition
- Minimizing administrative costs in design and enforcement
- Minimizing the loss of merger-induced efficiencies
- Efficient reallocation of assets (that is, selling them to the buyer who values them most).

He points out that only the first two are mentioned in the Commission Notice on Remedies (2000); this is appropriate because they represent the interests of the Commission and its objectives, while the second two are in the interests of the firms. Since the Commission encourages firms to propose appropriate remedies and to find an appropriate buyer for divested assets, they can presumably be relied on to achieve these criteria on their own.

Balto (2001) adds an important extra condition of certainty from his FTC perspective.[1] This is also a condition in the EC Remedies Notice, although Lévêque does not choose to highlight it. Balto's principles provide a strict hierarchy:

1. To make sure that a merger does not reduce competition 'to any significant extent'
2. To select a remedy that will preserve competition with as much certainty as possible
3. To preserve the efficiency-enhancing potential of a merger, 'to the extent that it is possible without compromising the obligation to preserve competition'.

Publication of the FTC Merger Remedies study has generated a legal debate in the USA, but there is little agreement over even the basic principles. Sims and McFalls (2001) argue that proportionality (of remedies to expected competitive effect) is important because merger regulation is not a 'zero-tolerance statute'. However, this is disputed by Boast (2001), who claims that firms proposing an otherwise illegal merger should not be entitled to a minimally intrusive remedy. In summarizing the debate, Blumenthal (2001, p. 978) writes:

> Those with a more libertarian outlook argue for enforcement standards derived from ancient Greek medicine – the government should be minimally intrusive and first do no harm. Those with a more activist outlook argue for standards that allocate commercial and regulatory risk to the merging parties and resolve uncertainty in favour of the government. Both arguments have merit. Neither is compelling.

Joskow (1991, 2002) observes that although the direct effect of, say, action in relation to a merger is felt by the merging parties, a possibly much greater effect of antitrust rules is contained in the signal they send to other firms and in their responses (that is, the deterrence effect). This deterrence effect may be beneficial, but if the wrong or unclear signals are sent, then there will be costs in either deterring beneficial mergers or promoting harmful ones. Not least because of bounded rationality, there will inevitably be mistakes. If the working hypothesis is that mergers are pro-competitive, the merger and remedy appraisal may make: Type I errors that prevent beneficial mergers; and Type II errors that fail to detect harmful mergers. These are inevitable, but the consequences can presumably be reduced if these are anticipated, and actions are chosen appropriately to take this into account. One implication might be that the competition authority (CA) should always consider the wider signalling effect of the choice of remedy in any particular case.

Jenny (2003) suggests three characteristics of a 'useful' merger remedy. 'First, they must be formulated in a non-ambiguous way. Second, the control of their implementation must be easy. Third, they must be relevant in the sense that they must alleviate at the lowest possible social cost the competition concerns identified' (2003, p. 163). Jenny's third principle of 'relevance' sounds more like a principle of proportionality, to which we shall return.

Turning to the procedure for negotiating remedies, Oldale (2002) argues that the procedure itself must be transparent and accountable. It should include a statement of objections that is updated through an inquiry, and justification by the Commission for why a remedy proposal is rejected. Procedural transparency with the main parties is desirable, but it may be difficult to be externally transparent given the commercial sensitivities of, for example, a divestiture. Nevertheless, the Commission's 'market testing' is important both for procedural transparency and for gathering information on expected effectiveness. This involves asking competitors, customers, suppliers and other significant third parties what they think of any proposed remedies. Remedies must be necessary and appropriate, or, briefer still, they must be proportional.

Wider principles can be gleaned from the considerable experience that has been accumulated on the regulation of privatized utilities and other traditionally controlled sectors. The Better Regulation Task Force in the UK suggests that in order to achieve legitimacy, the following attributes of 'good' regulation are desirable (Haskins, 2000, p. 60):

- transparency
- accountability
- targeting
- proportionality
- consistency.

There seems to be no clear definition of proportionality, though most authors think it is important. We suggest that there may be two competing definitions:

1. A cost–benefit analysis of the risk of loss of competition versus the gain in efficiencies or business freedom; or
2. A weighing of the risk of loss of competition versus the risk of failure of a remedy (with no account taken of efficiencies).

In part, the choice between these definitions may depend on one's attitude to the choice of welfare standard, which is discussed in the final section of this review. The former is consistent with a total welfare standard, including benefits for the merging parties, while the latter is more customer-focused.

In summary, Lévêque's four principles usefully highlight the main issues, though we would add procedural transparency. Proportionality is often mentioned by lawyers, but is not unambiguously defined and is not as obviously important in the context of mergers (where a change by the firms is being contemplated) as it is for Articles 81 and 82 (which review existing practices). Other general principles applied to wider legal issues, but which are not highlighted in the above literature, include: certainty (so firms can consider the consequences of a potential merger proposal); enforceability (see Section 2.4); deterrence (touched on by Joskow, 2002; see above); clear expectation in their effect; long-term effect without encouraging substitute practices; and restitution (which is a legal principle consistent with the consumer welfare standard discussed in Section 2.8).

Many of these principles are already incorporated in agency best practice. The Antitrust Division of the United States DOJ (Department of Justice) sets out six main principles in its policy guide;[2] these are that: it will not accept a remedy unless there is a sound basis for believing a violation will occur; remedies must be based upon a careful application of sound legal and economic principles to the particular facts of the case at hand; restoring competition is the key to an antitrust remedy; the remedy should promote competition, not competitors; the remedy must be enforceable; and the antitrust division will commit the time and effort necessary to ensure full compliance with the remedy. The UK Competition Commission (CC) Guidelines for divestitures[3] and the merger Guidelines[4] emphasize similar factors: comprehensiveness, reasonableness (proportionality) and practicability. By reasonableness the Guidelines mean the consideration of the costs of the chosen remedy (that is, from two equally effective remedies, the CC will always choose the one that imposes the least cost or that is least restrictive).

International organizations have picked up on lessons learned from experienced authorities with a view to disseminating best practice. The OECD's background note to the Roundtable on Merger Remedies[5] identifies four main principles: remedies should not be applied unless there is in fact a threat to competition; remedies should be the least restrictive means to effectively eliminate the competition problem(s) posed by a merger; reinforcing the previous point, competition authorities typically have no mandate to use merger review to engage in industrial planning; and competition authorities 'must be flexible and creative in devising remedies'. Similarly, the International Competition Network (ICN), a network of competition authorities from all around the world, recently prepared a comparative review on merger remedies in order to offer advice to authorities.[6] This review sets out four main principles: proportionality; effectiveness (that is, comprehensive impact addressing expected harm, acceptable risk of possibly not addressing competitive detriment, practicality, and appropriate duration); minimized potential remedy burdens and costs; and transparency and consistency.

Finally, the European Commission's written contribution[7] to the OECD study suggests that there are safeguards which the EC uses to avoid or to minimize the risk of overly strict remedies: pre-notification discussions to explore without the time pressure of procedures the potential competition concerns and solutions thereto; competition concerns founded in the results of a market investigation as well as a proper assessment of the concerns raised by third parties in order to distinguish between genuine competition concerns and comments driven by the vested interests of competitors, customers or suppliers which may be unrelated to issues relevant under competition law; the fact that, although remedies are the result of an intensive dialogue between the Commission and the notifying parties, they are eventually proposed by the parties and not imposed by the authority;[8] internal and external procedural safeguards (such as the involvement of the Remedies Unit, the Legal Service, and the national competition authorities); and 'stop-the-clock' provisions allowing for a more flexible timeframe, in particular for complex remedy negotiations.

2.2 CLASSIFICATION OF REMEDIES

Most classifications make the broad distinction between outright prohibition, structural and behavioural remedies. A structural remedy aims to restore the pre-merger market structure in markets where competition was expected to be impeded. A behavioural remedy aims to control the effect of any change in market structure (for example, price control, no-discrimination provisions, access agreements). It is also possible to classify structural and behavioural remedies according to various characteristics. For example, for structural divestment, depending on the use to which the taxonomy is to be put, it may be important to identify: the extent of divested activity; the relationship between divested activities and activities remaining in the merged firm; the nature of the buyer; and whether shareholdings and directorships are involved. Most of the existing literature makes few distinctions according to such characteristics. We develop these divisions and our 'clean break' principle in Chapter 3. In this section, we review the previous attempts to classify remedies.

Common practice, within both antitrust authorities and academia, is to make the simple structural/behavioural distinction. Lévêque (2001) attributes this to the early influence of 'structure–conduct–performance' in the 1970s, and Scherer in particular. Parker and Balto's (2000) refinement of this dichotomy is perhaps the best-known recent development. In addition to distinguishing between full- and part-divestments of ongoing businesses, they effectively split behavioural remedies into:

- contractual arrangements 'such as licensing of intellectual property or perhaps a supply agreement', and
- 'some sort of behavioural relief such as non-discrimination provision'.

Motta et al. (2003, p. 108) suggest a property rights definition of structural versus behavioural remedies:

- Structural remedies modify the allocation of property rights and create new firms: they include divestiture of an entire ongoing business, or partial divestiture (possibly a mix and match of assets and activities of the different firms involved in the merger project).
- Non-structural remedies set constraints on the merged firms' property rights: they might consist of engagements by the merging parties not to abuse certain assets available to them. They might also consist of contractual arrangements such as compulsory licensing or access to intellectual property.

For these authors, the telling differences are the irreversibility of the former (but note also that little can be done if a newly created firm fails or else coordinates its behaviour with the merging parties), and the need for *ex post* monitoring of the latter. They categorize remedies that transfer property rights by contract as 'quasi-structural': for example, Astra/Zeneca[9] licensing of Tenormin in Sweden and Norway for at least ten years, and Lufthansa/SAS[10] requirement to give up take-off and landing slots to facilitate entry.

Motta et al. (2003) review some recent cases in which the Commission has required behavioural remedies, which they suggest 'consist mainly of commitments aimed at guaranteeing that competitors enjoy a level playing field in the purchase or use of some key assets, inputs or technologies that are owned by the merging parties. Therefore, this situation mainly arises when the merged entity is vertically integrated' (p. 116). In Vodafone-Airtouch/Mannesmann (M1795, April 2000), the merged parties offered other mobile operators access to their pan-European network for three years, so a first-mover advantage in creating such a network would not get locked in. In Vivendi/Canal+/Seagram, the parties agreed that Canal+ would not get 'first-window' rights for more than 50 per cent of Universal Films for five years. Motta et al. also mention as a potentially important remedy the use of 'vertical firewalls' to protect sensitive information about downstream rivals. Although these have not yet been used by the Commission, they have been used frequently in the USA.[11]

Lévêque (2001) is less convinced of the value of the basic structural/behavioural distinction, arguing that it can sometimes be ambiguous. For instance, he argues that, in the Microsoft case, remedies relating to intellectual property rights (IPRs) were interpreted as structural by some commentators, but behavioural by others. He also suggests that it is restrictive to view structural remedies as purely synonymous with divestment. He cites, as examples, the EdF (Electricité de France) auction of 6000 MW supply contract and the EdF loss of business control in French electricity generator CNR (Compagnie Nationale du Rhône). He points out that neither remedy entailed divestment, but that both would lead to a change in industry structure. This leads Lévêque to advocate an alternative typology, which distinguishes the remedy's mechanism of action (how it works) from the component of the business it acts upon (that is, which business decision is affected). The instruments in the former can be separated into either:

- regulatory (command and control) or
- economic (incentives based);

and the latter can be either the firm's:

- 'outputs' (price, quantity, quality) or
- its 'organization' (size and internal organization).

Thus a full shares (equity) divestment would be an example of an economic remedy applied to the firm's organization, while a purchasing contract would be regulatory, applied to the firm's 'outputs'. While a four-way typology of this sort must logically be more flexible than a simple behavioural/structural dichotomy, in practice the distinction between organization and outputs may be unimportant since 'regulatory' appears to be largely synonymous with behavioural, and 'economic' with structural.

In principle, it is possible to identify a distinct category of 'contingent' remedies. These would be imposed *ex post* if some predefined criteria of continued competition were contravened.[12] Apart from specification and monitoring problems, most markets are subject to exogenous shocks and changing conditions that would severely undermine such remedies unless they were for a short period only. In the latter case, it appears likely that a behavioural remedy might be simpler to implement.

Overall, while we find some of these classifications to be helpful, it is often difficult in practice to classify particular remedies. For example, licensing a brand to another firm would clearly fall into the structural class if it were sold in perpetuity for a lump sum, but if it were licensed for a royalty that is renegotiated annually, the classification would be behavioural. It is hard to define a boundary across which a licensing agreement becomes structural or behavioural. A more general confusion surrounds the identity of whose behaviour is being referred to in 'behavioural remedies'. In terms of the 'structure–conduct–performance' approach of traditional industrial organization theory, a behavioural remedy should affect the conduct of the industry (for example, unilateral or cooperative pricing); but in terms of the property rights definition, a behavioural remedy directly affects the strategies available to the merging parties, only indirectly affecting the behaviour of others.

In this context, it is interesting to note the three-way classification used in the *UK Merger Guidelines* (UK Competition Commission, 2003). Apart from fairly standard structural and behavioural categories, a third category separates out remedies that are intended to increase the competition that will be faced by the merged firm, whether from existing competitors or new entrants. These include: requiring access to essential inputs/facilities; licensing know-how or intellectual property rights; dismantling exclusive distribution arrangements; and removing no-competition clauses in customer contracts. This group includes hybrid remedies that have both structural and behavioural elements and so are often difficult to classify in the standard dichotomy.

Most competition authorities have a strong preference for structural over behavioural remedies, particularly for horizontal mergers. This is due to the implementation costs of ongoing monitoring and the associated bureaucracy, and the belief that cunning firms can often avoid the impact of regulation. Also, behavioural constraints may limit potentially beneficial strategies (for example, some price discrimination) and restrict the ability of firms to respond to market conditions. However, not everyone agrees that structural remedies always have advantages (for example, Rey, 2003, discussed in the next section). Furthermore, small countries often do not have the power to impose effective structural remedies (for example, the merging multinational firms may simply withdraw from the country), in which case behavioural remedies come into their own.

2.3 ECONOMIC THEORY AND ECONOMETRICS OF REMEDIES

Farrell (2003) provides a preliminary analysis of a competition authority (CA) as a negotiator of remedies. He argues that the buyer of divested assets should be seen more as a 'team mate' of the merging parties than of the competition agency. This arises from standard cooperative bargaining theory, or equivalently from the Coase theorem. Two (or more) parties trying to reach agreement will try to maximize joint profits, then share the benefits of agreement in proportion to their bargaining power. Thus, if the merging parties *plus* the buyer of divested assets had a joint gain in, say, failing to use the divested assets in the most efficient way possible (from the social point of view), then they would ensure that the assets were run down. The buyer would be compensated, for example, by paying a reduced price for the assets, but this would be mutually beneficial.[13] If the appropriate behavioural model for the industry is one of unilateral effects, therefore, the relevant market share for evaluating whether assets would be utilized to the full would be the joint capacity of all three firms (that is, merging parties plus buyer of divested assets) and not just of the merging parties. This insight suggests that the CA must be particularly vigilant in ensuring that a package of divested assets is protected until the buyer can be reliably expected to act independently of the merging parties, particularly when the buyer already operates in the industry. The CA should also recognize the incentive for all parties to the divestiture to collude, and so be wary about accepting the buyer's advice at face value.[14]

The importance of the identity of the buyer of divested assets has been formalized for one type of market by Medvedev (2004), who develops a Cournot model of a market with fixed industry capital and firms of differing efficiencies. There is also a potential entrant. He finds conditions (that is, patterns of differing efficiencies between merging and non-merging firms) in which welfare would be enhanced by a partial merger accompanied by an appropriate divestiture. The main contribution of this paper is to highlight the sensitivity of welfare outcomes to the identity of the buyer (including their efficiency and whether or not they are a new entrant). His simulations suggest that it may be exactly the conditions under which the merging parties would like to sell to an incumbent that the CA would prefer a new entrant to buy, and vice versa. Vasconcelos (2007) develops a similar model, but with firms endogenously choosing between alternative merger opportunities. The possibility of divestiture widens the set of feasible mergers that would pass merger scrutiny. Also, with discrete, 'lumpy' divestitures and the CA pursuing a consumer welfare standard (see last section of this chapter), he finds that the most efficient mergers may be deterred and the CA can end up with 'excessive' divestitures.[15]

Cabral (2003, p. 609) shows that divestiture may have perverse effects on entry:

> By selling stores to potential rivals, merging firms may effectively buy them off, that is, dissuade them from opening new stores. This is good for the merging firms but bad for consumers: the latter prefer an asymmetric duopoly with more stores (no asset sales but nevertheless entry by the rival firm) to a symmetric duopoly with fewer stores (asset sales).

Fridolfsson and Stennek (2005) also identify a case where divestitures may be harmful to competition, at least in the short run. Their model applies to markets where there are greater benefits to non-merging firms than to the merging parties (for example, in Cournot markets, the merging firms have an incentive to reduce output, so encouraging non-merging firms to expand though by not as much – both benefit from the rise in price). In such cases, firms would be tempted to hold back from merger proposals in the hope that others will move first. This is beneficial in delaying anticompetitive mergers, even without regulatory intervention. It is then possible that merger control requiring divestiture allows non-merging firms to buy capacity and so to share the costs of output reduction, consequently hastening anticompetitive mergers.

A second major point made by Farrell (2003) starts from the observation that lengthy competition inquiries are costly and risky for the CA as well as for the parties. This means that there are joint gains from reaching a rapid agreement (for example, in Phase I rather than in Phase II). However, given that less than 100 per cent of the bargaining power lies with the CA, it is appropriate for the CA to focus on consumer welfare to balance the profit bias of the merging parties. It may even be appropriate to be positively hostile to efficiencies if the CA's bargaining power is sufficiently small – the greater the CA's power, the less it needs to compensate by biasing its negotiating stance in favour of consumers. A similar point can be made that the CA should also be biased in favour of rival firms, though this is much lessened inasmuch as the latter can lobby the CA quite effectively.

Lyons and Medvedev (2007) focus on the role of merging firms in making remedy offers. They consider how remedy negotiations between the merging firms and the CA are determined by the standard institutions of merger control (for example, how large a bundle of assets should be divested). They focus on the internationally standard two-phase investigation structure and remedy offers made by the firms. There is asymmetric information, with the merging firms initially knowing more about competitive effects than does the CA. They find that there are inherent biases in remedy outcomes, and identifiable circumstances where offers will be excessive and where they will be deficient. The key idea is that there is a trade-off between the firms' desire to avoid an expensive Phase II investigation, which encourages excessive remedy offers, and their desire to retain assets that would indeed harm competition. The fact that there are circumstances in which firms offer excessive remedies goes against a possible intuition that firms should expect to extract an information rent for possessing superior information about competition in the market.

Motta et al. (2003) develop Parker and Balto (2000) on why some theoretically appropriate remedies may not be effective in practice: information asymmetries between the merging parties and the CA; different incentives between the merging parties and the CA; and practical implementation difficulties. Also, as recognized in the EC Remedies Notice, hold-separate trustees are necessary because the merging parties have an incentive to weaken any package of assets (for example, by moving key personnel), as well as having an incentive to find a weaker buyer than the CA would like (for example, one with a record of non-aggressive, cooperative behaviour). A corollary of the latter is that the best buyer from the CA's point of view may not be the one willing to pay the most in an open auction.

A significant concern when divestitures are required will be that, if the CA is not very careful, by insisting on a strong buyer it can create the preconditions for collusion/collective dominance (for example, symmetric market shares, multi-market contact). This is because symmetric market shares are now understood to facilitate collusion, even though they may be more competitive than symmetric shares when behaviour is characterized by unilateral effects.[16] Motta et al. (2003) suggest that there may be a fundamental tension between strong buyers and a greater probability of collective dominance, so the CA should adopt a two-stage approach to remedies. Both unilateral and coordinated effects should be evaluated when considering a divestiture and buyer, and the remedy should be approved only if both hurdles are cleared. They also advocate a greater use of the requirement for an up-front buyer (though we suspect that this must also raise the possibility of coordinated effects).

Turning to behavioural remedies, Motta et al. (2003) point out the difficulty of making access remedies effective. It is insufficient simply to require access because the access price could be raised so high that competitors are effectively excluded or at least severely disadvantaged. A natural alternative would be access on non-discriminatory terms (as compared with the integrated firm's downstream activities), but this is often unenforceable because prices are not transparent and, even if they are, other intra-firm transfers can circumvent the effect. Technology transfer can also create problems, not least because it requires cooperation with an actual or potential competitor – either this is successful and coordination is possibly enduring, or it is imperfect as the merged entity has no incentive to create a successful rival.

Motta et al. (2003) further argue that the analysis required for the design of structural remedies is qualitatively different from that required for the initial merger appraisal. This is because the former 'require identifying and evaluating which are the competencies, assets, know-how, personnel and other common resources that must be packaged in the new entity to create a competitive enterprise', while 'whether the merged firm has the ability to make profits and survive in the market is never a relevant issue in the analysis of the original project' (p. 122). They go on to argue that the toolkit for structural remedies is, in fact, closer to that which has been developed for wider regulatory issues, such as identifying the appropriate industrial structure when privatizing electricity or the right number of licences for mobile phone spectrum auctions. Thus the CA needs to develop a new specialist expertise for administering structural remedies.

Rey (2003) provides a deeper analysis of how the experience of regulators can be used to identify the desirability of remedies. Structural remedies involve asset transfers that can significantly reshape an industry, while behavioural remedies typically relate to access (asset sharing), which appears to be less drastic. However, some form of price control is an essential adjunct to any access agreement. Rey points out that 'while both price regulation and industry restructuring are quite difficult jobs, regulators tend in practice to favour the former over the latter' (p. 130). While noting that institutional factors may influence this choice, Rey claims that 'this attitude also derives from the fact that asset transfers are more drastic and irreversible measures that involve greater risk of mistakes' (ibid.).

He also makes the important point that regulators are used to trading off the *ex ante* incentive to invest in assets against the *ex post* use of assets when setting an appropriate rate of return. Merger authorities might be more tempted to ignore the indirect effect on incentives because they do not have an ongoing responsibility for asset development. Furthermore, regulators have much more information, experience and expertise in their particular industries than can be expected of a mainstream competition authority. Taken together with the lack of resources to support ongoing price monitoring, these points go some way to explaining why behavioural remedies are unpopular with the CA. However, they should not be ignored, especially in industries characterized by high fixed costs and a limited number of participants.[17]

Rey (2003) also questions the conventional wisdom that structural remedies are more easily enforced (that is, simpler and easier to monitor) than behavioural remedies. He acknowledges that simplicity reduces transaction costs, and irreversibility reduces monitoring costs, and these may generally favour structural remedies, but this is not always clear cut. It is often difficult to impose a clear divestiture as neither human resources nor customers can be tied to the package, and shared physical assets can be reallocated. Conversely, behavioural remedies need not be too difficult to enforce. The CA is not the only possible monitor, and customers, suppliers and competitors can be effective alternatives. For example, competitors will be vigilant monitors of an access price, and arbitration procedures can be set up. Note, however, that for this to be effective, there must be a powerful agency which can act on any complaints (or an extremely effective legal system willing to act on the spirit of the remedy contract).

An important law-and-economics issue of principle is to what extent complementary legislation on abuse of dominance and anticompetitive agreements can be relied on as a safety net, such that greater leniency can be afforded in the form of more limited merger remedies. Jenny (2003) suggests four factors to consider when comparing *ex ante* merger remedies with the alternative of *ex post* enforcement of Articles 81 and 82. First, whereas *ex post* enforcement might pick up explicit collusion and predation, it would be ineffective against coordinated effects. Second, the deterrent effect of *ex post* controls would be greater if they included the ability to unwind a merger if the merged entity abused its market power. Third, monitoring costs must be taken into account, and this may be particularly relevant for complex behavioural remedies associated with high-tech mergers. Fourth, a competition authority will be happier about taking efficiencies into account if it believes *ex post* controls on potential anticompetitive behaviour will be effective. The implicit conclusion is that stronger remedies are necessary if tacit collusion is a concern, if *ex post* control has weaker powers of remedy, if behavioural remedies are difficult to monitor, or if *ex post* control is thought to be ineffective.

Finally, we mention three papers that have tried econometrically to explain the incidence of merger remedies adopted by CAs. As it happens, all three relate to decisions by DG Competition. The aim of these papers is to identify some consistencies in the main factors that determine whether or not remedies are required by the CA. A significant weakness is that they each focus on the Phase II decisions, to the exclusion of both Phase I remedies and the part played by merging parties making offers. Lindsay et al. (2003) 'look for the probability that the Commission would accept an undertaking to divest rather than some other form of undertaking or none at all' (p. 680).[18] They find that divestments are more likely if post-merger market share is large and there are barriers to entry (according to the Commission), and when there are more geographic markets involved. Bergman et al. (2005) investigate a slightly larger sample, but still fewer than 100 markets. They ignore Phase I remedies and focus on the combination of decisions requiring Phase II remedies and prohibitions ('negative decisions'). Negative decisions are found to increase with combined market share, especially when there is a large change, with the fear of coordinated effects and with barriers to entry. Various political factors were not found to be significant, though US firms were somewhat less likely to face a negative decision. There was slight evidence that vertical mergers were more, rather than less, likely to face a negative decision. Bougette and Turolla (2006) claim to find an additional effect that the size of merging parties encourages the Commission to demand remedies, though this is supported by only one of the statistical approaches they use.

2.4 REMEDIES IN HIGH-TECHNOLOGY MERGERS

Rubinfeld (2003) discusses the use of access remedies in vertical mergers.[19] Drawing on the lessons from AOL/Time Warner (where access to broadband was a key issue, especially in relation to foreclosure), and extrapolating from the Microsoft Explorer case (where access of alternative browsers to the Windows operating system was the key issue, especially in preserving incentives for innovation and opening the possibility of 'middleware' competition for the operating system), he concludes that such remedies should only be used when the merger would itself create a problem akin to the essential facilities doctrine developed in non-merger cases: 'it must be seen as a necessary cure to the anticompetitive harm likely to be created by the merger' (p. 157). In AOL/Time Warner (TW), there was a time limit by which TW would have to strike deals with two other Internet providers, and a similar access agreement for TW content. These were protected by 'most favoured nation' clauses relative to AOL access. In the Microsoft case, the initial structural remedy (separating the operating system from applications) was rejected on appeal (following arguments that this would have been inefficient and would not have guaranteed increased competition in operating systems). The compromise included allowing OEMs (original equipment manufacturers) to remove the Explorer icon and install icons for non-Microsoft middleware.

Jenny (2003) identifies three features of high-tech industries that make merger remedies particularly difficult to devise. First, the rapidly evolving technology means that new goods and services appear regularly, and compete with older-generation products such that the definition of the relevant market also changes. The CA must guard against sacrificing a potentially efficiency-enhancing merger in order to protect competition in a market that may be irrelevant in a few years. Second, technologies protected by intellectual property rights (IPRs) can deter entry, and licensing may be an appropriate remedy (though care should be taken if a complex arrangement is required, because the merged entity might act strategically against licensees). Third, many high-tech industries exhibit network effects, which can put a sharp focus on the trade-off between enhanced efficiency and reduced competition.[20] Overall, the appropriateness of a merger remedy depends on the ability to forecast the future of the industry. Because the future of high-tech industries is so uncertain, and behavioural remedies are relatively flexible, they may be preferable because they do not have the long-term effects of structural divestitures.[21]

Le Blanc and Shelanski (2003) consider merger remedies in the context of telecommunications mergers, for which there were 16 merger decisions under the ECMR between July 1998 and September 2001. Each was cleared subject to remedies, with an increasing proportion agreed in Phase I, presumably as the merging parties learned what would be required. The merging parties claimed many potential sources of efficiency. For example, Vodafone-Airtouch/Mannesmann (November 1999) announced expected synergies of £500 million due to purchasing and operating economies, creating a global brand, and the more efficient introduction of Internet and data products, all in the context of a network industry. With this background, they turn to an appraisal of remedies required by the Commission, which were mainly structural (see their table 11.7, p. 199). Le Blanc and Shelanski observe that both US and EU competition authorities were concerned with the competitive credibility of buyers, and within this constraint preference was given to smaller competitors in the same market, firms operating in neighbouring or related markets, or those with a good track record for operating similar assets. While all divestitures were eventually completed, there were frequent delays as the economic downturn set in, and some delays exceeded a year.

2.5 THE FTC (1999) REPORT ON THE EFFICACY OF REMEDIES

The first serious work on the efficacy of remedies was the FTC Divestiture Report[22] for the USA. Lévêque (2001) put it clearly at the time: 'The FTC study (1999) is the single *ex post* assessment ever made on remedies.'[23] The study covered 35 divestiture orders for the years 1990–94. It was interview-based (37 of the 50 buyers were interviewed). In summary form, the main findings were as follows:

- Almost all required divestitures occurred (in the sense that an acquirer of the divested assets was able to enter the market)
- However, only 75 per cent of the divestitures were successful, in the sense that the acquirer was still in the market one year after and was independent from the seller
- The probability of success was much higher if an ongoing business was divested (that is, divestiture of selected assets was significantly more problematic).

Various factors were identified which complicated the divestiture process and lessened the likelihood of success. Notably, sellers of assets have incentives to:

- offer a divestiture package that is too narrow
- propose a weak buyer
- engage in strategic behaviour to impede the success of the buyer; or, at least to not assist/cooperate with the buyer during the transition phase.

Other problems identified included:

- Continuing relationships between seller and buyer after divestiture (for example, a supply arrangement or technical assistance requirement) increased the buyer's vulnerability to seller behaviour. Of the 19 such divestitures, in six the ongoing relationship was so detrimental that the buyer could not operate effectively, and in a further seven the ongoing relationship was competitively harmful.
- Buyers often have a serious informational disadvantage compared with the sellers (that is, merging firms). They may not fully know what assets they need to succeed or whether the assets offered are 'up to the task'.
- Buyers may not have the same objectives as the Commission, so the remedial purposes of the order may not be met.
- Divestitures that include technology transfers bring together many of the above problems (incentive to limit the asset package, buyer's informational disadvantage, buyer's reliance on the seller for technical assistance and transfer of know-how, and the seller's incentive to engage in strategic behaviour). Another difficulty, because technology transfers often involve the divestiture of less than an ongoing business, is that the buyer may be at the bottom of the learning curve and thus starts with a disadvantage.

The FTC review has been very influential and has served to strengthen the emphasis on the identity of the buyer and tight control of the transfer process (for example, use of trustees, hold-separate agreements, up-front buyers, rejection on inappropriate buyers, 'crown jewel' provisions, broader divestiture packages). The significant impact on recent European practice is summarized in Monti (2003). However, it does have some significant limitations: the small sample size and short time period caution against robustness of results, the interview methodology was not amenable to rigorous statistical analysis, and, perhaps most importantly, the single-minded emphasis on success of entry (that is, survival one year after) is extremely limited.

2.6 THE DG COMPETITION (2005) REPORT[24]

DG Competition of the European Commission conducted an in-house study of past merger remedies, which was published in 2005. The study analysed 40 decisions containing 96 different remedies, adopted by the Commission between 1996 and 2000. These cases were sampled to pick up on a range of alternative remedies and different industrial sectors, as well as Phase I and Phase II agreements. The study used interviews with the parties selling and purchasing divested assets and trustees, carrying out a total of 145 full interviews. These were supported by access to the original files of the case and a quantitative questionnaire, although the assessed effectiveness of remedies is based in some cases essentially on the subjective judgement of those interviewed.

Four types of remedy were identified:

1. Divestiture (total of 68 remedies) of a:
   (a) previously 'stand-alone' business (15 remedies);
   (b) 'carve-out' business that was previously integrated with another (37);
   (c) 'mix-and-match' of assets from both pre-merger firms (8);
   (d) long-term exclusive licence of indefinite duration or until expiry of patent (8).
2. Exit from a joint venture (JV) (15).
3. Access to infrastructure, technology or other exclusive agreement (10).
4. Other (3).

If we consider exit from a JV as a form of divestiture, there are a total of 83 divestiture remedies, and 13 non-divestiture.

Out of the analysed cases, 80 per cent involved horizontal competition concerns, 14 per cent involved both horizontal and vertical concerns and

6 per cent were purely vertical mergers. As expected, divestiture remedies were mostly associated with horizontal concerns and access with vertical concerns. Eighty-four per cent of remedies were aimed at single dominance concerns, and were mostly addressed by divestitures, and 12 per cent at collective dominance,[25] where exit from a JV was prevalent.

The first set of findings relates to the design and implementation of divestitures. The most frequent problem was the scope of assets transferred, which afflicted 80 per cent of the divestitures, one-third of which remained unresolved after three to five years. Carve-out was mentioned about half as much. Transfer issues and inadequate interim preservation of assets pending transfer were the next most frequent problems, together afflicting up to two-thirds of divestitures though most such problems were resolved in three to five years. The unavailability of a suitable purchaser was problematic in around one in five cases.

The UK Competition Commission (2004) Divestiture Guidelines neatly summarize these design and implementation problems into

> three broad categories of risks that may possibly impair the effectiveness of divestiture remedies . . . :
>
> - Composition risks – these are risks that the scope of the divestiture package may be too constrained or not appropriately configured to attract a suitable purchaser or may not allow a purchaser to operate effectively and viably in the market.
> - Purchaser risks – these are risks that a suitable purchaser is not available or that the merger parties will dispose to a weak or otherwise inappropriate purchaser.
> - Asset risks – these are risks that the competitive capability of a divestiture package will deteriorate prior to completion of divestment, for example through loss of customers or key members of staff.

Returning to the DG Competition report, its second set of findings relates to access and other non-divestment remedies. The sample was small, but three out of four infrastructure remedies failed due to the market developing very differently from what had been anticipated. Technology access agreements were often flawed due to the licensor being able to limit transfer of essential support technology. Overall, however, the fundamental difficulty of setting suitable access terms was the single most important element impeding access as an effective remedy.

Finally, combining the above findings with a limited number of market indicators such as market share, the study was able to provide a basic assessment of the effectiveness of remedies. On the simple FTC criterion of whether divested assets were still in business three to five years later, the DG Competition study found that 94 per cent were (7 per cent of which had been transferred to new ownership). Market share evolution could be estimated for two-thirds of the divestitures. Of these, 4 per cent had disappeared, 44 per cent had reduced market share and 18 per cent increased market share, with a third remaining the same. Compared with the market share performance of assets retained by the merging parties, only 23 per cent of divestitures did better, with 57 per cent doing worse. Finally, each remedy was placed into one of four categories: effective; partially effective; ineffective; or unclear (due to lack of evidence or simultaneous events such as a major liberalization). Overall, 57 per cent were considered effective, 24 per cent partially effective, 7 per cent ineffective and 12 per cent unclear. Exit from a JV was the most effective remedy type and access remedies were least effective. Perhaps surprisingly, slightly more Phase I remedies were effective compared with Phase II, which the authors of the study put down to the greater complexity of such cases.[26]

2.7 UK STUDIES

The UK Competition Commission (2007) recently published an internal review of remedies in four mergers. These were chosen to highlight difficult cases and to cover divestiture, remedies to restrict vertical behaviour, and behavioural remedies. In relation to divestitures, they found that potential purchasers need to be carefully vetted for competitive ability and intent, the package of assets needs careful construction and sellers should be incentivized by appointing trustees with the ability to sell at no minimum price if the sellers procrastinate. In relation to behavioural remedies, they find that these are sometimes the only option where multinational firms are concerned. This problem does not come through in the US and EC studies because of their enormous economic size, but will presumably be much greater for countries smaller than the UK. The report finds that behavioural remedies (for example, 'Chinese walls') are complex and resource-intensive to monitor, especially when compared with divestitures, but that they can work well particularly where the firm has a compliance culture.

Moving outside the specific merger literature, there are a few studies on the efficacy of remedies put in place by competition authorities in cases of monopoly abuse. Shaw and Simpson (1986 and 1989) conducted a statistical analysis on a sample of 28 UK markets. They compared the market shares and profitability of the investigated firms against control groups before and after the intervention of the Monopolies and Mergers Commission (MMC). The evidence tended to suggest little or no influence on market shares and, at most, a marginal downward effect on profitability.

Clarke et al. (1998) also investigated the effectiveness of remedies put in place after MMC investigations of monopoly abuse in the UK (1973–95). They employed a case study methodology, combining hard statistical evidence and interviews. In the 14 cases considered, no general pattern emerged, although in some cases antitrust intervention appears to have had some limited effectiveness.

2.8 TRANSACTION COST ECONOMICS OF MERGER REMEDIES

'Transaction cost economics adopts a contractual approach to the study of economic organization' (Williamson, 1996, p. 54) and is underpinned by two behavioural assumptions: bounded rationality (so complete contracts are not feasible); and opportunism (so firms must be assumed to be led by managers who are self-interest seeking and act with guile). Contracts are interpreted broadly to include all forms of organization, including firms. These aspects of behaviour are particularly troublesome for contracting in the presence of investment in specific assets. Firms are expected to organize governance structures whose main purpose is to encourage specific investments and economize on costs, including those associated with contractual hazards and the operation of the governance structures themselves.

This complements a market power approach to industrial organization. Williamson (1996, ch. 11) is concerned that antitrust in the USA swung between unreasoned expectation in the 1960s that any non-standard business practice was for monopoly purposes, and a later over-simplistic adherence to the Chicago critique, along with a revisionist view that firms should be allowed a strong benefit of the doubt. While he believes firms are strongly motivated to organize so that they produce and invest efficiently (so *per se* prohibitions are generally a bad idea), the world is complex and businesses are instinctively opportunistic; thus the authorities should always look out for strategic behaviour. While he does not address remedies directly, he does propose three principles of antitrust enforcement. First, economizing by firms (as opposed to seeking monopoly power) should be taken as the 'main case'. Second, strategic behaviour in all its forms should be taken seriously. Third, these strategic considerations should provide exceptions to the main case as long as: the structural preconditions are in place (for example, entry barriers, substantial market share); the strategic logic withstands scrutiny in the particular context; and due allowance is made for 'the operational infirmities of enforcement process' (ibid., p. 306).

Joskow (2002) develops the transaction cost approach in the context of antitrust remedies. He does not find the results of the FTC remedies study at all surprising (and he would presumably say the same about the DG Competition study).

> Firms subject to 'voluntary' divestitures to mitigate market power should be expected to behave strategically; ongoing businesses that have been divested are likely to fare better post-divestiture than are assets that require the creation of a complete new business organization to be used effectively; buyers negotiating divestiture agreements in which they are dependent on the seller and have not protected themselves against *ex post* hold-ups are likely to face the consequences of those hold-ups; contractual arrangements for input suppliers between competing firms can soften competition between them; it is not the size of the acquirer but its ability to utilize the assets effectively that matters. (Ibid. p. 27)

He therefore argues for considerable caution before approving a divestiture remedy, even if made 'voluntarily'.

Le Blanc and Shelanski (2003) provide an interesting example of the transaction costs of divestiture, drawing on the testimony of the CEO of Cable and Wireless (C&W) at US Senate hearings. C&W was buying MCI's Internet business as part of an agreed divestiture to allow the MCI/Worldcom merger. One year on, there were numerous breaches of undertakings relating to staff transfers, customer contracts, non-solicitation of transferred customers and support services. In retrospect, this seems almost inevitable given that the divested business had been highly integrated with other telecom services, sharing engineers, sales staff, billing and databases. The economic consequences were substantial. Pre-divestiture in 1998, MCI's Internet market share had been 40 per cent, but C&W was left with less than 10 per cent market share in 2000.

It is difficult to specify a clear and unambiguous contract between the Commission and the merging parties. The merging firms are likely to act opportunistically because they have an incentive to run down assets, retain key staff, divest a mishmash of assets that form an incomplete business, sell to the weakest or most collusive buyer, etc. In the absence of an enforceable contract that addresses these problems in a satisfactory way (which is almost impossible), the solution is to find appropriate 'penalty clauses' that can be triggered by easily monitored events (for example, legal transfer of business by a certain date). These issues were discussed in the FTC divestiture study (though not in explicit transaction cost terms), and resulted in the guidelines on preference for an up-front buyer, divestiture of complete businesses, and 'crown jewel' provisions (Parker and Balto, 2000; Baer et al., 2001).

2.9 REMEDIES IN THE CONTEXT OF AN ENDOGENOUS INDUSTRIAL STRUCTURE

This section is very brief because the current literature on the evolution of industrial structure does not directly address merger remedies. Nevertheless, we believe that it draws attention to some important long-term forces in the economy that are very relevant in the present context.

While much early literature on the determinants of concentration focused on the role of mergers (for example, Prais, 1976; Hannah and Kay, 1977), the recent literature has stressed the underlying technical and behavioural factors in competition: economies of scale; endogenous sunk costs; innovation; and entry (for example, Sutton, 1991, 1998; Bresnahan and Reiss, 1990).[27] This does not mean that mergers are unimportant, but they are only one way of achieving a particular structure. The implication is that if a merger is not allowed, this may have little long-run effect as endogenous growth and exit will eventually reach a similar outcome. Put another way, artificial changes in market share due to either merger or divestiture will be undone by market processes. Structure matters more than how it is achieved.

An intermediate view is that there is no single equilibrium market structure, but a range of feasible structures.[28] The implications for mergers are developed in Lyons (2001). If there is an exogenous shock to an industry, it will need to adjust if the shock takes the structure out of the feasible equilibrium set. If the shock is common across firms, this may cause a merger wave. For example, Andrade et al. (2001) suggest that the shock of deregulation in the 1990s was a major cause of merger activity as firms adjusted to a shock to the industrial structure.

The lesson for the current literature review is that remedies agreed by a CA may be subject to 'unwinding' by market forces if they do not create a market structure that is a feasible equilibrium. However, it would be far too strong to proceed to argue that merger remedies do not matter. An equilibrium market structure is necessarily a long-term tendency, and any attempt to identify it would have to be very speculative. The CA cannot be expected to operate on that timescale. Wood (2003) points out that the US Merger Guidelines set out a time frame of just two years, while she believes 'some EU decisions reflect a greater willingness to take a stab at a longer-term prediction about competitive consequences' (p. 73). The more modest conclusion is that they should conduct a 'reality check' of any proposed remedies so as to avoid any instability where powerful changes in the underlying determinants of structure are at work. For example, this is likely to be relevant in the presence of rapid technical change or where knock-on mergers can be predicted.

2.10 REGULATORY OBJECTIVES OF MERGER CONTROL

An explicit welfare criterion is the prerequisite to providing a measure by which any proposed merger remedy can be appraised. Practitioners need to know what they want to achieve before making any intervention. Unfortunately, the objectives ascribed to regulators in much existing economic analysis differ significantly from those set out in legislation (in particular, ECMR, 1989, and its recent revisions) and presumably pursued by the European Commission. The EC is not unique in this respect, and the same applies to legislation and competition authorities across the globe.

Farrell and Katz (2006) provide an excellent review of the emerging literature in relation to wider antitrust issues. In the context of appraising an existing industry structure, the economics literature nearly always adopts the total welfare standard. Total welfare is defined as:

$TW = CS + \pi$, where CS = consumer surplus,[29] and π = industry profits.

For example, in comparing perfect competition with a monopoly structure, if €1 of consumer surplus is transferred to profits without affecting the pattern of consumption, then TW is unchanged – the only welfare detriment is the 'deadweight loss triangle'. From the perspective of TW, the only problem is that price distortions create a Pareto loss because a €1 gain in profits can be achieved only by, for example, a €1.50 loss in CS. This welfare indifference between CS and π might be challenged as failing to take account of income distribution, particularly since shareholders as a group are likely to be wealthier than consumers. The economist's standard riposte is that a government has many redistributive tools at its disposal (for example, direct taxation), and merger policy is likely to rank very low for effectiveness in the range of such tools.

A practical problem with welfare measurement derives from the vertical interdependence of industries. The partial equilibrium approach of measuring welfare in the relevant input market alone is fine if downstream markets are competitive. However, if the downstream market is oligopolistic, greater care is needed. For example, double marginalization can exacerbate distortions, and buyer power can ameliorate such an effect.

In the context of a merger, the total welfare standard compares total welfare pre- and post-merger (see, for example, Williamson, 1967), and states that the merger should be allowed if total welfare does not fall:[30]

TWS: allow merger if and only if TW(post-merger) $\geq$ TW(pre-merger).

The ECMR (1989) is less clear in stating a welfare criterion, but it is usually taken to adopt a consumer welfare standard:[31]

CWS: allow merger if and only if CS(post-merger) $\geq$ CS(pre-merger).

Thus mergers are allowed provided consumers do not lose out as a consequence. With a given downward-sloping demand curve and costs unchanged by the merger, the TWS and CWS will give identical results for a horizontal merger. However, if the merger creates synergies, there will be mergers that would satisfy the TWS but not the CWS. In practice, such mergers are most likely to be referred for Phase II investigation, so the distinction is likely to be crucial.[32]

Farrell (2003) provides a directly remedies-related reason why a CA should be unsympathetic towards efficiencies in mergers that create competitive harm, even when the merger might pass a simple TWS. The CA is sometimes accused of requiring a package of remedies that not only restores competition, but either creates more competition than there was before the merger or incorporates assets not tied to the narrow market in which harm had been identified. In part, this may be necessary to create a viable competitor.[33] However, the temptation for a CA may be to go beyond this. A positive effect of such a policy may be that it allows the gainers (that is, the merging parties) actually to 'compensate' the losers (that is, consumers in the market where competition has been lessened), whereas the TWS involves only a potential Pareto improvement. The downside of such 'excessive' remedies might be that, because they confiscate the rents, they deter firms from searching for potentially efficiency-enhancing mergers in the first place. They may also be more difficult for the CA to evaluate inasmuch as they involve assets outside the appraised market. Furthermore, the actual 'compensation' may be biased towards rival firms that are more active in lobbying the CA than are final consumers.

An alternative welfare standard suggested by Armstrong et al. (1994) in the context of price regulation is to adopt a weighted welfare function:

$$WW = CS + \alpha\pi, \text{ where } 0 \leq \alpha \leq 1,$$

and α reflects the weight society puts on €1 of profit as compared with €1 of consumer surplus. If $\alpha = 1$, then $WW = TW$, and if $\alpha = 0$, then $WW = CS$, so this is a simple generalization. The weighted welfare standard in the context of a merger would be:

WWS: allow merger if and only if WW(post-merger) $\geq$ WW(pre-merger).

Armstrong et al. (1994, p. 17) make three further observations on the use of a weighting factor. First, the tax/benefit system is imperfect, so 'in theory and with an idealized regulator' one would wish to take distributional issues into account, in practice 'the regulation of private firms is a tool ill suited for redistributive policy'. Second, if a greater proportion of consumers than of shareholders lies within the area of jurisdiction (Europe), then $\alpha < 1$ can be justified in nationalistic terms. Third, 'taking a more "political" viewpoint we could see the regulator as mediating a bargain between consumers and shareholders of the firm over their shares of the gains from trade [merger], with α representing the relative weakness of shareholders in the process' (ibid.). We would add a fourth item to this list if the relevant market sells a necessity to the poor or vulnerable (for example, utility industries). In such markets, the argument for distributional concerns becomes much greater.

The discussion so far has considered distributional issues between either consumers as a group and shareholders as a group, or (briefly) between consumers. We also need to consider the distribution of profits across firms. There is very little economics literature on this point, although it has been important in the history of competition policy in the USA (Neale, 1970; Whish, 1989, pp. 13–14), and arguably has had some influence in the application of the ECMR (Neven et al., 1993). There are two sets of issues here. First, there has sometimes been a concern with the dispersal of economic power and preservation of small and medium-sized firms as a socially desirable institution,[34] though this seems to have little influence now. Second, and more importantly, it is sometimes argued that competitors need protecting even at the cost to current welfare (however measured) because this preserves a competitive presence that may be important for the future. The argument might be particularly relevant in an emerging industry where the nature of future technical progress is uncertain and where it would be difficult for a completely new entrant to catch up.[35]

We do not propose to review regulation objectives founded in the protection of national firms from foreign takeover, regional policy, etc. since these do not appear to have any serious current relevance for the operation of the ECMR. A possibly more important omission is any review of the objective of single market integration in the EU.

So far, our review of welfare standards has emphasized price effects. In some mergers, there will be an issue of appropriate variety or quality of products, and the implications of mergers on these dimensions are notoriously hard to predict (see Chapter 3 in relation to simulation studies). It becomes even harder to predict the effects on technical progress, and so the distribution of welfare over time. Evans and Schmalensee (1999, p. 16), make the point that

> although static competition is rarely vigorous in new-economy industries, the key determinant of the performance of these industries is the vigor of dynamic competition – an issue that is ignored in traditional economic analysis. An explicit investigation of present and future dynamic competition is essential to sound economic analysis of Schumpeterian industries.

Finally, we raise the important issue of the extent to which merger remedies should be used only to reinstate competition (to a level appropriate to the *TWS*, *CWS* or *WWS*), or whether it is appropriate to try to improve on the pre-merger position. Put another way, should the standard be a threshold that the merger must pass (allowing the parties to appropriate any surplus beyond that), or should it be something to be optimized using whatever tools are available to the CA and subject only to not making a desirable merger unprofitable? Most authors who mention this issue (for example, in Lévêque and Shelanski, 2003), argue that merger control should only reinstate the original position, with the minimum remedies necessary to achieve that – the CA should not attempt to optimize market structure or behaviour, not least because it does not have the information and resources to do so. Moreover, any attempt at optimization could have negative effects on incentives for firms to create the most efficient form of organization (see Section 2.3 on the economic theory of remedies). Note that this view is quite consistent with the need to establish a viable remedies package which may require, for example, a full ongoing business that includes assets outside the narrow market that is the cause for concern (see Baer and Redcay, 2003, pp. 55–6; Winckler, 2003, p. 83).

NOTES

1. Balto is a co-author of the FTC Merger Remedies study – see below.
2. USDOJ Antitrust Division (2004).
3. Application of divestiture remedies in merger inquiries: Competition Commission Guidelines, December 2004.
4. Merger references: Competition Commission Guidelines, June 2003.
5. OECD (2004), p. 17. In fact, these comments were based on a speech from Deborah Majoras, Deputy Assistant Attorney General, United States DOJ (Antitrust Division).
6. ICN Merger Working Group: Analytical Framework Subgroup, Merger Remedies Review Project, Report for the fourth ICN annual conference Bonn, June 2005, downloaded from: http://www.internationalcompetitionnetwork.org/ICN_Remedies_StudyFINAL5–10.pdf.
7. OECD (2004), p. 253.
8. Interestingly, although it is overwhelmingly normal practice to simply accept or reject the offer by the parties, this is not always the case. In both MAN/Auwärter and Shell/Enterprise, the parties submitted commitments during the first phase, but both cases resulted in an unconditional clearance decision. Two related examples are Cargill/Cerestar and Compass/Restorama/Rail Gourmet, in which the parties submitted

first-phase commitments to the Commission before the case was referred to the UK competition authorities, who granted unconditional clearances.

9. This case (M1403, 1999) is investigated in detail in Chapter 9.
10. Adopted under Article 81, before full function joint ventures were treated under the ECMR (IV35.545 January 1996).
11. They have also been used by the UK Competition Commission in Centrica/Dynegy (Cm 5885; August 2003). A recent internal review suggests that these have been effective in achieving their purpose. See also Wilcox (2005) on behavioural remedies and vertical mergers.
12. See OECD (2004) for a discussion of a market share threshold and Werden et al. (2005) for a model of an output threshold with fines or rewards for failing to meet or exceeding the threshold.
13. Note that this argument does not rely on the asset buyer being ignorant or fooled into buying a weak set of assets – this is an outcome that is mutually beneficial.
14. A recent paper by Medvedev (2004) provides a theoretical investigation of divestiture in a Cournot framework, based on the analysis by Farrell and Shapiro (1990).
15. Cosnita and Tropeano (2006) argue that a larger divestiture should be required from a merging firm that creates lower efficiency gains. The problem for the CA is that the firms are better informed about their cost savings. The authors suggest that the CA could induce the optimal divestiture by regulating the sale price of divested assets.
16. Closely related to this, a detailed study of the Nestlé/Perrier merger by Compte et al. (2002) is discussed in a later section.
17. Rey illustrates this point by reference to the Decision in relation to Telia/Telenor (since abandoned), the original national telephone operators for Sweden and Norway. Given that the 'enlarged footprint' was the cause for concern, he supports the Decision that open access would be much more effective than any divestiture could have been.
18. Unfortunately, it is not at all clear how this has been operationalized in constructing their dependent variable. Their sample is also small, being a one-in-four sample of mergers from January 2000 to June 2002, and they only look at the 'first affected horizontal market' in identifying characteristics of the merger. No summary statistics are provided in the paper.
19. He claims that divestiture or intellectual property licensing can usually resolve horizontal concerns.
20. He discusses AOL/Time Warner and Vivendi/Canal+/Seagram (October 2000) in this context. Remedies for the latter included both structural divestments and behavioural commitments for five years (first window rights to Universal Films, and access to online music content).
21. Jenny argues that the pre-2004 ECMR was biased against efficiencies, and that this led to drastic prohibitions in Aérospatiale/de Havilland and GE/Honeywell. It remains to be seen to what extent the recent revisions of the ECMR will change things.
22. FTC (1999); see also Cary and Bruno (1997) and Baer and Redcay (2003).
23. There was some *ad hoc* work which assesses specific cases. An example of this (cited by Foer, 2001) is Cotterill's finding that supermarkets divested by Royal Ahold sometimes performed 25 per cent below stores not divested. For context, Rakovsky (2000) provides a very brief summary of European Commission practice. Morgan (2002) provides a useful descriptive account of remedies used by the Commission, examining them from the managerial perspective of the merging parties.
24. This major report was conducted alongside our own work described in this book, and access to data was shared, as was the design of questionnaires. Earlier commentaries on the ECs merger remedy policy can be found in Drauz (1997) and Elliott (1999).
25. The remaining 4 per cent are difficult to classify.
26. In an informal insider opinion based on recent (at the time) experience, Kemp and Pitkänen (1999) offer three conditions for Phase I remedies to be appropriate. First, the product and geographic dimensions of the market should be easily identified. Second, the merging parties should recognize the competition problem early and be willing to negotiate seriously to resolve it. Third, they should be able to identify and offer viable

divestitures (or other relevant remedies). The second and third problems can persist into Phase II if the Commission is slow to identify the precise competition problem or if the parties are uncooperative.

27. For European empirical evidence see Lyons et al. (2001).
28. The most sophisticated take on this is Sutton's (1991, 1998) 'bounds approach'.
29. There are some well-known problems with consumer surplus as a measure of consumer welfare. In particular, the strict equivalence breaks down when there are income effects, though these can usually be dismissed as *de minimis* as long as the merger results in only relatively small knock-on price changes (Willig, 1976).
30. In the context of a merger remedy, we can say that a remedy is *proportionate* if the post-remedy welfare standard is met without penalizing the profit gains by the firms more than is necessary. Of course, this begs the question of what is 'more than necessary'. See also the end of this section.
31. For example, the Commission is required to take into account 'the development of technical and economic progress *provided that it is to consumers' advantage* and does not form an obstacle to competition' (Art.2.1(b), italics added). See also DG Enterprise paper by de la Mano, No 11 on Merger Efficiencies.
32. Strategic arguments in defence of the *CWS* or at least a weighted welfare standard are provided by Besanko and Spulber (1989), Neven and Roller (2000) and Lyons (2002). For example, firms have private information on the benefits of mergers, and also have free choice of their merger partners, while the CA only has veto power or the ability to impose a remedy that is intended to restore pre-merger competition. Such factors create incentive imbalances that can, at least partially, be corrected by modifying the welfare standard. See also Werden (1996) on how basic simulation is made much easier to implement under the consumer welfare standard.
33. Motta et al. (2003) suggest that Unilever/Bestfoods (M1990, September 2000) and Total Fina/Elf Aquitaine (M1628, February 2000) illustrate how the Commission appropriately required wider packages to satisfy viability. The latter followed 'market testing' (that is, asking third parties). MCI Worldcom/Sprint (M1741, June 2000) found that no separable package of assets could be divested so as to create a viable competitor. Viability depends on the buyer as well as the bundle of assets. Motta et al. identify the Bosch/Rexroth case (M2060, December 2000) as the first to require an up-front buyer – a strong buyer was necessary to prevent customers drifting back to Bosch.
34. Compare the similar arguments for small and medium-sized farms in the context of agricultural policy. The US legal literature contains numerous commentaries on the infamous Brown Shoe case of 1962, where the courts were protecting competitors rather than competition (for example, Posner, 1976, ch. 6).
35. We have not located any explicit references that make this point.

3. Classification of merger remedies

3.0 INTRODUCTION

This chapter begins by summarizing the empirical classification of EC remedies, mainly into structural and behavioural, but also according to competitive concern. We go on to consider the value of this simple dichotomy and focus on two issues: the need to understand how any particular remedy affects competition in the market; and the details of remedy design as revealed by the clean break principle.

3.1 EMPIRICAL CLASSIFICATIONS OF REMEDIES

The DG Competition study (2005) analysed in depth a sample of 40 of its merger decisions over the period 1996–2000. Because most European mergers involve more than one market, the number of markets in which remedies were applied was 96. The full population of its merger cases over these years involved 227 remedies. Although this is only a five-year sub-period, it includes disproportionately high shares of the full-period mergers and remedies, because of the intense activity in the late 1990s (see Figure 1.1). Table 3.1 lists the main types of remedy used. Broadly speaking, this taxonomy can be aligned with the structural/behavioural dichotomy: transferring a market position and exit from joint venture (JV), being divestment, are structural; granting access is behavioural; and long-term exclusive licences straddle the two, depending on the details of the agreement.

'Transferring a market position', or divestment in common parlance, is most frequent. The Commission says this is 'aimed at re-creating the competitive strength of a business in the hands of a suitable purchaser who exercises a sufficient competitive constraint on the merging parties' (ibid., p. 18). The Commission further splits this into three sub-categories, by the extent and scope of the divestment. Commitments to exit from a JV 'required the committing parties to give up their joint control over a business by transferring it to a suitable purchaser'.

On the behavioural side, commitments to grant access are 'measures to provide other market participants with access to key assets and thus reduce

Table 3.1 EC remedy types, 1996–2000

	Population (%)	Sample (%)
Transfer a market position of which:	56	65
Stand-alone business	15	17
Extensive carve-out	34	40
Package of assets	7	8
Exit from JV	17	15
Long-term exclusive licences	11	8
Grant access	10	9
Others	6	3

Source: DG Competition (2005), Chart 6, p. 19.

Table 3.2 An alternative classification of EC remedy types, 1991–2005

	Structural	Behavioural	Both	Total
Phase I	62	36	17	115
Phase II	26	18	28	72
Total	88	54	45	187
% of total	47	29	24	100

Source: Bougette and Turolla (2006).

barriers to entry' (ibid., p. 18). The Commission highlighted three types of access remedies: (1) granting of access to infrastructure or technical platforms; (2) granting of access to technology via licences or other IPRs; and (3) termination of exclusive vertical agreements. Granting of long-term exclusive licences is a category that we discuss below.

An alternative summary derived by Bougette and Turolla (2006) is shown in Table 3.2. Their own analysis (presumably with less detailed information on the precise nature of individual remedies) is based on a sample of 229 cases, 1991–2005. Apart from the period, this differs from the DG Competition summary in that each merger is taken to be the unit of observation, as opposed to each market affected by a merger. Because of this, they find that nearly one-quarter of all cases involve both behavioural and structural remedies. Nevertheless, structural remedies are confirmed as the most frequent type of remedy.

Two other features of the DG Competition findings that are important for our own approach to remedy analysis relate the type of remedy to type of competition concern and theory of harm. Table 3.3 shows that, quite

Table 3.3 Remedy by type of competition concern

Type of concern	Type of remedy				Total
	Transfer market position	Exit from JV	Access	Other	
Horizontal	58	13	3	3	77
Horizontal and vertical	10	1	2	0	13
Vertical	0	1	5	0	6
Total	68	15	10	3	96

Source: DG Competition (2005), Table 4, p. 20.

Table 3.4 Remedies by theory of harm

	Transfer	JV	Access	Other	Total
Single dominance	60	10	9	2	81
Collective dominance	4	5	1	1	11
Cooperation effects	4	0	0	0	4
Total	68	15	10	3	96

Source: DG Competition (2005), Table 5, p. 21.

reasonably, divestitures are associated with horizontal concerns, while access remedies are more likely for vertical concerns. Perhaps more surprising is that access is sometimes used in the case of a horizontal merger. Table 3.4 confirms that single dominance is far more frequently a source of expected harm than is collective dominance. Consequently, the sample of the latter is too small to draw any conclusions with respect to remedy choice.

3.2 COMPETITIVE CONTEXT AND THE STRUCTURAL/BEHAVIOURAL DICHOTOMY

The broad structural/behavioural dichotomy is well entrenched in the literature and policy circles, and there is no strong case for discarding it. However, it is all too often too easy to claim that 'structural remedies are always better than behavioural remedies'. This glib proposition is faulty for two important reasons. First, the competitive context of the remedy is often more important than whether it is structural or behavioural. It is possible, for example, for a structural remedy to do more harm than good. Second, the implementation of an apparently structural remedy may be ineffectual. The former issue is developed in this section and the latter in the next.

A given remedy will not always have the same effect regardless of the competitive context. For example, a given divestment may have very different effects depending on whether the sale is to an existing competitor or an entrant; or the difference may result from a market with the potential for collective dominance as compared with one in which there is a singly dominant firm.[1] In other words, understanding the context of a remedy is more important than attaching a particular label to it.

Aspects of context which may be significant in any case are:

1. Nature of the market and the competitive process: are products homogeneous or differentiated?; nature of technology and cost curve; the distribution of market shares; barriers to entry; vertical linkages and relationships etc.
2. Nature of the merger: characteristics of the merging firms and third parties; is the merger vertical or horizontal?
3. How might the merger affect competition, with and without remedies: unilateral or coordinated effects; what is the scope for subsequent anti-competitive strategic behaviour by the merged firm?

Box 3.1 shows the sort of information on context that it is necessary to have before an informed judgement can be made on likely impact; it is illustrative rather than exhaustive.

BOX 3.1 REMEDIES IN CONTEXT

Divestment

- Nature of assets: tangible or intangible for example, brand names, landing slots?
- Existence of market: current or future (pipeline)?
- Extent of divestment: stand-alone, extensive carve-out, or bundle of assets?
- Relationship between sold and retained assets: same or different horizontal/vertical markets?
- Nature of buyer: incumbent or entrant?
- Any dependence between buyer and seller?

Other structural

- Divestment of shareholdings/directorships: complete or partial; how large were overlaps?
- Joint ventures: extent/dissolution, or JV remains but merged firm withdraws?

Behavioural

Vertical

- Access to essential facilities: no price control, non-discrimination, other price control?
- Bundling?
- Licensing: short or long term? Exclusive or not?
- Termination of other exclusive agreements – by type?

Horizontal price undertakings

- Not to predate?
- Not to price excessively (for example, RPI−X[2])?

Precise nature of information agreements

3.3 INTERPRETING STRUCTURAL/BEHAVIOURAL REMEDIES USING THE 'CLEAN BREAK' CRITERION

The neatest definition of structural/behavioural remedies in the literature reviewed in the previous chapter (Section 2.2) is provided by Motta et al. (2003), who argue that the key distinguishing feature is property rights: structural remedies will entail a change in property rights, while behavioural remedies imply controls on how those property rights are exercised. Another highlighted suggestion was that structural remedies are typically irreversible, while behavioural remedies require *ex post* monitoring and can be modified over time as market conditions change or as new information is received on the effectiveness of the remedy.[3] However, the property rights of some assets are not always clear-cut; and their transfer may be of only limited duration. Examples include: reduced shareholdings and directorships; landing slots; divestment/transfers of brand names; temporary licensing or transfer of brand names; and licensing.

Indeed, the dichotomy may be characterized in other similar, but not identical, ways. For example:

- Structural remedies typically create a new player in the market, or at least materially increase the market share of an incumbent, while behavioural remedies at best give the opportunity for smaller firms or entrants to compete more effectively.
- Behavioural remedies may be modelled as an attempt by the competition authority to influence marginal costs (for example, access prices), while structural remedies affect fixed costs.
- Structural remedies attempt to influence competition by changing the structure of the market, while behavioural remedies leave structure unchanged and operate on the conduct of firms (this is probably the closest to the original SCP conceptualization).

Each of these approaches provides some insights. However, as a practical guide to policy, we suggest that one of the most important characteristics of a remedy is identified by asking: 'Does the remedy impose a "clean break" from pre-merger to post-merger?'

A clean break remedy should not create relationships between the merged firm and other market players (including upstream, downstream and horizontal); or a regulator. Clean break remedies are naturally associated with structural remedies. Divestments, requirements to reduce/remove shareholding/directorships and to disband JVs can all be 'clean breaks'. Equally, the implementation and monitoring of behavioural remedies typically create relationships that continue post-remedy. More importantly, the clean break principle can be used to clarify cases that are difficult to classify.

A good test case is licensing remedies.[4] These may differ from case to case in a number of different dimensions:

- Exclusive or non-exclusive (that is, undertakings to provide universal access by third parties to license post-merger, as opposed to undertakings to provide a specific competitor with access to a unique licence).
- Geographical reach: is the remedy confined to just some, or all, member states?
- Duration: is access indefinite, or for a finite period of time?
- Are access payments a one-off or are there ongoing royalties?
- Does the licence relate to ongoing research, or to a technology to be incorporated in a commercial product?
- Relatedly, does it refer to a process or product?

Consider, for example, payments associated with a licence. Any remedy entailing a one-off payment would be structural, as opposed to 'behavioural' royalty payments which provide an ongoing financial relationship between firms and can be used to influence marginal costs. Similarly, indefinite access is a clean break, but a short-term licence would not be. In between, access for only a finite number of years remains a grey area. A practical distinction might be possible by identifying a duration long enough for firms to plan significant subsequent investment strategies or, where relevant, when a patent runs out.

The clean break principle will not always correspond exactly to the conventional structural/behavioural dichotomy. For example, even a divestiture, with full transfer of property rights for an indefinite duration, will not imply a clean break if the buyer of the divested assets is still dependent on the merging parties for key supplies in the future. The importance of the clean break principle is that it focuses attention on an important aspect of a remedy that simple classification would fail to pick up.

3.4 CONCLUSIONS

We accept the standard structural/behavioural dichotomy as a helpful starting point for categorizing remedies. However, we do not agree that a structural remedy is necessarily better than a behavioural remedy, though it often will be. We argue that the central issue is to form a view of how the remedy is expected to affect the competitive process, once it is imposed. Because of this, remedies – however they are labelled – should always be examined on a case-by-case basis, in the context of the particular market and merger in which they are agreed. The detail of any remedy is crucial. In that respect, the 'clean break' principle should prove helpful.

NOTES

1. See, for example, Compte et al. (2002), who argue that the outcome of the Nestlé/Perrier merger remedies might be coordinated, as opposed to unilateral, effects – depending on the identity of the buyer of the divested assets.
2. This is where the parties are required not to raise the price by more than the general increase in prices (for example, the retail price index) minus an allowance (set by the regulator) for anticipated cost reductions due to technical progress. This approach was pioneered in the UK in the context of regulation of previously nationalized firms, but it has also been used by the competition authorities; see Clarke et al. (1998, ch. 5).
3. Here, we should stress the word 'typically'. We admit that some divestments, for example, may be reversible: the Commission informs us that firms can request either to buy back or to be discharged from remedies in certain circumstances.
4. The treatment of brand names and copyright is analogous.

4. Methodology for assessment of mergers and remedies

4.0 INTRODUCTION

The purpose of this chapter is to introduce our proposed methodology for assessing the efficacy of merger remedies: 'basic' simulation founded in oligopoly theory.

We start from the position that any remedy should be assessed in terms of how far it succeeds in restoring the market to a level of competition equivalent to that existing before the merger. This requires an understanding of: (a) the pre-merger nature of competition; (b) what would have happened post-merger, had the remedy not been imposed; and (c) what can be expected to happen post-remedy. The initial finding of an adverse effect of the merger is based on comparison of (b) with (a). Remedy appraisal is associated with a comparison of (c) with (b). We argue that these alternative outcomes are best identified by simulation of the market.[1] The *ex ante* efficacy of a remedy can be judged by the extent to which it yields an outcome that is at least as good as pre-merger.

We begin with an informal description of the basic idea. The essence of the methodology is as follows. Faced with any merger and proposed remedy, one first forms an opinion of the nature of competition in the market concerned. This is then formalized into a relevant oligopoly model. The analytical implications of the merger are then derived within the model – both with and without remedies. In order to quantify those implications, one needs to calibrate (that is, attribute numerical values to) certain key parameters, most notably: market shares; demand elasticities; and claimed efficiency savings. Thus simulation requires both formal theoretical analysis and a practical reading of market conditions.

We believe that this process of simulation of remedies fits naturally into the analysis that any CA should undertake anyway when assessing a proposed merger. Either implicitly, or, it is hoped, explicitly, the authority must form an impression of how the merger might lead to a lessening of competition in the markets concerned. In this context, the process of constructing a simulation model serves as a beneficial discipline on the case team in how they think competition would be affected by an unremedied merger. Even without completing any simulations, the methodology would still force the case team to ask the 'right questions'; for example, to quantify the relevant demand elasticities. Beyond this, using simulation to appraise alternative candidate remedies provides a very natural link between the competitive harm and remedy.

As we shall argue later, full-blown simulation methods are typically very expensive and time-intensive to implement. It is for this reason that we advocate more basic simulation, using simplified methods. This makes the methodology eminently practicable even within the constraints of a Phase I case, where the pressure on time can be intense.[2]

In principle, this methodology can be applied to all cases – so long as the analyst is able to identify an appropriate oligopoly model which is determinate in its predictions, and where the key parameters are amenable to calibration. However, these conditions will not always be met. As a generalization, it tends to be easier to model structural remedies (as long as they provide a 'clean break' in the sense we have defined in Chapter 3) because they can usually be reduced to comparing the impacts of different structures within a given oligopoly game. Behavioural remedies will typically involve more judgement because they affect, sometimes in an unpredictable way, firms' behaviour and therefore the very nature of the oligopoly game. Because they do not involve a clean break, one-off change, they may also introduce an additional layer of strategic behaviour. Moreover, some types of merger will be difficult to model because oligopoly theory does not provide precise predictions. As explained in Section 4.5, vertical mergers are an example where existing theory is rather less certain.

We do not pretend that simulation, especially what we call basic simulation, is a well-developed science; too much judgement and uncertainty are involved to make such a claim. Ultimately, however, the benefits of simulation must be compared with what is the current practice. In its decisions, the Commission's reasoning starts from an analysis of market shares as the primary quantification of market power. Although many other factors may be taken into account, this focus on market shares inevitably leads to a preference for remedies that eliminate market share overlaps if there is expected to be a significant impediment to effective competition. In nearly all the cases we look at in detail in this book, this means that the remedy is equivalent to 'prohibition within the market'[3] if combined market share would exceed 40 per cent. Although such divestitures are categorized as a remedy short of prohibition, this is only because the merging parties are diversified across a number of relevant markets. In principle, simulations can distinguish the competition effects of partial divestiture (for example, to take the merger just below the 40 per cent threshold), although this also raises important questions about the viability of a carved-out business.

The remainder of the chapter develops these opening remarks. First, and because the simulation methods we advocate are based on formal oligopoly models, Section 4.1 provides a brief targeted summary of the relevant parts of the existing academic literature on oligopoly theory. Section 4.2 then explains the basics of simulating mergers, and Section 4.3 describes some of the 'basic' methods currently available. The following three Sections, 4.4–4.6, turn to the specific task in hand – simulation of remedies. Section 4.4 explains how simulation of alternative equilibria is used to assess the effects of different remedies; Section 4.5 identifies which types of merger and remedies are most, and which are least, likely to be suited to this methodology; and Section 4.6 proposes a practical checklist that can be applied to collate the various data required for identifying and calibrating an appropriate model.

4.1 OLIGOPOLY THEORY AND THE EQUILIBRIUM ANALYSIS OF MERGERS

This section highlights those parts of oligopoly theory that are most relevant to the simulation methodology when applied to mergers.

4.1.1 The Basics[4]

A convenient reference point is to start with the structure–conduct–performance (SCP) paradigm for oligopolistic behaviour. Broadly speaking, within this traditional paradigm, the main concern was that a merger, leading to increased concentration, would raise the chances of collusion – what we now refer to as coordinated effects. This was enshrined in the original US merger guidelines with their structural emphasis on market shares and concentration.

Over the last 20 years, however, the emphasis in the literature has switched to unilateral effects. A unilateral effect occurs without a qualitative change in behaviour, but as a consequence of individual firms choosing to revise their price/output/product positioning etc. choices as a consequence of the post-merger market structure of the industry. It will occur even without any change in the mode of conduct, since equilibrium price(s) will typically change post-merger.

The catalyst for deeper reflection on the unilateral effects of mergers was a paper by Salant et al. (1983), which showed that under certain restrictive assumptions, mergers were typically unprofitable for the merging parties. These assumptions were (1) Cournot behaviour (firms setting output to maximize their profits, taking as given the output decisions of their rivals);

(2) homogeneous product; (3) symmetric firms, (4) constant marginal costs; (5) not merger to monopoly, and (6) no efficiency effects from the merger. This result is often referred to as the 'merger paradox'. With hindsight, it is not this headline result that was so significant – others quickly established how the merger paradox could be overturned by modifying the assumptions. What was more influential was the understanding it provided on *why* a merger might be unprofitable for the interested parties – in particular, the behaviour of the non-merging firms (the outsiders). More specifically, in the Cournot equilibrium after the merger, the insiders will choose to contract their output (that is, the merged firms supply less post-merger than the sum of their outputs pre-merger). In itself, this would raise price and the merged firm's profits. However, in response, the outsiders choose to *increase* their output, thereby ameliorating the price increase – and typically this leads to lower profits for the merged firm (and higher profits for the outsiders).

This literature was taken forward significantly by Farrell and Shapiro (1990). Generalizing by extending the model to asymmetric firms, they established a number of important results. Crucially, they showed that unless the merger leads to cost savings (and/or entry), it must result in increased price. Moreover, even where there are cost savings, these need to be very significant if they are to offset the forces working towards an increased price. Thus, typically, consumer welfare will fall. However, this is not to say that aggregate welfare (that is, the sum of consumer and producer surplus) will necessarily fall, because the realignment of market shares following the merger may lead to a higher proportion of industry supply now in the hands of low-cost firms. In turn, this leads to various predictions about welfare enhancement in terms of the market shares of both the merging and non-merging firms. For example, if the non-merging firms are relatively more efficient, then the reallocation of output post-merger will lead to a lower weighted average marginal cost, and thus higher producer surplus. Given that more efficient firms have larger market shares in the Cournot model, it is more likely that aggregate welfare will increase the smaller are the market shares of the merging firms, and the more concentrated are the non-merging firms.

Subsequent work on homogeneous products has explored the conditions under which a merger may yet be profitable for the merging firms. Much depends on the ability of outsiders to expand output post-merger. For example, if outsiders are capacity constrained, then they will be unable to increase their output post-merger and the price raising effects will be higher.[5]

One further issue is worth highlighting. Because we can expect firms to be, at least approximately, maximizing profits, this offers a degree of freedom in data collection. In other words, it makes up for the lack of data on one apparently crucial parameter. This can be illustrated in a very simple example. If the pre-merger market is thought to be well characterized by a Cournot model with N firms each having identical marginal costs, c, the equilibrium price–cost margin (that is, the result of profit-maximizing behaviour) is

$$[p - c]/p = 1/Ne, \tag{4.1}$$

where e is the industry elasticity of demand and p is market price. First, suppose we have data only on p, N and c, then e can be estimated by rearranging this profit-maximizing (equilibrium) margin condition to give

$$1/e = N[p - c]/p. \tag{4.2}$$

Alternatively, if an independent estimate of e is available, but marginal costs are hard to measure, we can rearrange the same condition to provide the estimate:

$$c = p[1 - (1/Ne)]. \tag{4.3}$$

This technique is used widely in simulation models. The implied estimates can then be used in the equilibrium margin equation to predict what will happen post-merger (that is, when N falls to $N - 1$).

4.1.2 Product Differentiation

Most research in recent years has been directed towards mergers in markets characterized by product differentiation. In this context, it is more sensible to think of firms as price setters (rather than the output-setting firms that all supply the same good at a single price in the Cournot model), and the literature has tended to work within a Bertrand (price-setting) framework. Another early paper, Deneckere and Davidson (1985), established two important results: (1) without cost savings or entry, the merger must lead to a price increase, but (2) in this case, the non-participants also raise their prices. The first is consistent with the above Cournot result, but the second underlines an important difference between Cournot and Bertrand models: the outputs of merging and non-merging firms move in opposite directions (best response functions slope downwards) in the former; whereas prices move in the same direction post-merger (best response functions slope upwards) in the latter.

Theory

Broadly speaking, theoretical models of product differentiation can be grouped into three types:

1. In one-dimensional spatial models,[6] competition between brands is local: each firm competes only with immediate neighbours – these are the only non-zero cross-price elasticities.
2. In global models, deriving from Chamberlin's monopolistic competition,[7] all brands compete with each other, with identical cross-price elasticities.
3. Intermediate depictions, for instance, the 'characteristics approach', inspired by Lancaster (1991),[8] allow brands to compete on several dimensions. As the number of characteristics increases, so does the number of neighbours, and competition becomes less local.

Underlying any demand system, there is, at least implicitly, a model of consumer preferences that might give rise to that system. In this respect, models differ in their assumptions about how many brands consumers can purchase – in spatial models, consumers buy only one brand, giving rise to the so-called 'discrete choice' approach. Product variety matters only indirectly in that it allows more consumers to buy their most preferred brand. In global models, consumers are allowed to buy more than one brand each, opening up an individual consumer preference for variety.

Empirical models of product differentiation

In this subsection, we describe five different models that have been used in the empirical literature to estimate demand systems in which there is competition between differentiated brands:

1. Random utility discrete choice model of consumer behaviour
2. Multinomial logit model
3. Nested multinomial logit model
4. Localized spatial models
5. Multi-stage budgeting.

The models differ in their generality and, therefore, their practicability. While we attempt to provide an intuition in each case, the interested reader is referred to the source articles for more detail.

Random utility discrete choice model Probably the most general (that is, making fewest restrictive assumptions) available model is the 'random utility discrete choice model' of consumer behaviour. This makes very explicit the link between consumer preferences and the demand function (Berry, 1994). It also serves as a useful encompassing way to survey some of the standard empirical models.

For consumer *i*, the utility (net of the disutility of price) from buying the particular brand *j* (U_{ij}) is assumed to be a function of the characteristics (vector X_j) of the brand and (negatively) its price (p_j):

$$U_{ij} = b_{ij}X_j - a_{ij}p_j + u_{ij}, \tag{4.4}$$

where *a*, *b* and *u* represent the individual consumer's 'tastes', and the model is general in that these parameters are allowed to vary between consumers.

To illustrate, consider the case of newspapers. Here, the characteristics (the *X* vector) might include: the proportion of the newspaper devoted to sports coverage; the ratio of advertisements to text; the number of photographs, column inches of gossip, cartoons, TV coverage etc. The *b* parameters reflect how much utility the consumer derives from each of those characteristics – the model is general, in that different consumers may differ in how much they value those characteristics (for example, some may like heavy sports coverage while others may not). The *a* parameter reflects the lost utility to the consumer from price, and this is also allowed to vary between consumers – for example, richer consumers will typically lose less than poorer consumers. The disturbance term, *u*, represents the effects of unobserved characteristics and all other factors that would influence the individual consumer's utility from consuming a particular brand.

The consumer selects the brand that yields him/her the highest utility (that is, consumer *i* chooses product *k* where U_{ik} is higher than all other U_{ij}). The taste parameters are assumed to vary randomly across different consumers (hence the term 'random' utility), so different consumers may choose different brands.

In principle, this model could be estimated using data on individual consumers, but in practice, we are usually more interested in estimating the aggregate demand curve. To do this, we need to introduce assumptions about how the taste parameters are distributed across consumers. As a general rule, the assumptions tend to become more specific and restrictive the less rich is the data source at the disposal of the econometrician.

We turn next to two specific models that impose very restrictive assumptions. On the other hand, those restrictions yield much-simplified estimating equations, with much-reduced data requirements.

Special case I: the (multinomial) logit model[9] This is very much the 'base' model, widely used, very easy to estimate, but very restrictive in its assumptions. For clarity, we describe a simplified version.[10] First, we conflate all the characteristics of a given brand into a single parameter, *b*. Second, we assume that all consumers have the same *b* and *a* values, and that only *u* can vary between them. In other words, consumers are still allowed to derive different utilities from a given brand, but variations are captured by including a random disturbance term. Thus the utility function simplifies to

$$U_{ij} = b_j - ap_j + u_{ij}. \qquad (4.5)$$

From this, we can calculate the probability that a given consumer will choose any particular brand. This depends on the *b* and *a* parameters for the brand (and those of all others) and the price of that brand (and all others).

The attractive feature of this simple model comes when we aggregate across all consumers. It can be shown that it generates a particularly simple empirical relationship between the market share gained by a particular brand (s_j) and its own price (p_j), both of which will be directly observable in many real-world cases:

$$\ln(s_j) - \ln(s_0) = b_j - ap_j + u_j \qquad (4.6)$$

Here, 0 refers to an 'outside good' that helps capture the size of the 'potential' market. Consumers who choose not to purchase any of the brands on offer are assumed to purchase the outside good.[11] A huge attraction of equation (4.6) is that parameters *a* and b_j can be estimated from data only on a product's market share and price. These are readily available to any CA.[12]

However, this simplicity is only achieved at a major cost: a key limitation of the logit model is that it imposes a sort of symmetry with respect to all brands (more correctly, substitution is proportionate to market shares). So, for example, if the price of one brand were to rise, the implication is that consumers would switch to other brands in proportion to those other brands' shares of the market. In turn, this means that, if all brands are priced identically and have equal market shares, all cross-price elasticities are identical. Thus, in this model, there are no local neighbours, as in the spatial models. Instead, all brands are equal substitutes for each other (as in Chamberlin-type models). Obviously, it is undesirable to *impose* this property on a demand system; ideally, one would like to test (econometrically or with consumer survey data) whether it appropriate, rather than implicitly assuming so. To return to our case of newspapers, it would imply that, *ceteris paribus*, consumers see two different broadsheets as no more substitutable for each other than a broadsheet and a tabloid.

Special case II: the nested (multinomial) logit This is a slightly more general form of the logit, with less inbuilt symmetry. Here the brands are first classified into groups of 'like brands' (for example, broadsheet and tabloid newspapers, or adult and children's breakfast cereals). The indirect utility function is made slightly more general by allowing for the possibility that a given consumer may have a general preference ordering of those groups, but not so strong that the consumer would always prefer brands from one group to those from other groups, regardless of the price.

In this case, the basic relationship between market share and price still holds, but the estimating equation (4.6) is revised to include an additional variable that identifies the group to which the individual brand belongs. The results from the estimation reveal whether the nesting adds to the explanatory power, because, by estimating a nested logit, one does not rule out the possibility of the special case in which the nests are unimportant, that is, the simple (multinomial) logit.

Relating this back to the localized/global spectrum of product differentiation models, this model allows for intense competition within groups but not necessarily across groups. Thus it is as if the market is populated by a number of families of brands, with stronger localized competition within families, and lesser global competition across families.[13]

Localized spatial models There is a different strand to the empirical literature that is more obviously related to the local competition part of the theory. For instance, Bresnahan's model of vertical differentiation in the car market (1981 and 1987) has a single parameter that reflects brand quality. Here, it follows that each brand competes directly only with its two immediate neighbours in the vertical spectrum. Consumers are located along a taste distribution which is assumed to be uniform. The vertical quality of a brand is assumed to depend (in a very restrictive way) on its observable characteristics, and, as in simple spatial models of horizontal differentiation, the brand competes only with its immediate neighbours. Feenstra and Levinsohn (1995) offer a natural extension of Bresnahan, in that they assume that utility depends on a vector of characteristics, not just a single quality measure.[14] Since there are a number of quality dimensions, brands may compete with more than just two immediate neighbours, but only so long as they share a common market boundary (that is, they are neighbours in at least one of the dimensions of quality). Nevertheless, if brands do not share a boundary, they do not compete.

Multi-stage budgeting In all of the above models, it is assumed that the consumer buys just one brand (if at all). The discrete choice model has been generalized (for example, Hausman et al., 1994; Hausman and Leonard,

1997) to allow consumers to purchase several brands. Their model has three levels of demand for a differentiated product:

- top level, in which consumers decide how much to spend on the product group;
- medium level, in which they allocate aggregate expenditure on the product into broad types/segments; and
- low level, in which they select specific brands within the type.

To continue with our newspaper example, the demand for 'all newspapers' would be the top level; the medium-level sectors might be broadsheets and tabloids; and the brands within the tabloid sector might be, in the UK context, *The Sun*, *Daily Mirror* etc. This is similar to the nested logit, but is more general in that non-symmetry is allowed within groups.

4.2 MERGER SIMULATION

Against this backcloth of theoretical and empirical models, we now explain the rudiments of the merger simulation methodology.

4.2.1 The Rudiments of Merger Simulation

Stage 1: choice of model and derivation of a pre-merger equilibrium for the oligopoly game in the market concerned

Are products homogeneous or differentiated? Do firms act unilaterally or in a coordinated (collusive) way? If products are indeed differentiated, are they symmetrically so, or is competition more localized?[15] This stage requires the choice of a particular model of differentiation, for example, logit versus nested logit.

Stage 2: calibration of the model's parameters

It is necessary to attach specific numerical values to the parameters of the model. These will sometimes be derived from direct observation (for example, existing market shares, prices and extraneous estimates of demand elasticities). In other contexts, it may be necessary to undertake full-blown econometric estimation of the demand system in order to derive estimates of those parameters. By substitution of these 'known' parameters into the equilibrium conditions derived in stage 1, one can then recover (that is, solve for) other, unknown, parameters.[16] In some cases these unknowns might be the firms' marginal costs; in others they might be parameters that summarize the extent of 'market power'.[17]

Stage 3: simulation of the post-merger equilibrium

The equilibrium is recomputed, using the calibrated parameters, but now allowing up to three things to change: (1) coordination in the price setting of the brands of the newly merged firm; (2) any claimed synergy effects (for example, reductions in the marginal costs of the merged firm); (3) reactions by outsiders (that is, competitors).[18] In principle, one might also simulate a switch in the prevailing behaviour of firms as a consequence of the merger; for example, if it is suspected that the merger would result in a coordinated effect between merging and non-merging firms, one could compute alternative collusive post-merger equilibria. Rather more difficult are the possibilities that firms might want to reposition their products, or where the potential for new entry becomes important.

4.2.2 Examples of Merger Simulation in Practice

Simulation by the US authorities

Simulation is often used by the US authorities, and they are clearly in the vanguard of this technology. Many examples are not in the public domain, but probably the best-known, and most widely cited, case is the proposed (but actually blocked) merger between Interstate Bakeries and Continental Baking (reported and discussed by Shapiro, 1995). This involved brands of bread, and copious scanning data were available. In this case, simulations suggested price increases of between 5 per cent and 15 per cent in the Los Angeles and Chicago areas. Two other well-known cases are Van de Kamp's acquisition of Mrs Paul's and L'Oréal's acquisition of Maybelline. Shapiro also confirms that simulation is commonly used by the Antitrust Division's economists. He cites two other examples: the Gillette pens case (1993) involving potential substitution between pens, ball-point pens etc, and the proposed cereals merger between Kraft and Nabisco.[19] Outside of the public domain, Greg Werden of the DoJ presented a two-day workshop to the UK CAs (29–30 April 2003, DTI Conference Centre, London), at which he presented verbally a wide range of theoretical models he has employed in practice. Broadly speaking, these are as follows:

- Homogeneous products
  - Dominant firm, with a competitive fringe
  - Cournot without capacity constraints (constant marginal costs)
  - Cournot with capacity constraints (constant marginal costs up to capacity constraint)
- Differentiated products
  - Logit model
  - Nested logit model

Two illustrative examples from the academic literature

Nevo (2000): mergers with differentiated products, US ready-to-eat breakfast cereals This study covers the period 1988–96 and pays particular attention to the econometric estimation of product differentiation parameters in the most general model possible. The industry is highly concentrated, with the top three firms, Kellogg, General Mills and Post, accounting for about three-quarters of the market, which comprises about 200 brands. All leading firms are multi-brand, and this, in itself, has led to antitrust concerns over a number of years. The market is clearly characterized by differentiation between brands. During this period, there were a number of significant mergers, notably (Post's owner) Kraft's acquisition of Nabisco's cereal lines in 1992. Amongst other things, the purpose of Nevo's article is to evaluate the effects of this merger.

To estimate the demand system, Nevo used scanner data on retail prices and quantities, as routinely collected by supermarkets and retail stores. The database covers 24 different brands in 45 cities over 20 quarterly periods. In terms of the variance of price, inter-brand differences account for the largest proportion (revealing a wide range of brands included), and the variance across cities is rather greater than that across time.[20]

On the demand side, Nevo employs a random utility discrete choice model of consumer behaviour, as in Section 4.1.2 above. The utility that a consumer is assumed to derive from a particular brand of breakfast cereal is determined by a set of characteristics such as calories, sodium and fibre content, etc. The consumer then chooses the brand that offers the maximum utility net of price. While the actual characteristics offered by any particular brand are identical for all consumers, the consumers are allowed to have different preferences for those characteristics.[21] Of course, preferences for characteristics by individual consumers are not observable, so assumptions are required for the general way in which they will vary across consumers. These assumptions also allow estimation at the aggregate market level. The unobserved components are modelled by assuming that they may vary between brands and over time (captured by time and brand-segment dummy variables).

This leads to a demand model in which the explanatory variables include the characteristics mentioned above, dummy variables representing the broad segment of the market in which the brand lies ('all-family', 'kids', 'adult'), and time dummy variables. The econometric model also provides estimates of the extent of variability across consumers in tastes and importance attached to price. In effect, this model amounts to a more general and flexible form of the nested logit. As always with models of this type, there are econometric issues of identification and simultaneous bias. As such, it is essential to have access to sensible instrumental variables. In this case, Nevo exploits the independence of markets in geographical space to good effect (ibid., p. 405).[22]

The model generates estimates of the own-price and cross-price elasticities of brands – most own-price elasticities are in the range −1.5 to −2.2, while cross-price elasticities vary considerably in the range 0 to 0.5. In contrast to the logit, or even the nested logit, this model leaves it to the data to tell us which brands are close, and which are distant, substitutes.

Of course, estimation of demand equations is not the ultimate purpose: they are required as an input into the simulation of the effects of mergers. To complete the analysis, he therefore needs a model of the oligopoly game. He assumes that firms compete non-cooperatively in a one-shot Bertrand game (in other words, they choose price to maximize their own profits, taking the prices of rivals as given). The first-order conditions imply, for each brand, a relationship between the price–cost margin and market share. This relationship involves demand elasticities, which have now been estimated in the demand system. Therefore, by substituting these into the first-order condition, it is possible to estimate the (unknown) marginal costs of each brand.

Armed now with estimates of marginal costs on the one hand and the parameters of the demand system on the other hand, Nevo turns to simulating the hypothetical post-merger equilibrium. In every respect but one, this will be identical to the pre-merger situation. The difference is, of course, that the prices of the brands now under the single ownership of the newly merged firm are set, not in competition with each other, but in coordination so as to maximize the joint profits generated by those brands. In turn, outsider firms will also want to adjust their prices.

The simulated price increases following the Kraft (Post) acquisition of Nabisco are 3.1 per cent for Nabisco's Shredded Wheat and 1.5 per cent for Post's Grape Nuts. These estimates are based on various assumptions about the post-merger equilibrium: (1) no change in costs; (2) no change in the nature of the oligopoly game (that is, no coordinated effects); and (3) no change in marketing strategies (for example, product repositioning and/or increases in advertising). The last assumption is, of course, debatable in an industry such as breakfast cereals, although it might be a reasonable approximation in the short run (perhaps the one or two years following the merger).

Ivaldi and Verboven (2005): mergers with differentiated products, the EU truck market[23] More briefly, this is a study of the proposed merger between Volvo and Scania in 1999. It assumes a geographically segmented (by national boundaries) European market, in which two distinct parts of the product market are identified. The model of demand used is a nested logit, extended for multi-brand firms. The demand system is estimated using a panel of two years for 16 countries. Assuming non-cooperative Bertrand pricing before and after the merger, they estimate that Volvo and Scania would have raised their prices by more than 10 per cent in several countries (particularly Scandinavia and Ireland). Outside firms would also raise price, but usually by not much (typically less than 1 per cent). Against this backcloth, the authors then consider what synergies would be necessary to offset these price increases: if the merger led to reductions of 5 per cent in costs, this would remove the price increase in eight of the 16 countries. In practice, this paper is a fairly conventional application of nested logit, albeit with a novel feature: it includes a simulation of what would have happened, had the EC agreed to the merger, and if this had led to subsequent mergers by other leading players in the market.

4.3 'BASIC' SIMULATION

The advocates of simulation often stress the increased accessibility of these techniques, given the speed of present computing technology. Considerable developments have indeed been made, conceptually as well as logistically. Nevertheless, simulations of the type conducted by Nevo or Ivaldi and Verboven are both data- and time-intensive, calling for high technical competence in economic and econometric modelling. As Nevo (2000, p. 396) explains: 'The analysis was performed without time pressure and using (almost) ideal pre-merger data. Time and data constraints might limit the ability to perform this analysis in real time.'

This does not deny the value of in-depth (or what we shall call 'full-blown') simulation models in the context of specific merger investigations. But in the context of this book, exploring a methodology that might be applied across the board in a potentially comprehensive assessment of the efficacy of remedies over a large number of different mergers is clearly too time- and cost-demanding.

As such, there is a case for developing simple versions of simulation, which might be applied much more quickly, and with less demanding data requirements, to generate approximate ball-park magnitudes. Here we describe three examples, each of which will be applied in our later case studies:

- Homogeneous products
- Product differentiation: the diversion ratio
- Proportionality-calibrated almost ideal demand system (PCAIDS).

4.3.1 Homogeneous Products

Given a genuinely homogeneous product, there is only one price, and one price elasticity. Using a standard linear Cournot quantity-setting model, it is easy to derive an equilibrium ratio between the price–cost margin, the market elasticity and market share (at the firm level) or the Herfindahl index (at the industry level). Absent capacity constraints, simple algebraic manipulation of the equilibria pre- and post-merger derives an expression for the change in price which depends only on the number of firms, elasticity and market share (or margin) of the acquired firm. Assuming market shares (or margins) and numbers are observable, simulation requires only an estimate (or expert opinion) of the elasticity. In algebraic modelling terms, things are a little less straightforward when firms are capacity-constrained, but the mechanics of the simulation remain straightforward.

Davies and Majumdar (2002, pp. 101–6) present an example case study of simulating mergers in homogeneous product industries (flour), and one of the paper case study mergers later in this book (Chapter 6) provides another example.[24]

4.3.2 Product Differentiation: the Diversion Ratio

The diversion ratio is the basic approach to simulating the effects of a merger between firms producing differentiated products. It is described by Shapiro (1995) in his address to the American Bar Association. Having discussed the very detailed work which was possible in the Interstate Bakeries/Continental Baking Co. case, mentioned above, he goes on to explain: 'The reality is that data are rarely available to do this type of full-blown simulation analysis with assurance . . . [but there are still] . . . some rough and ready quantitative procedures that can be used when hard data are scarce.' These can be explained in terms of the following four-step procedure (where A and B are two merging brands):

1. Estimate what fraction of Brand A's sales would be captured by Brand B, following an increase in the price of Brand A. Call this the diversion ratio.[25] Shapiro's preferred methods (in descending order) for estimating the diversion ratio are econometric estimation of elasticities, consumer survey data, and company, or other, documents concerning consumers' first and second brand choices. If all else fails, market shares might be helpful.
2. Use the estimated diversion ratio, along with pre-merger margins, to give a rough prediction of post-merger prices, absent cost savings or rival response.

3. Try to anticipate product repositioning and entry. Here, the history of brand entry, exit and repositioning might be helpful.
4. Allow for any genuine cost savings likely to ensue, but only conceding those that are truly merger-specific and marginal cost-reducing.

Not much can be said, in general, about steps 3 and 4, as they will be very case-specific. But on steps 1 and 2, he offers the following basic approach.

Assuming that the elasticity of demand is constant, the firms are single-brand, and the two are symmetric in terms of pre-merger market shares and mark-ups, it can easily be shown (see Box 4.1) that the profit-maximizing proportionate price increase resulting from the merger is:

$$(p^*-p)/p = mD/(1-m-D), \tag{4.7}$$

where p^* and p are post- and pre-merger prices respectively, m is the pre-merger mark-up, and D is the diversion ratio.

BOX 4.1 PROOF OF EQUATION (4.7)

A profit-maximizing firm facing its own demand curve which has an elasticity of e will set a price–cost margin, given by

$$m = (p - c)/p = 1/e.$$

Consider the reasons why demand for the brand declines if the firm raises price: some consumers leave the market altogether, but some (most?) will switch to other brands, assuming that there are close substitutes. Now consider the demand relationship between two brands, A and B, which are produced by two firms that are about to be merged. Suppose that, when the price of A is raised, a fraction, D, of the lost demand is diverted to Brand B. It follows that, once the firms merge, and A and B are priced in a parallel way, this part of the market for A will no longer be lost as the price of A is raised. So instead of demand falling by e per cent following a price rise for A, post-merger it will only fall by $e(1-D)$ per cent.

Thus, assuming no change in costs, the post-merger margin is given by:

$$m^* = (p^*-c)/p^* = 1/(1-D)e.$$

Combining the two expressions, substituting out for c, and rearranging gives:

$$(p^* - p)/p = D/\{e(1 - D) - 1\},$$

and substituting $1/m$ for e gives:

$$(p^* - p)/p = mD/\{1 - m - D\}$$

The intuition behind this result is that the effective elasticity faced by each brand post-merger has decreased because the prices of A and B will now be coordinated to remove competition between the two brands. Where D is low, the brands are not seen as alternatives by consumers, and the effect will be negligible; but where D is high, a significant amount of switching is avoided by raising the two prices in tandem. For example, suppose the pre-merger mark-up is 40 per cent, and the diversion ratio is 0.2: it will be optimal for the firm to raise price by 20 per cent (because the effective elasticity has changed from 2.5 to 2).

If one is prepared to make additional assumptions about the nature of differentiation, there is a simple way of linking the diversion ratio to observed market shares. In particular, suppose (1) that the dominant reason why firms face downward-sloping demand for their brands is competition between brands (that is, when the price of a brand is raised, nearly all the lost custom is because consumers switch to other brands, rather than leaving the market altogether), and (2) that all brands within a given market or sub-market are equally close or distant substitutes for each other. In these special circumstances, one can approximate the diversion ratio from A to B by the proportion of demand for non-A brands accounted for by B. Thus, if A has a market share of 50 per cent and B 25 per cent, $D = 0.5$. In other words, if the price rise of Brand A persuades a consumer to switch to another brand, there is a 50 per cent chance that he will choose Brand B (because B already accounts for 50 per cent of all consumers who currently prefer another brand to A).

In effect, this is the proportionality assumption implicit in the logit model. Just as for the logit, it will underestimate diversion to the extent that A and B are closer than average substitutes, while overestimating it to the extent that they are weaker than average substitutes and/or some consumers would leave the market entirely following a rise in price of their favourite brand. Nevertheless, it provides a ball-park figure around which to discuss relative preferences.

As an illustration of how this works out in a particular case, let us return to the Post acquisition of Nabisco analysed by Nevo above. In this case, at the time of the merger, the firms' market shares were in the regions of 11 per cent and 3 per cent respectively, so Post accounted for 11/97 = 11.3 per cent of the non-Nabisco share of the market, and Nabisco accounted for 3/89 = 3.4 per cent of the non-Post share of the market.

We have no direct evidence on margins in this case, but Nevo does impute and report marginal costs, from which we can derive estimated pre-merger price–cost margins for Shredded Wheat and Grape Nuts (the two brands which were, apparently, the closest substitutes). Depending on the exact form of Nevo's model we use, these computed margins are either 0.22 or 0.39 for Shredded Wheat and 0.26 or 0.44 for Grape Nuts. For illustrative purposes, we shall use the lower estimates.

Substituting these estimates of m and D into (4.5), we have, for Shredded Wheat, $D = 0.113$ and $m = 0.219$, yielding a predicted price increase of 3.7 per cent. For Post, $D = 0.034$ and $m = 0.258$, and the predicted price increase would be 1.2 per cent. Interestingly, although Shapiro's basic diversion ratio model clearly relies on a number of questionable and restrictive assumptions (see above), in this particular case it yields estimated price increases that are remarkably close to Nevo's own estimates from a much more sophisticated and general model, namely 3.1 per cent and 1.5 per cent respectively.

A second illustration is less encouraging. This comes from Hausman and Leonard's paper (1997), applying the multi-stage budgeting model (see above) to the Kimberly-Clark/Scott merger in paper tissues. As it happens, this is one of our Chapter 6 case studies, but in a European context. For the USA, they predict low post-merger price increases, including 2.4 per cent for Kleenex. According to LECG (OFT, 1999), when the Shapiro formula is applied to the data in this case, it predicts a much larger increase of 12.7 per cent. LECG concludes: 'the use of diversion analysis to simulate price increases resulting from mergers can lead to very biased results when the products in the market are not perceived by consumers as equally substitutable' (p. 101).

This is a classic example of the sort of problem that can arise with the proportionality assumption in the diversion ratio. As with the logit model, it imposes an assumption that all goods are equally differentiated – equally 'distant' from each other. However, the formula can be very misleading if A and B are not close substitutes because even if B has a large market share, there may be little incentive to increase price post-merger. The multi-stage budgeting model is more flexible and so is better placed to allow cross-elasticities to differ. Of course, this interpretation rests on the premise that Hausman and Leonard's model has correctly estimated the 'true' values of the elasticities, and this itself may or may not be so. Nevertheless, the example does illustrate the potential danger in applying the formula without any regard for the nature of the brands concerned.

4.3.3 PCAIDS (Proportionality-Calibrated Almost Ideal Demand System)

This provides a simple alternative approach to the diversion ratio for differentiated product industries. In some ways, it is wrong to describe PCAIDS as a simple approach, since it derives from a sophisticated demand system known as AIDS (almost ideal demand system). On the other hand, readily accessible software enables the practitioner to use it with minimal data requirements and in a matter of minutes. Thus it is a serious candidate for our purposes because it is remarkably modest in its demands on time and data.

A clear exposition is provided by Epstein and Rubinfeld (2002), so here we summarize only briefly. In the traditional AIDS model, a demand system that covers all brands in a market can be written as a set of equations, where the market share for any brand depends on the price of that brand and the prices of all other brands in the market. This model is general in that it makes no assumptions about which brands are close substitutes, and which are not. Therefore it encompasses both local and global competition. However, a major problem with AIDS in this context is that it includes a very large number of unknown parameters (corresponding to all the brands' own-price elasticities and the cross-price elasticities between brands). The full model can only be implemented econometrically, which would require access to large quantities of data.

Proportionality-calibrated AIDS (PCAIDS) is a highly simplified form of AIDS, in which various restrictions are imposed on the relative values of key parameters in order to make the model tractable with fewer data. Some of these restrictions are fairly conventional, often made in the traditional AIDS literature, and uncontroversial in this context. However, one assumption is unconventional: that of proportionality. This is similar to the proportionality assumptions underpinning both the diversion ratio, above, and the logit model: 'the share lost as a result of a price increase is allocated to the other firms in the relevant market in proportion to their relative shares'.

If one is prepared to accept this proportionality assumption, Epstein and Rubinfeld show that all that is required to predict the effect of a merger on price is information on (1) the aggregate market price elasticity of demand, (2) the own-price elasticity of any one brand, and (3) market shares. These can be inserted into a user-friendly Excel spreadsheet (provided on request by Epstein and Rubinfeld). The software also reports the implied own-price and cross-price elasticities of all brands. These provide a useful reality check. Importantly, one also has the option to investigate the impact of efficiency savings, and to modify the model by introducing nesting structures which loosen the proportionality assumption between groups of brands.

The upside of this model is its ease of use; the downside is similar to that of the logit (or nested logit) and diversion ratio. The proportionality assumption has come in for criticism from various quarters.[26] Although the option to nest is a partial answer to this critique, it undoubtedly relies on the judgement of the practitioner.

A major advantage of PCAIDS over the simple diversion ratio is that it considers the effects of the merger not just on the prices of the merging parties, but on all brands in the market. Metaphorically speaking, one might think of it as a general equilibrium, rather than partial equilibrium, approach. We employ PCAIDS in a number of the case studies that follow.

4.4 SIMULATING REMEDIES

Simulation of merger remedies, as opposed to the mergers themselves, has attracted little attention in the existing literature, but much of the above discussion carries over.[27] In principle, simulating a merger with remedy is similar to simulating a merger: one must first form an opinion on the nature of competition in the market before modelling how the merger (and now also remedy) may change things. However, this is not to deny that remedies introduce additional potential sources of error into the simulation: (1) divestments can usually be modelled by changing the structure (market shares) in the industry, but it is less clear how behavioural remedies will affect behaviour; and (2) the process of asset transfer and change of ownership may affect costs in difficult-to-predict ways.

The basic idea is simple. We are interested in at least three and possibly more equilibria:

1. Pre-merger
2. Post-merger without remedies
3. Post-merger with remedies
4. Post-merger with alternative remedies (if applicable).

4.4.1 The *Ex Ante*/*Ex Post* distinction

In a retrospective study such as the one we are conducting, (1) and (3) are actual market outcomes, for which information is (in principle) available. (2) and (4) are hypothetical outcomes, which were never observed. However, the nature of merger appraisal by the European Commission is inevitably *ex ante*, so (3) remains hypothetical at the time of the decision. For this reason, much of the emphasis in the following chapters is on *ex ante* evaluation. Of course, (4) is always hypothetical, but of interest in order to appraise whether the chosen remedies might have been improved upon. Note that as far as a simulation is concerned, a prohibition is the same as (1) – the *status quo*.

Having calibrated the simulation model using information observed from the *status quo*, the chosen model allows us to simulate (2), to assess whether the merger without remedy would have led to a substantial impediment to effective competition, and (3) whether the proposed remedy should be expected to eliminate this impediment.

Prohibition turns out to be more important in our case studies than we had originally anticipated. While none of our cases entailed outright prohibition of the merger as a whole, the agreed remedy much more often amounts to what we shall call 'prohibition within the market'. By this, we mean that the merged firm was required to divest, *entirely*, all the assets of one of the parties in a particular geographical or product market. In these cases, if the buyer of the divested assets was previously non-active in that market, the divestment effectively leaves the market structure, in terms of market shares, exactly as it was pre-merger (although there has been a change in the ownership of the divested assets). It is as if the merger was prohibited *in that particular market*. Therefore, unless we have reason to believe that the change in ownership will have some predictable impact on the performance of the divested assets, the 'simulation' of the merger with remedy is no more than assuming the pre-merger *status quo* in that particular market. In other words, for prohibition within the market, (3) is identical to (1).

Ex post evaluation is less straightforward. Realistically, in the period elapsing since a merger, other things will have changed in the market. These changes may be 'endogenous' (resulting directly or indirectly from the merger and/or remedy), or they may be 'exogenous' (unrelated to the merger and possibly unanticipated at the time of the Commission's decision). Examples of exogenous events include the unrelated entry of a major new competitor or unanticipated down-/upturns in demand, cost changes, etc.[28] Such problems do not afflict our *ex ante* appraisal, because we wish to conduct the *ex ante* assessments exactly as if they were undertaken at the time of the original merger decisions. For these simulations, then, we rely almost exclusively on the information reported in the confidential versions of the original Commission decision, supplemented by documents made available to us and to which the investigation had access at the time.[29]

On the other hand, our *ex post* assessments have benefited from the simultaneous, but independent, *ex post* survey of merger remedies undertaken by DG Competition (2005) and summarized in Chapter 2 above. This entailed interview/questionnaire answers from various parties (the merged firm, buyers of divested assets, etc.) for a large number of cases, drawn from across the industrial spectrum, but including five mergers in pharmaceuticals and one in paper, which we therefore included in our own case studies in Chapters 6 and 8 below.[30] Alongside our simulations and the necessary background work done to develop them, the qualitative and quantitative information provided by DG Competition have given us a rich source on which to base our *ex post* evaluations, especially in pharmaceuticals.

4.5 SOME LIMITATIONS OF MERGER AND REMEDY SIMULATION

The general 'pros' and 'cons' of merger simulation have been widely discussed, especially in the policy literature.[31] Moreover, some of the strengths and weaknesses of the methodology when applied to merger remedies will be illustrated in the case studies of Chapters 6 and 8. An overview is included in Chapter 9. Necessarily, however, these case studies constitute only a very small sample of the population, and before becoming too embroiled in the specific detail of particular cases, we make the following general observations.

4.5.1 Type of Merger

As mentioned in the introduction to this chapter, a necessary condition for simulating any merger and/or remedy is that one should be able to capture the main features of the market in an appropriate oligopoly model. Where existing oligopoly theory is incomplete or unconvincing, simulation will be speculative.

Horizontal mergers and horizontal divestiture are relatively straightforward to model – at least the basic techniques for modelling a merger are now well known (see above). If it is reasonable to assume that prevailing market conduct does not differ pre- and post-merger, simulation is tantamount to comparative statics (that is, comparing the impacts of different structures within a given oligopoly game). If it is feared that merger without remedy might result in coordinated effects, this can be modelled by comparing a collusive outcome with the non-cooperative outcome.

Modelling *vertical mergers* presents rather more problems, because economic theory is less settled on their competitive impact. The baseline model (sometimes known as Chicago, and assuming fixed coefficient production functions and unchallenged monopoly at one stage of production) is that vertical merger has no competitive impact, other than to eliminate double marginalization. However, there are at least two important exceptions to this benevolent view. First, integration may create an entry barrier.[32]

Second, more recent work has investigated how integration may allow a firm (or colluding firms) credibly to price monopolistically without the expectation of hidden price cuts undermining this strategy. There are also important reasons to expect integration to reduce costs and enhance efficiency (for example, by promoting the incentive for specific investment). A further problem with modelling vertical remedies is that it is often difficult to specify exactly how the four equilibria in Section 4.4 differ (of course, this is revealing in itself). For example, the elimination of double marginalization can only take place if pre-merger firms were originally using a linear pricing structure; but if double marginalization is a problem, it would be surprising if firms did not develop non-linear pricing as a relatively straightforward way to solve the problem. In general, a large number of alternative contracts can mimic full vertical integration. Many of these are entirely legal (and for good reasons). This contrasts with the sharp horizontal merger effect of removing a competitor from the market, which cannot legally be mimicked due to the prohibition on cartels (which is for extremely good reasons).

We also need to be able to evaluate the efficiency advantages of vertical mergers and their alternative remedies. We expect these efficiencies to be far more significant than in horizontal mergers, at least relative to any potentially adverse market power effects. Incomplete contracts fail to internalize the investment payoffs to market transactions, and an integrated enterprise may be able to sustain a higher level of specific investment. However, certain forms of market contract may be able to substitute for full integration. It is a very subtle issue to distinguish efficiency from market power effects of alternative remedies, and we acknowledge that it would be extremely difficult to use formal modelling to do so.

None of this means that simulation is impossible in cases with a vertical dimension. However, because vertical modelling would have to be very finely tuned to the specifics of the industry in question, it is less likely that one will be able to develop a library of off-the-shelf ready-made models.

In industries in which *new products are developing rapidly*, or where there are major quality improvements, competition between existing suppliers may be much less important than 'competition for the market'. Theory is still better equipped to deal with 'competition in the market', rather than 'for the market'. In Schumpeter's terms, the most important factor in 'new economy' industries may be creative destruction.[33] It is far more difficult to predict the impact of remedies in this context, as compared with their effect within an existing market. Schumpeterian thought suggests that a more profitable current market will attract entrepreneurial and innovation resources in that direction. However, it will also make it more attractive for incumbents to try to protect their market, maybe by innovating first themselves, but perhaps by erecting entry barriers (for example, multiple patenting; that is, a proliferation of patents, some of which would not be exploited, but nevertheless would narrow down the options for potential rivals). In these circumstances, the likely effects of mergers and remedies become much more speculative, and choosing any particular model may be, to some extent, arbitrary. Therefore it may sometimes be more prudent to adopt a less formal approach to modelling such competition and the effect of remedies (for example, compulsory product licensing; unbundling or no-tying agreements). It also suggests very different data requirements for appraising remedies. Some of these issues are encountered in some of the pharmaceuticals case studies.

4.5.2 Type of Remedy

Many of the above remarks carry over to the likely difficulties in simulating different types of remedy. For example, in principle, horizontal divestitures are probably the most straightforward. More generally, we would expect that 'clean break' remedies should be easier to model because they allow us to compare the effects (for example, on price) of two or more different market structures. As we argued in Chapter 3, this is more likely with structural remedies. In contrast, behavioural remedies will typically involve more judgement because they affect, sometimes in an unpredictable way, firms' (and sometimes the regulator's) behaviour and therefore the nature of the oligopoly game. Because they do not involve a clear-cut, one-off, change, this may introduce an additional layer of strategic behaviour.

Nevertheless, some aspects of horizontal behavioural remedies can be modelled. For example, if the fear of predatory pricing leads to a remedy of the form, say, that price is not allowed to be cut more than 2 per cent *per annum*, then this could be incorporated as a constraint in the oligopoly game. In vertical mergers, an appraisal of behavioural remedies with respect to upstream suppliers or downstream retailers of a particular brand needs to consider two quite different effects: (1) the effect on intra-brand competition (between alternative retailers of a particular brand), and (2) the effect on competition between brands (inter-brand), and the ability of entrants with a new brand to compete for the market.

4.5.3 Errors of Judgement: Choosing the 'Wrong' Model

It would be wrong to suggest that simulation, especially basic simulation, is a well-developed science. Too much judgement and uncertainty are involved to make such a claim. For example, we have already cited an instance (Section 4.3) when an inappropriate choice of a symmetric model of product differentiation would lead to potentially large errors. This is obviously more likely in those cases where information on how the market works is limited.

Similarly, a basic model may sometimes be too rough an approximation to full-blown simulation, based on detailed econometric estimation of the demand system. On the other hand, the sheer simplicity of basic simulation helps to keep it in an appropriate perspective alongside other more traditional evidence. The same might not be true for a full-blown simulation that gains undue prominence merely because of the effort and resources that it demands.

4.5.4 Insufficient Data

Although we advocate the use of only basic models, even these require reliable estimates of key parameters, such as the market elasticity. These estimates may not always be available – though this is far less likely if the requirement to obtain relevant information is included in the tasks of the merger investigation team. This chapter includes an appendix containing a checklist of the sort of information that an inquiry team might gather fairly routinely in order to be well placed to select, modify and calibrate a basic simulation. As we have said before, such information has intrinsic value beyond any narrow simulation exercise.

4.6 CONCLUSION

The purpose of this chapter has been primarily expositional: to explain, describe and illustrate what we mean by 'basic simulation': a methodology for appraising mergers and the efficacy of remedies. We have also tried to point out some of the limitations. The 'proof of the pudding' is in the two case study chapters below.

It should be clear from our exposition that we believe that simulation should be used with care and without raising false expectations of a spurious certainty. Even those with enormous experience and commitment to merger simulation frequently emphasize the need for caution.[34] Simulation of both mergers and remedies requires careful thought about the nature of competition in any particular case, considerable attention to collecting the right data, and sufficient sensitivity analysis to establish the robustness of results.

NOTES

1. There will be some cases (for example, due to discreet divestitures) where the post-remedy outcome is superior to the pre-merger position.
2. For example, in Chapter 8, we encounter a pharmaceuticals merger with in excess of 100 relevant markets with competition concerns. It would not have been impossible to use our proposed methodology even in this case.
3. This concept is defined below in Section 4.4. In brief, it is when the merging firm is required to remove an overlap in a particular market, by divestment, even though the merger is allowed to proceed as a whole.
4. A longer exposition of the material covered in this subsection can be found in Davies and Majumdar (2002, ch. 6).
5. For example, see Perry and Porter (1985).
6. For example, Hotelling's linear product space (1929), Salop's (1979) circular model (both referring to horizontally differentiated products), and Gabszewicz and Thisse's (1979) vertical model.
7. As initially developed, for example, by Dixit and Stiglitz (1977).
8. Lancaster (1991).
9. For example, Werden and Froeb (1994). The reader is referred to this source for details.
10. In versions of the model that explicitly distinguish the different characteristics of the brands, b is replaced by a vector of characteristics, each with its own coefficient, as in (4.4).
11. This can present empirical problems in that a more or less arbitrary judgement is required on the size of the non-purchasing part of the market, that is, consumers who could, but do not actually, purchase. Predictions can be very sensitive to this.
12. Though a single price is often difficult to specify, for example, when customers get quantity discounts or some pay delivery charges, etc.
13. It is worth noting here that the analyst has to exercise discretion in choosing these groups (nests), and necessarily this involves *a priori* assumptions.
14. Consumers are assumed to be uniformly distributed in their tastes for each of the various characteristics.
15. The fact that many markets, even when supplying basically homogeneous products, have a geographically localized dimension means that differentiation models are by no means confined to obvious cases where there are strong brands.
16. See the last paragraph of Section 4.1.1.
17. Note that the term 'market power' depends on the context of the model. It may be an attempt to parameterize the extent to which behaviour deviates from the norm of completely non-cooperative behaviour (Bertrand). Sometimes 'conjectural variations' are used – these are meant to represent the degree of interdependence of firms' decisions, with higher values of the conjectural values parameter equivalent to more tacitly collusive conduct.
18. In general, they will now want to change their prices, and in response to the price changes of the merged firms. These are predicted when the new equilibrium is computed.
19. Other examples we are aware of (not all by the authorities themselves) include: Werden and Froeb's (1994) exposition of their own simulation approach in the (hypothetical) context of long distance carriers; a merger of two HMOs in Minneapolis (Feldman, 1994) uses a nested logit to estimate that prices would increase by 19 per cent; and Kimberly-Clark and Scott (tissues) – Hausman and Leonard (1997) estimated the merger would lead to price increases in the range of 1–2 per cent (see Chapter 6 below).
20. This property of the data turns out to be important when selecting appropriate instrumental variables (see note 21).
21. This model allows for both horizontal and vertical differentiation – horizontal because consumers attach different weights to the characteristics, and vertical because the coefficient on price can also vary across consumers (so, for instance, richer consumers will be less deterred by a high price for high-quality brands; they will therefore derive a higher utility from these brands compared to less well-off consumers).

22. The identification problem arises whenever it is unclear whether an estimated relationship between price and quantity refers to the demand curve or the supply curve, or both. Simultaneous bias occurs when there is two-way causality: not only do the X variables affect the Y variable, but also the reverse is true. Instrumental variables are a standard method for overcoming simultaneous bias; they involve replacing X variables with other variables (instruments) which, while closely related to the replaced X variable, are not determined by the Y variable. In this case, he uses prices from other cities as instruments for price in a given city – they will be closely related, but he argues that price in New York, for example, will not be determined by quantities in Chicago.
23. Apparently, this research was undertaken on behalf of the Commission during Phase II of the merger (M1672, 15 March 2000).
24. See Option 1, Chapter 6, Section 6.2.4. Option 2 develops this model to allow for capacity constraints.
25. Formally, it can be shown that this is the ratio of the cross-price elasticity between the two brands to the own-price elasticity.
26. For example, L. Wu, in NERA 'Antitrust Insight', January/February 2003.
27. See also Jayaratne and Shapiro (2000).
28. See Peters (2006) for an attempt to distinguish what we call 'endogenous' from 'exogenous' in the context of merger simulation in the US airline industry.
29. In principle, additional firm-level and industry data might be available from more general, published sources. However, we found that freely available data were rarely accessible on exactly the right market definitions. Usually, published data only relate to too aggregate markets, and more appropriate disaggregate data can only be accessed at some cost from specialist consultancies.
30. We should stress that we had no direct contact with the firms. In an ideal world, direct contact would have been desirable inasmuch as the questionnaires/interviews would have been easier to target on the specific issues of concern to us. Having said this, we were extensively consulted on the format and content of the questionnaires. We also drew, to a small extent, on publicly available sources, for example, newspapers, company reports, etc.
31. An interesting example, reporting a discussion between three influential antitrust practitioners, can be found in Antitrust Source (2004).
32. The same could be true of a tie-in contract that integration replaces. Alternatively, it is quite possible that a remedy in the form of a commitment not to tie products may result in a higher price for consumers.
33. Evans and Schmalensee (2001) put it thus: 'In particular, the analysis of market power in new-economy industries must consider the vulnerability of leading firms to entry powered by drastic innovation, not just to the entry of firms producing equivalent products with known processes. Analysis of this sort of fragility may require difficult judgements about the likelihood of disruptive innovations in the future, but simply to assume such innovations cannot occur is to ignore history and to impart substantial and obvious bias to market power analysis in important sectors' (p. 47).
34. See Werden and Froeb in Antitrust Source (2004).

APPENDIX A CHECKLIST OF DATA REQUIREMENTS

A necessary condition for the application of simulation of remedies is that the analyst should first assemble a set of focused 'facts'. Once assembled, these facts will be used to inform:

- the choice of broad type of oligopoly model (for example, Cournot, PCAIDS);
- any modification/restriction of the model to reflect the institutional detail of the market (for example, capacity constraints, brand segments);
- calibration of the model (for example, estimates of elasticities and market shares);[1]
- simulation of what would happen if the merger were prohibited (the calibrated model) or allowed (identification of the SIEC) or remedied in some other way.

In the case study chapters, we begin each case by using a standardized checklist we designed and which is set out below. This, or something similar, could easily be used in Phase I investigations.

Standardized Data Checklist

Product

- Nature of product: homogeneous or differentiated? If latter, what type?
- Product life cycle: creative destruction? Demand changes?

Costs

- Overall cost structure (shares of revenue): manufacturing, marketing, R&D, operating profit, transport, other items
- Nature of manufacturing costs: short- and long-run; significance of capacity
- Nature of R&D costs: time from idea to market, etc.
- Nature of marketing: advertising or sales reps
- Overall economies of scale: extent? Exogenous or endogenous?

Demand

- Nature of demand curve: appropriate own and cross-price elasticities

- Who are the buyers?
- Idiosyncrasies of demand: for example, separation of consumer, chooser, and payer

Market

- Market definition: product and geographic
- Import competition: actual and potential
- Vertical structure
- Spot market, auctions or contracts?
- Regulation
- Importance of patents

Structure

- Number and size distribution of sellers
- Cooperative agreements between sellers: JVs, co-marketing, licensing, etc.
- Potential for entry
- Number and size distribution of buyers

Conduct

- Main competitive weapons? Is it just price/quantity? Or are advertising, R&D, innovation, brand positioning important?
- Type of R&D competition: patent race, independent trajectories, etc.
- Innovation market? Product pipeline?
- Type of marketing competition
- Nature of behaviour: unilateral or coordinated?
- Buyer power

Merger and remedy

- Claimed efficiency enhancements pre-remedy: manufacture, marketing, R&D, transport
- Type of remedy: is it a clean break?
- A judgement of the competitive strength or weakness of the buyer of the divested assets
- Impact of remedy on merged firm's efficiency claims.

NOTE

1. This might require either econometric estimates (perhaps from previous studies) or expert opinion from within the industry. If the latter, this might be in the form of questions such as: 'If you raised your price by 10 per cent, by how much do you estimate demand would fall?', and similar questions to extract industry elasticity and cross-elasticity. Such questions should be asked of both main parties (merging firms) and third parties (customers and competitors) for a balanced picture if no econometric estimates are available. Note that this extra information should not be costly to collect.

5. Structure and competitive process in paper and board markets

5.0 INTRODUCTION

This chapter provides the background setting for detailed analysis of specific individual merger cases and remedies in what follows. There are seven sections. The first three set the scene: Section 5.1 defines the appropriate NACE broad industry/sector (21), and identifies all merger interventions by the EC over this period; Section 5.2 provides some brief information on broad aggregates and trends, and an assessment of the standing of the European industry in the world as a whole; and Section 5.3 identifies the leading firms. The following four sections turn more specifically to those features of market structure and the competitive process that are likely to influence our choice of oligopoly models. Section 5.4 establishes market definition. Section 5.5 discusses the key features of the product: on the demand side, the nature of the product and product differentiation; on the supply side, costs and technology. Section 5.6 surveys available data on industry structure, notably, leading market shares and concentration. Section 5.7 concludes with a preliminary assessment of the implications for the nature of the oligopoly game and the competitive process.[1]

5.1 DEFINING THE SECTOR

It was agreed with the Commission that this case study sector should be defined as pulp, paper and paper products (NACE 21). Table 5.1 shows the NACE definitions at the 2, 3 and 4-digit levels. There is a clear vertical sequence, running from pulp (21.11), the main input into paper, through paper and board (21.12), to manufactured articles of paper and board (21.2).

Table 5.1 also shows the number of EC merger investigations (and interventions) in each part of the sector over the period covered by this project, that is, 1990 to the end of 2004. This serves to establish two points of importance at the outset. First, while 16 mergers can be identified within reasonably specific 4-digit industries (for example, corrugated paper and paper containers), many more (50) straddle 4 digits – either to the 3-digit

Table 5.1 NACE 21 pulp, paper and paper products

		EC merger investigations 1990 to end of 2004	
		Total	Interventions
21	Manufacture of pulp, paper and paper products	22	2
21.1	Manufacture of pulp, paper and paperboard	15	4
21.11	Pulp	1	0
21.12	Paper and paperboard	5	0
21.2	Manufacture of articles of paper and paperboard	13	3
21.21	Corrugated paper(board) and containers	6	0
21.22	Household and sanitary goods and toilet requisites	2	1
21.23	Paper stationery	0	0
21.24	Wallpaper	0	0
21.25	Other articles nec	2	0
	Total*	64	9

Note: * Two cases (including one intervention) appear in two different categories.

Source: Compiled from EC merger database http://europa.eu.int/comm/competition/mergers/cases/.

level (28), or even to the aggregate 2-sector digit (22). This reveals that many firms are integrated/diversified across the stages; and that some of the distinctions in NACE are blurred in practice (for example, between the paper and board used in packaging articles, and the articles themselves). Second, the pulp industry had only one specific merger (and this had no remedies).

Table 5.2 reinforces both points. It focuses on the nine mergers in which remedies were imposed, identifying the precise markets in which these remedies were applied. As can be seen, pulp does not feature at all. For this reason, we shall only discuss pulp hereafter in so far as this aids understanding of paper and board. Note also that, in two cases, the remedies were applied in adjacent industries outside this sector, and these will not be considered in the remainder of the project.

Three of the merger cases straddle the production of paper and board used in packaging, and the packaging products themselves (21.12 and 21.21). This suggests that we should look beyond the NACE for additional sources of disaggregation. For this purpose, we turn to a richer industry data source, provided by the Confederation of European Paper Industries

Table 5.2 Merger interventions classified by markets in which remedies imposed

	NACE	Precise market involved	
		Product	Geographical
Printing and writing paper, 21.12			
UPM-Kymmene/ Haindl (2498) 2000		Newsprint, magazine paper	All
Paper and board for packaging, packaging products, 21.12 21.21			
Repola/Kymmene (646) 1995	21.21	Paper sacks	Finland
Enso/Stora (1225) 1998	21.12	Packaging board (for liquids)	All
SCA Packaging/Metsä Corrugated (2032) 2001	21.21	Corrugated boxes	Denmark
Tissue paper and tissue products, 21.12 21.22			
Procter & Gamble/ VP Schickedanz (430) 1994		Sanitary towels	Germany, Spain
Kimberly-Clark/Scott Paper (623) 1996		Toilet tissues, kitchen towels, facial tissues	UK, Eire
SCA/Metsä Tissue (2097) 2001		Toilet tissues, kitchen towels, wiping tissue	Sweden, Norway, Denmark, Finland
Outside this sector			
KNP/Bührmann Tetterode/ VRG (291) 1993		Distribution and servicing of printing presses	Belgium, Netherlands
Metsä/Modo (2020) 2000		Paper merchanting	Sweden

Source: Compiled from EC merger database on http://europa.eu.int/comm/competition/mergers/cases/.

(CEPI), which classifies the subsectors in a more illuminating manner than the NACE (Table 5.3).

Table 5.3 shows that, in volume terms, graphic papers account for around 50 per cent of total paper and board production, packaging paper for about 40 per cent, and hygiene and specialty papers for about 10 per cent. It is helpful to paraphrase CEPI's definitions of each of their categories.

- *Graphic papers (also referred to as publication papers)*
  - Newsprint, used mainly for printing newspapers

Table 5.3 Paper production and consumption by grade, 2001: CEPI classification (million tonnes)

		Production	Consumption
Pulp		37.9	43.9
Total paper and board		88.2	81.3
Total graphic paper		43.7	39.8
Of which:	Newsprint	10.7	11.0
	Uncoated mechanical	6.0	4.7
	Coated mechanical	8.4	6.5
	Uncoated woodfree	9.8	9.3
	Coated woodfree	8.8	8.4
Sanitary and household		5.4	5.6
Total packaging		35.1	32.7
Of which:	Case materials	20.3	20.1
	Carton board	7.3	6.3
	Wrappings	3.5	3.1
	Other paper for packaging	4.0	3.2
Other		3.9	3.2

Note: EU15 accounts for over 93% of the total.

Source: CEPI Annual Statistics 2001.

- Uncoated mechanical (groundwood or wood containing paper), used for magazines
- Uncoated woodfree, used in office papers, such as business forms, copier, computer, stationery and book papers
- Coated papers are coated on one or both sides with minerals such as china clay, calcium carbonate etc., suitable for printing or other graphic purposes

- *Sanitary and household* This covers a wide range of tissue and other hygienic papers for use in household or commercial and industrial premises. Examples are: toilet paper and facial tissues, kitchen towels, hand towels and industrial wipes. Tissue is also used in the manufacture of nappies, sanitary towels etc. CEPI's production statistics refer to the 'parent reel stock', that is, the paper from which these products are manufactured (converted).

- *Packaging*
  - Case materials (kraftliner, testliner and fluting), used mainly to manufacture corrugated board

- Carton board, used mainly in cartons for consumer products (for example, frozen food, liquid containers)
- Wrappings include sack kraft, other wrapping krafts, greaseproof paper
- Other – includes papers and boards for industrial purposes, and cigarettes.

Relationship to the NACE

This classification seems to correspond fairly closely to NACE 21.12, 'Manufacture of paper and paperboard'. It does not appear to include 'Manufacture of paper articles' (21.2) *per se*, but there is obviously a very close input–output relationship between CEPI's 'Packaging' and 'Household and sanitary' and the two major categories of NACE's 21.2: Packaging products (21.21) and Household and sanitary goods (21.22). The column for apparent consumption in Table 5.3 should therefore give a good indication of the sizes of these two manufactures subsectors.

Henceforth, our industry definitions and disaggregations of paper and board will follow the CEPI categories. It will often prove convenient to distinguish the three broad categories: graphic papers, tissues and packaging; and sometimes it will be helpful to focus on their component parts, for example, newsprint. Of course, once we move on in the next stage of the report to individual mergers, sometimes even finer disaggregations will be necessary, for example, paper sacks.

5.2 BROAD CONTEXT AND PERFORMANCE

We start with a bullet point précis based on CEPI's commentary from its annual report for 2002. It provides a rough idea of the key dimensions of the broad sector in the CEPI countries:

- Annual turnover of 76 billion euros. It is a vital part of an economic cluster – the paper and forest cluster – that generates an annual turnover of more than 400 billion euros.
- Employment for about 251 000 people.
- Capital investment (annual flow) is 4 billion euros.
- It uses 42 per cent of recycled fibres, 42 per cent of virgin pulp and 15 per cent of non-fibrous materials.
- Germany is the largest paper producer, followed closely by Finland, Sweden and France. The main pulp-producing countries are Finland and Sweden.

Table 5.4 Some indicators of structure and performance

	Pulp	Paper and board
Capacity (mn tonnes)		
2001	43.4	98.6
Production (mn tonnes)		
2001	37.9	88.2
1990	31.7	61.5
average % change p.a., 1990–2001	1.6	3.4
Share of world production (%)		
2000	20.8	28.1
1990	19.1	25.6
Net trade balance with rest of world (mn tonnes)		
2001	−6.4	5.7
1995	−6.6	6.1
Mills (number)		
2001	219	1045
1991	250	1090
Average plant size (capacity, th. tonnes)		
2001	198	94
1991	144	63

- CEPI member countries account for 28 per cent of world paper and board production, slightly behind North America (32 per cent) and Asia (30 per cent).

Table 5.4 draws on various tables from the CEPI report to present a concise series of indicators of how the sector is structured and of how it has changed over the last decade (1990–2001).

Thus, in 2001, the sector was producing well within capacity: pulp (87 per cent) and paper and board (90 per cent). It has grown steadily throughout the last decade – rather slowly for pulp (1.6 per cent p.a.), but more healthily for paper and board (3.4 per cent). It accounts for well over a quarter of the world's production of paper and board, and about one-fifth of pulp production; its 'market share' has grown significantly for both subsectors over the last ten years. Further evidence from the world stage is given by the net trade balance: Europe is a sizeable net exporter of paper and board, but a net importer of pulp.

There are over 200 pulp mills, and their average capacity has increased by over one-third in the last decade; the paper and board sector has over

Table 5.5 Geographical distribution of production by broad product category, leading countries' shares (%) 2001

	Pulp	Paper	Graphic	Tissue	Packaging
Finland	29	14	20	3	8
Sweden	29	12	12	6	14
Germany	6	20	20	19	19
France	6	11	10	11	12
Italy	1	10	7	23	12
UK	1	7	6	14	7
Remainder*	27	26	24	25	27

Note: * No other country has a share greater than 10% in any product category.

Source: Authors' own calculations, based on various tables and editions of CEPI's annual report.

1000 mills – they tend to be much smaller than pulp mills, but their average size has grown even more dramatically, by almost a half.

Table 5.5 shows the shares, within the total, of each country, by broad product category, focusing only on those countries that have a market share of at least 10 per cent for at least one product type. Only six countries satisfy this criterion: the two Nordic countries, Finland and Sweden, and the largest four member states, Germany, France, Italy and the UK. The picture differs significantly between pulp, and paper and board. As can be seen, Finland and Sweden dominate the pulp sector (29 per cent each), but for paper and board, although their shares are still sizeable (12–14 per cent), Germany now has the highest market share (20 per cent), with France and Italy both recording 10 per cent.

The last three columns break down the aggregate paper and board figure by type of product. It is noticeable that Finland is strongest in graphics, with only relatively minor shares in tissue and packaging, while Italy is the leader in tissues (UK also records its highest share in tissues).

5.3 EUROPE'S LARGEST FIRMS

Given Europe's prominent position in the world, it is perhaps unsurprising to find that many of the world's largest 100 firms in this sector are European.

As can be seen from the first column of Table 5.6,[2] Europe has three of the world's 10 largest companies, seven of the top 20, and 16 of the top 50. Unsurprisingly, given the finding in Table 5.5, this list includes 11 firms

Table 5.6 European firms in the world's top 100

World rank		Origin	Sales, 2002 ($ bn)	Mergers	
				Total	Interventions
5	Stora Enso	Finland	12.1	3	1
7	UPM-Kymmene	Finland	9.9	6	2
10	Svenska Cellulosa (SCA)	Sweden	9.1	7	2
11	Metsäliitto	Finland	8.4	7	1
15	Anglo American (Mondi)	UK	4.8	2	
16	Jefferson Smurfit	Ireland	4.5	3	
17	Worms & Cie	France	4.2	5	
26	Norske Skog	Norway	3.0	4	
28	Kappa Packaging	Netherlands	2.8	1	1
30	David S. Smith	UK	2.2		
39	Ahlstrom	Finland	1.7	4	
41	Holmen	Sweden	1.7		
44	Cartiere Burgo	Italy	1.6		
48	Sonae Industria	Portugal	1.4		
49	Myllykoski	Finland	1.4		
50	The Lecta Group	UK	1.3		
56	Södra	Sweden	1.2		
57	Mayr-Melnhof Karton	Austria	1.2		
63	Andritz	Austria	1.1	2	
65	Portucel	Portugal	1.0		
67	Ilim	Russia	1.0		
74	AssiDomän	Sweden	0.9	3	
77	Billerud	Sweden	0.7	1	
81	Kinnevik (Korsnas)	Sweden	0.6		
84	Groupe Gascogne	France	0.6		
87	Reno De Medici	Italy	0.6		
91	Exacompta Clairefontaine	France	0.5		
97	Ence	Spain	0.4		
99	Otor	France	0.4		
Total sales ($ bn) of European firms in top 100			80.1		
% sales of European firms in world's top 100			27.0		
Non-Europeans with sizeable European operations*					
4	Kimberly-Clark	USA	13.6	1	1
6	Procter & Gamble	USA	11.9	2	1

Note: * As with all firms in this table, sales figures refer to worldwide sales.

Source: Global Forest & Paper Industry Survey, PricewaterhouseCoopers, 2002.

from the two Nordic countries, Finland and Sweden; more surprisingly, although France (4), UK (3) and Italy (2) are well represented, there are no German firms in this listing. Evidently, Germany's dominance in the graphic grades, noted in Table 5.5, reflects the fact that it has a large number of medium-sized more specialist firms and/or there are important German subsidiaries of the leaders from the other member states.

Table 5.6 also serves as a sort of 'cast list' for the remainder of this project. In effect, it introduces on to the stage all the main players in the rest of the story. The two columns on the right of the table record, for each firm, the number of mergers investigated by the EC. In total, these firms account for 52 investigations, out of a total of 66;[3] and, of our nine case studies of merger interventions, eight involve firms now in the world's 11 largest.

A comparison of the corporate structures of the leading players reveals some common features: notably, all (1) are vertically integrated to a lesser or greater extent, and (2) have extensive cross-border operations. On the other hand, each one has different foci. The largest, Stora-Enso, is the most diversified, having leading positions in publication, tissue and packaging papers; SCA is also significantly diversified, and is also a leader in tissues and packaging, but with lesser operations in publications. UPM-Kymmene tends to be more specialized in publication papers; Metsäliitto is strong in pulp and publication papers; Norske-Skog is strongest in publication papers, especially newsprint. The two main US companies with large European operations, Kimberly-Clark and Procter & Gamble, hold leading positions in tissues.

5.4 MARKET DEFINITION

Against this backcloth, this and the following two sections provide an overview of the intrinsic nature of the various types of market that populate this broad sector.[4] This will help us to form a judgement of the nature of the competitive process itself, which will be needed to inform the subsequent simulation stage of the research. The obvious starting question is: 'What are the appropriate market definitions?'

Returning first to Table 5.1 and the NACE, we have a three-way distinction between pulp (21.11), paper and paperboard (21.12), and manufactured articles of paper and paperboard (21.2), and then the five four-digit industries within 21.2. At the very least, then, this would provide five distinct (although typically vertically related) industries.[5] However, in addition, within 21.12, there is the three-way distinction, used by the industry itself (CEPI, as reproduced in Table 5.3) between graphic paper, sanitary and household, and packaging. This means at least seven 'industries'.

In fact, as we move down one further level of disaggregation in Table 5.3, within graphic paper, fairly obviously, newsprint is not demand-substitutable for other printed papers (but, say, uncoated mechanical and woodfree papers *may* be substitutable). Within packaging, the paper and board inputs, case materials and carton board are obviously used to produce different packaging products. Thus there are at least seven distinct industries (and probably more) on the demand side:

- Newsprint
- Other graphic papers
- Tissue (sanitary and household, including tissue articles thereof)
- Packaging: case materials (including articles thereof)
- Packaging: carton board (including articles thereof)
- Packaging: wrappings (including articles thereof)
- Pulp.

This is also likely to be the case on the supply side. Paper machines are specialized, typically producing only one category of paper (Pesendorfer, 2003, reports that, in the USA, 80 per cent of all capacity is allocated to plants producing a sole category of paper). Substitutability across these seven 'industries' is therefore also likely to be very limited – especially in the short run.

In fact, it is highly likely that even some of these seven 'industries' will be too aggregate, in the sense that they themselves comprise a number of different markets. The Commission's assessments of the relevant markets in the individual merger cases shows that this is indeed the case: even more narrowly defined market definitions are required (Table 5.2 above). However, we shall leave these finer distinctions until the analysis of the individual mergers. Suffice it to say at this stage that there is a relatively large number of sub-categories of paper and board and manufactured articles thereof that each form distinct markets.

We shall also leave discussion of the geographical scope of the market until the analysis of individual mergers in the next chapter. But, to anticipate, for some products, the appropriate geographical market appears to be Europe-wide, or even global, but for others, national markets can be identified.[6]

5.5 THE NATURE OF THE PRODUCT, CAPACITY, COSTS AND TECHNOLOGY

Assuming then that one has correctly identified the relevant markets, what should we expect about the nature of the product within each market? On the demand side, is the product homogeneous or differentiated? On the supply side, what does the technology imply about the nature of the cost curve and the role of capacity?

The intuition is that the product will be fairly homogeneous; for example, the newsprint from one producer is more or less identical to that from any other. This is certainly the working hypothesis used by Pesendorfer in his econometric work on the US industry (2003, p. 9): 'Products within a category are largely homogeneous', and on the supply side 'we expect little spillovers, or externalities, in production between paper categories and assume that individual paper categories constitute independent markets'. There is, however, one important exception: tissue products, where brand names are important, and the nature of differentiation (between, say, different brands of tampon, or different brands of paper handkerchiefs) will need to be acknowledged in modelling.

It would be premature to make definitive, specific, judgements on the nature of technology and costs within individual finely defined markets within the sector. (That is done in the course of our detailed analysis of the specific mergers in the next chapter.) Nevertheless, certain general observations can be made, partly on the basis of our reading of industry sources, and partly on the modelling assumptions made by Pesendorfer in his study of the US industry.

The typical size of plant has increased dramatically in recent years (see Table 5.4), and production scale economies are considered to be significant. Capacity utilization tends to be high, typically in the region of 90 per cent. (See Table 5.7 for the example of graphic paper.) This means that output expansion will often require an increase in installed capacity (although there is some scope for speeding up the rate at which machines are operated). Indeed, Pesendorfer characterizes capacity as the key competitive weapon: 'investment decisions are the main strategic choice variable in the paper industry' (2003, p. 1).

Table 5.7 Capacity utilization in the graphic paper sector

	1995	1996	1997	1998	1999	2000	2001	Average
Newsprint	96	88	92	91	93	94	91	92.1
Uncoated mechanical	93	85	89	92	92	92	88	90.1
Coated mechanical	96	83	92	93	94	96	87	91.6
Uncoated woodfree	91	92	94	90	87	92	89	90.7
Coated woodfree	81	84	88	88	92	98	87	88.3
Total graphics	91	87	91	91	92	94	88	90.6

Source: CEPIPRINT Demand and Supply Report, Newsprint and Magazine Paper Grade, 2002–4.

5.6 MARKET STRUCTURE: LEADING MARKET SHARES AND CONCENTRATION

There are a number of reasons why one might expect this sector to be fairly highly concentrated. Not least, there has been a major wave of mergers and acquisitions (M&A) over the last decade, many mergers involving the leading firms identified above (see Table 5.8).

Table 5.8 Main mergers/JV proposals by the largest firms

Ahlstrom	**M1431 – Ahlstrom / Kvaerner** M1792 – Ahlstrom / Capman / Folding Carton Partners M1930 – Ahlstrom / Andritz M2441 – Amcor / Danisco / Ahlstrom
Andritz	M1736 – UIAG / Carlyle / Andritz M1930 – Ahlstrom / Andritz
Assidomän	M1884 – Mondi / Frantschach / AssiDomän M2243 – Stora Enso / AssiDomän / JV M2391 – CVC / Cinven / AssiDomän
Jefferson Smurfitt	M499 – Jefferson Smurfitt / St-Gobain M613 – Jefferson Smurfit plc / Munksjo AB M1208 – Jefferson Smurfit / Stone Containers
Kappa Packaging	**M291 – KNP / Bührmann Tetterode / VRG** (the merger that formed Kappa)
Kimberly-Clark	**M623 – Kimberly-Clark / Scott Paper**
Metsäliitto	M1356 – Metsä-Serla / UK Paper M1744 – UPM-Kymmene / Stora Enso / Metsäliitto / JV **M2020 – Metsä-Serla / Modo** **M2032 – SCA Packaging / Metsä Corrugated** **M2097 – SCA / Metsä Tissue** M2234 – Metsäliitto Osuuskunta / Vapo Oy / JV M2245 – Metsä-Serla / Zanders
Mondi	M210 – Mondi / Frantschach M1884 – Mondi / Frantschach / AssiDomän
Norske Skog	M1296 – Norske Skog / Abitibi / Hansol M2493 – Norske Skog / Abitibi / Papco M2499 – Norske Skog / Parenco / Walsum M2552 – Norske Skog / Peterson also, the proposed buyer of divested assets in M2498
Procter & Gamble	M398 – Procter & Gamble / VP Schickedanz **M430 – Procter & Gamble / VP Schickedanz (II)**
Sappi	M526 – Sappi Warren

Table 5.8 (*continued*)

SCA	M549 – Svenska Cellulosa / PWA Papierwerke
	M1556 – Mo Och Domsjö / SCA
	M1996 – SCA / Graninge / JV
	M2032 – SCA Packaging / Metsä Corrugated
	M2097 – SCA / Metsä Tissue
	M2522 – SCA Hygiene Products / Cartoinvest
	M3102 – Thomesto / SCA Holz JV
Stora Enso	**M1225 – Enso / Stora**
	M1744 – UPM-Kymmene / Stora Enso / Metsäliitto / JV
	M2243 – Stora Enso / AssiDomän / JV
UPM-Kymmene	**M646 – Repola/Kymmene**
	M871 – UPM-Kymmene / Finnpap
	M1006 – UPM-Kymmene / April
	M1744 – UPM-Kymmene / Stora Enso / Metsäliitto / JV
	M2498 – UPM-Kymmene / Haindl
	M2867 – UPM-Kymmene Corporation / Morgan Adhesives
Worms	M25 – Arjormari/Wiggins Teape
	M750 – IFIL / Worms / Saint Louis
	M909 – Worms / Saint Louis
	M1010 – Artémis / Worms & Cie
	M1023 – IFIL / Worms & Cie

Note: Mergers shown in bold are our intervention cases.

Source: Compiled from EC merger database on http://europa.eu.int/comm/competition/mergers/cases/.

Moreover, the typical scale of plant is large, and increasing, relative to the size of the market, and we should expect to observe typically high, and increasing, levels of producer concentration. Strong evidence that this is indeed the case is provided by the data in Tables 5.9–5.11, which report leading market shares and concentration in various sub-sectors at the European level.

Graphic (Publication) Papers

Four of the five paper categories in this sector are highly concentrated (Table 5.9): the five firm concentration ratio exceeds 70 per cent, the ten firm concentration ratio exceeds 90 per cent, and the HHI index exceeds 0.12. In terms of the merger guidelines of the USA, EC and UK, such a level is taken to indicate a concentrated, if not highly concentrated, market.[7] In fact, such concentration levels at a still fairly aggregate level of

Table 5.9 Leading market shares and concentration in the graphic paper sector

	Origin	Firms' capacities (th. tonnes pa) in EEA, 2001				
		Newsprint	UWC	CWC	UWF	CWF
UPM-Kymmene	Finland	2315	2245	2960	920	1495
Stora Enso	Finland	2625	1413	1815	1505	1617
Metsäliitto	Finland			355	1440	2700
Norske Skog	Norway	2070	735	790		
Sappi Ltd	S. Africa			455		2025
Cartiere Burgo	Italy			1115		1010
Myllykoski	Finland	700	695	1035		
Holmen	Sweden	1310	385			
The Lecta Group	UK					1414
Svenska Cellulosa (SCA)	Sweden	525	495	430		
Palm Group	Germany	465				
Abitibi Consolidated	Canada	270				
Papresa SL	Spain	250				
Mondi	S. Africa	200			364	
Golzern Holding	Germany		110			
Arctic Paper	Sweden		65			
Matussiere & Forest S.A.	France		65			
Cartiere Paolo Pigna S.p.A	Italy		45			
Marchi Group	Italy			165		202
Steinbeis Holding	Germany			152		
Portucel Group	Portugal				1082	
International Paper	USA				627	
Arjo Wiggins (Worms)	UK				373	644
Felix Schoeller	Germany				300	
Papierfabrik August Koehler	Germany				290	240
Papelera Guipuzcoana de Zicunaga	Spain				250	
Ahlstrom	Finland					162
Industry capacity total		**11285**	**6574**	**9873**	**11160**	**12655**

Table 5.9 (continued)

	Origin	Firms' capacities (th. tonnes pa) in EEA, 2001				
		Newsprint	UWC	CWC	UWF	CWF
Measures of concentration						
Concentration ratio, 10 firm	CR10	95	95	94	64	91
Concentration ratio, 5 firm	CR5	80	85	78	50	73
HHI index	Herfindahl	0.152	0.196	0.160	0.058	0.124

Note: Figures are only reported for the scale of a firm's capacity in any industry if it is within the top ten in that industry. Thus it excludes any relatively minor market shares of these firms, in markets in which they are not leaders. This means estimates of the HHI will be slight underestimates. A further factor leading to HHI underestimation is that these calculations take no account of the shares of the unreported smaller firms in each industry.

Source: The market structure and competition in the European printing and writing paper industry, confidential report for DG Enterprise, Jaakko Poyry Consulting, March 2003.

industry definition typically conceal much higher concentration in individual product markets within these aggregates.

Equally significant, in each case, there is a 'natural break' in the size distribution between the sizes of the top two (UPM and Stora Enso for UWC and CWC; Metsäliitto and Sappi for CWF) or the top three producers (UPM, Stora Enso and Norske Skog for newsprint) and their smaller rivals. Such markets are often associated with tacitly collusive markets, and mergers therein with coordinated effects.

Tissues

The tissues sector is also very concentrated. Table 5.10(a) refers to the production of tissue papers, and 5.10(b) to two important categories of articles manufactured with that paper. While neither part of the table is definitive,[8] together they are illustrative of a concentrated sector, dominated by multinational firms.

Packaging

Table 5.11 shows the market leaders in the two most important parts of packaging. Again, both markets are dominated by a small number of firms: SCA, Jefferson Smurfitt and Kappa. Mergers have played an important role in this part of the sector (Table 5.8 above): Kappa was formed as the

Table 5.10 Leading market shares and concentration in the tissues sector

Tissue paper production capacity, 2000

	Mn tonnes	Share (%)
SCA + Metsa Tissue	1.5	30.0
Kimberly-Clark	0.9	18.0
Fort James	0.7	14.0
Cartoinvest	0.4	8.0
Sofidel	0.26	5.2
Procter & Gamble	0.23	4.6
Tronchetti	0.2	4.0
Wepa	0.14	2.8
Cartiera Lucchese	0.13	2.6
Kartogroup	0.12	2.4
Zeritis Group	0.11	2.2
Annunziata Group	0.10	2.0
Athens Papermill	0.08	1.6
Paloma	0.07	1.4
Duni	0.06	1.2
Subtotal	5	
Concentration measures		
CR 5		75
CR 10		91
HHI		0.16

Source: Confidential report for DG Enterprise, Jaako Poyry Consulting, November 2000.

Leading market shares in tissue products

	Market shares (%)	
	Europe	North America
AFH (away from home)		
SCA	17	20
Kimberly-Clark	17	26
Georgia-Pacific (Fort James)	12	36
Incontinence products		
SCA	41	18
Hartmann	18	2
Procter & Gamble	6	–
Paper Pak	5	10
Tyco/Kendall	3	29
Kimberly-Clark	2	26

Source: SCA web pages.

Table 5.11 Leading ten market shares in packaging

	Capacity, mn tonnes, 2002	
	Corrugated board	Containerboard
SCA	4.9	2.7
Jefferson Smurfitt	4.5	2.8
Kappa	3.7	2.1
International Paper	1.5	0.0
D. Smith	1.2	0.8
Mondi	1.2	0.0
SAICA	1.1	1.5
Otor	0.6	0.7
Rossman	0.6	0.0
Bauernfeind	0.6	0.7
Palm	0.0	0.8
M-Real (Metsäliitto)	0.0	0.6
Emin Leydier	0.0	0.5

Note: Comparable data on total industry capacity for these two sectors are not reported in this source, so we are unable to calculate reliable measures of concentration, such as HHI and CR5/10.

Source: SCA current web pages.

result of the KNP/Bührmann Tetterode/VRG merger, and three mergers involving Jefferson Smurfitt have been examined by the Commission.

Apart from concentration, entry barriers are the other major structural variable we shall want to consider in the merger cases. Since these are not really quantifiable with proxies available from public sources, a detailed qualitative examination will be delayed until the merger cases. However, again, a general overview observation is possible. Barriers to new entry are typically high across most of the industries within the sector. Scale economies are typically pronounced, and significant capacity creation is costly and time-consuming. In some cases, vertically integrated incumbents enjoy a significant advantage over *de novo* entrants. Strong brand names also offer incumbents a major first-mover advantage in the tissues sector. The potential for import competition is patchy because of the high volume–value ratio.

5.7 CONCLUSIONS

This sector includes a number of well-defined subsectors. Even within the manufacture of paper and board (as opposed to pulp, and articles made from paper and board), there is an important distinction to be made between publication papers, tissues and packaging. Although some of the leading players (including most of those involved in our specific merger cases) are diversified and integrated across those sectors, it is important to acknowledge that these subsectors are quite separate markets. More correctly, they are separate clusters of related markets. As will be seen in the merger cases themselves, the economically meaningful market definitions are often even more disaggregated than the broad subsectors identified thus far.

However, within each correctly defined market, the product will be largely homogeneous. The one exception is tissue products, where brand names, product differentiation and product innovation are likely to be important competitive weapons.

Mills tend to be large, capacity is largely fixed in the short run, and scale economies are significant. In the terminology of game theory, modelling will require a two-stage framework, with capacity decided in the first stage, and price in the second.

Concentration is typically high. Even at the relatively broad levels of aggregation reported here, many subsectors are dominated by two or three main firms. Once we move down to the level of individual well-defined markets within those subsectors, concentration is likely to be even higher.

The combination of homogeneous products, competition via capacity, and high concentration means that we should not necessarily confine our attention to non-cooperative oligopoly models: there is the potential for joint dominance and mergers with coordinated effects.

NOTES

1. This is only preliminary, however: as will be seen, the markets identified in most merger reports are typically more disaggregated than even the subsectors identified in generally available public data. In-depth analysis in the next modelling stage will undoubtedly lead to a richer and more detailed picture
2. It also includes two major non-European firms with substantial European operations.
3. This involves a small amount of double counting, since some mergers (and joint ventures) have involved two of these leading firms.
4. They draw upon our reading of the [non-confidential versions] of the merger decisions themselves, a number of confidential documents made available to us by the Commission, publications of CEPI and its CEPIPRINT associate. Two recent sources, more obviously in the public domain, which have proved very useful, are Pesendorfer (2003) and Christensen and Caves (1997).
5. Given its miscellaneous nature, it is unlikely that 21.25 (Other articles nec) can be analysed as a distinct market.
6. One telling point, in defining geographical scope, is the fact that most larger firms locate their production facilities across member states. It is likely that transport costs are high relative to the value of the product, and this will often mitigate towards national markets (as will be clear in our analysis of the specific mergers in the next stage of the work).

7. A helpful way of thinking about the HHI value is that its reciprocal gives the number of equal-sized firms that would generate such a value. Thus HHI = 0.12 is equivalent to just eight equal-sized firms.
8. Part (a) is taken from a report in 2000, anticipating what would be the effect of a merger between SCA and Metsa Tissue (one of our merger cases); part (b) is taken from SCA's web page and therefore highlights two areas of particular strength for SCA. AFH tissues refers to the market for tissue products consumed away from the ultimate consumer's home, for example, in restaurants and hotels.

6. Assessment of remedies adopted by the EC in paper mergers

6.0 INTRODUCTION

This chapter uses the simulation methodology to assess the efficacy of remedies for two of the mergers in the paper sector (see Table 5.2): Kimberly-Clark/Scott (KC/S) in tissues, and SCA/Metsa (S/M) in corrugated packaging. These were chosen as examples, respectively, of differentiated and homogeneous products.

Unfortunately, the DG Competition questionnaire/interview survey (2005) which was being conducted simultaneously with our project included only one of these mergers, KC/S, and so a full *ex post* assessment of S/M is not possible.

The chapter is in two main sections, one for each merger. The two sections follow the same structure, starting with filling in the checklist from Chapter 4, supplemented by some ancillary analysis to derive estimates of demand elasticities. The simulation proper starts with some introductory remarks on how we intend to characterize the merger and remedy, and what this will entail for *ex ante* and *ex post* assessment. We then set out what we believe to be the appropriate oligopoly model. The merger and remedies are then simulated *ex ante*, with sensitivity analysis on the assumptions about nesting, capacity and efficiency savings. This generates our main predictions and simulation results. We close the *ex ante* simulations with a discussion of alternative remedies that might have been used. Finally, we turn to *ex post* developments in the market, including, in the KC/S case, information from the DG Competition survey.

6.1 KIMBERLY-CLARK/SCOTT PAPER (1996) – M623

6.1.1 Applying the Checklist

The first task is to summarize the key features of the merger and remedies – key, that is, to our subsequent modelling. To achieve this, we apply the general checklist presented in the Appendix to Chapter 4.[1] The main source is the EC's final decision document (where appropriate, specific references are indicated by the relevant paragraph number(s) in the form EC, x).

Decision: Article 8(2) = Phase II, 16 January 1996

Competition concerns – products and markets that raised concerns The UK and Eire consumer paper tissue product markets for:

(i) toilet paper
(ii) kitchen paper
(iii) handkerchiefs/facial[2] tissues

The significance of the word 'consumer' is to exclude the AFH ('away from home') part of the industry (see below under market definition).

Had the merger been allowed without remedies, this would have led to a structure in each of the three markets in which the merged firm was effectively the only supplier of branded products.

Market definition: product and geographic As just mentioned, AFH was considered to be a separate market.[3] The buyers of AFH (industrial and institutional purchasers, for use in factories, offices etc.) are typically not final consumers, and are less affected by brand image, and more prone to consider alternative materials as substitutes (for example, plastics, hot-air dryers).

More controversially, in each case, the market was defined to include both branded and private (that is, supermarket) labels. The Commission noted (EC, 48) that 'in retail stores private label products are priced relative to leading branded products and at least some consumers are willing to switch between branded and private label products in response to promotional campaigns'. Superficially, this would appear to be in contrast with the Commission's conclusion (EC, 2001, 28) in the subsequent S/M tissue case: 'for the purpose of the present case, branded and private label consumer products are separate relevant product markets'. However, there is no contradiction, despite this wording. In S/M, the Commission (EC, 27) makes a deliberate (and well-founded) distinction between retail and wholesale: 'branded and private label consumer tissue products can compete with each other at the retail level, whilst being in separate markets at the wholesale level'. We return to the importance of this distinction below, under 'buyer power', but, for the moment, we take forward the conclusion that branded and private label products do compete in the retail market, and are (albeit imperfect) substitutes.

Geographically, the Commission identified the UK and Eire as forming a separate market from continental Europe. This was justified on a number of grounds. First, UK consumers were reputedly more sophisticated, with a stronger preference for high-quality products, reflected in the higher average prices paid by UK consumers. Second, in general, patterns of consumption, particularly with respect to the purchase of handkerchiefs as opposed to facial tissues, differ by country. The UK and Eire appear to be outliers: in continental Europe, consumption of handkerchiefs is very high, while in Eire and particularly in the UK it is very low. For facial tissues this position is reversed. Third, finished tissue products are bulky and of low value. As such they are expensive to transport. For example, the cost of transporting toilet paper from Northern Germany to the UK exceeds 15 per cent of the sales value and for kitchen towels exceeds 25 per cent. Fourth, in the UK, the predominant brand of toilet paper is Andrex (sold by Scott). Kimberly-Clark only uses the Kleenex Double Velvet brand for toilet paper in the UK and Eire. These brands are not used to any significant extent in continental Europe. Number 3 in the UK market for branded toilet paper, Jamont, uses the Dixcel brand almost exclusively in the UK.

Table 6.1 (derived from EC Annex Table 4) summarizes the relative sizes of the three segments, and the relative importance of Eire. As can be seen, (1) toilet tissues are obviously the largest segment, and (2) Eire accounts for an almost trivial proportion of the total.

Competition from other member states: actual and potential The fact that UK prices are higher than in other member states, while transport costs for finished tissue products are lower, provides compelling evidence of the difficulty of new market entry by import of finished goods from continental Europe. Retailers were apparently unanimous in identifying difficulties of overseas supply.

Product

Nature of product In all three cases, we deem the product to be differentiated. This is indicated by relatively high advertising spends, consumer survey evidence of brand loyalty, and price premia on leading

Table 6.1 Dimensions of market, 1994

Product	% share	UK and Eire market size (mn ECUs)	Eire share (% of previous column)
Toilet tissue	71	996	2.9
Kitchen towels	15	215	3.3
Facials	14	193	4.1
Total	100	1404	3.1

brands. In the eyes of the consumer at least, and probably also in terms of objective assessments of 'quality', the brand leaders are vertically differentiated from private labels and lower-priced branded products. Brands are also probably horizontally differentiated – different consumers having differing preferences for attributes such as thickness, absorbency, softness and, in some cases, a preference for recycled paper. In terms of the theoretical discussion in Chapter 4, this might be described by a model such as the nested logit, with separate nests for branded and private labels.

Product life cycle: creative destruction or demand changes? In all three cases, the product is mature and well established. The market is therefore stable and not prone to large demand shifts in aggregate. However, within the aggregate, the relative shares of the branded and private label segments have changed noticeably in favour of the latter,[4] and, within toilet tissues, superpremium brands have gained at the expense of premium.

Elasticities of demand The confidential version of the decision document includes the following table (Table 6.2) of own-price and cross-price elasticities. Unfortunately, no elasticities are reported for either towels or facials, and none at all for individual brands.

Interestingly, these estimates are typically lower than those provided by Hausman and Leonard (1997) in their modelling of the same market for the USA: they estimate the overall elasticity as −1.17 and the own-price elasticity of private labels as −3.13. We have no explanation for these differences, although we should note that the configuration of market shares is very different between the two countries – for example, private labels account for only 7.6 per cent of the market (as opposed to 45 per cent in the UK).

Costs

On the production side (as always in the paper sector), scale economies are only exhausted at a non-trivial minimum efficient scale, capacity imposes a very definite upper limit on production, and high capacity utilization is

Table 6.2 Estimates of price elasticities for toilet tissue

Overall market elasticity	−0.67	
Own-price and cross-price elasticities		
	Branded	Private labels
Branded	−1.47	0.64
Private labels	0.61	−1.16

required (EC, 40–41 and Table 1). Exogenous and endogenous sunk costs (production and advertising scale economies) render entry difficult for any firm without the requisite physical production capacity and established brand loyalty.

Demand: who are the buyers?

Consumer tissues products are sold through the retail distribution sector, with about three-quarters accounted for by the large supermarket/hypermarket chains.[5] The UK supermarket sector is, itself, concentrated: in 1993, the top five firms accounted for about 45 per cent of the market (Sainsbury 13 per cent; Tesco 12 per cent; Asda 8 per cent; Safeway 7 per cent; and Somerfield 4 per cent; see Clarke et al., 2002, pp. 72–3).

Vertical structure

On the production side, apart from preliminary stock preparation, there are two major stages: (1) paper preparation on a paper machine, the end product of which is a 'parent reel', and (2) converting the reel into the final product. All the majors are integrated – producing both reel and the products thereof. In addition, there is a number of small converters (accounting for about one-sixth of converting capacity): they tend to concentrate on AFH, and are sourced by, *inter alia*, KC.

On the retail side, producers have no retail operations of their own. Importantly however, as already noted, many of the largest retailers sell their own private labels. Not only do these account for a large proportion of the retail market (see below), but also they are sourced by, among others, KC and Scott. The joint KC/S share of total private labels sourcing in 1994 was 36 per cent, 37 per cent and 21 per cent in the three sectors (EC Annex Table 7). We return to the significance of this later when discussing buyer power.

Spot market or contracts? Price is negotiated with the supermarket chains. However, evidence supplied by the parties suggests that contracts are typically only short term (for example, three months). While the leading brands have a 'must stock' status, retailers frequently switch between alternative sources of supply for their private labels. In the S/M decision (EC, 2001, 25), the Commission explains that

> for private label products, however, the supermarket determines the quality and quantity of the product, and the supplier produces to order . . . this process allows supermarkets more readily to switch private label volume between tissue manufacturers with spare capacity . . . In this respect, a private label contract could be viewed as a toll-manufacturing arrangement where the contract is awarded through a bidding process. As the termination period is short, this bidding process may be repeated quite often, even every few months.

Structure

Table 6.3 shows the number and size distribution of sellers. As can be seen from this table, in each of the three parts, KC and Scott were the leading suppliers of branded products. Private labels clearly accounted for the largest share, and, given our earlier figures on retail market shares, we would expect that three firms (Tesco, Sainsbury and Asda) would account for a leading proportion of the total. Note that the shares for KC and Scott exclude their sourcing of private labels.

Potential for entry The Commission clearly saw advertising and brand loyalty as the primary barriers:

> Any new entrant to the branded sector who does not enjoy the strength of an existing major brand would have to compete with the financial strength and resources of the combined KC/S entity. Moreover, advertising expenditure and market share is self-reinforcing. (EC, ibid.)

Table 6.3 Number and size distribution of sellers

	Market shares (by value), 1994		
	Toilet tissue	Kitchen towels	Facials
KC	13.7	7.3	27.7
	Kleenex	Kleenex	Kleenex
Scott brands	29.1	12.4	6.3
	Andrex	Andrex	Andrex
	Scottonelle		
		Scottowel	
			Scotties
		Fiesta	
Jamont	4.2	4.5	6.1
Fort Sterling	3.4	2.6	0.7
Gulp		3.2	
Kent Paper		0.5	
SCA/PWA		0.1	
Others	49.6	69.4	59.2
Of which private labels	44.9	61.3	51.6

Note: These statistics relate to shares in the total market, but do not attribute to the named firms those parts of private labels which they source. For example, some private label toilet tissues may be sourced by KC. The 13.7 per cent shown does not include those sourced supplies.

Source: Papers made available to us by the European Commission.

Other barriers include:

- *Market growth*: the UK and Irish toilet-tissue markets are relatively saturated. Low rate of growth renders market entry less attractive in general terms.
- *Advertising sunk costs*: establishing a new brand would require heavy investment in advertising and promotion to persuade brand-loyal customers to switch. This is a sunk cost and adds to risk of entry. One competitor estimated the costs to launch a new product in the UK market could be ECU 40 million for the first year alone (EC, 212).
- *Distribution difficulties*: tissue paper products are bulky, have low value and require substantial shelf space. Entrants will therefore find it difficult to secure adequate distribution with retailers. As a result of merger, KC/S would be the unchallenged market leader for branded consumer products. This would provide them with a strong influence on product layout and display within a retailer.
- *Physical production*: a new entrant would experience major difficulties with the physical manufacture of the paper tissue products required to enter.

Conduct

Main competitive weapons In the long run (stage 1 of the game), the main strategic variables are capacity (as always in the paper sector) and advertising (less usual); in the short run, there is price competition.

In 1994, almost £13 million was spent, by all competitors, on advertising toilet tissue, and £3.3 million on facial tissues; spending on kitchen towels was lower and more variable. Advertising outlays are concentrated, of course, on the branded products. But even within branded products, Andrex (Scott) is by far and away the most advertised brand, especially in the toilet tissue sector. On the other hand, in facials, Kleenex dominates. Surprisingly, none of the other branded products are significantly advertised, with the sole exception of Dixcel in toilet tissues. In essence, then, significant advertising competition is confined to just the two market leaders in two of the three sectors; see Table 6.4.

R&D and product innovation competition Firms are able to differentiate the quality of brands by additives in the production process and/or through the relatively new 'TAD'[6] production process. However, opinions are divided about the competitive advantage proffered by this technology. In any event, it is no longer new (introduced into Europe in the 1980s). Having said this, there is no doubt that certain Kleenex brands are seen by

Table 6.4 Advertising spends, 1994 (£000)

	Toilet tissue	Kitchen towels	Facials
Kleenex	3706	304	3209
Andrex	8401	255	
Dixcel (Jamont)	644		
Others	161	18	97
Total	12922	577	3306

Source: EC, Table 5.

the consumer as of superior quality (especially in their softness). On a blind test, consumers prefer Kleenex Double Velvet to Andrex by seven to three. Kleenex has the only TAD factory in the UK (which was part of the divestment package).

Nature of behaviour: non-cooperative or cooperative? There is no suggestion in any of the papers that behaviour is anything other than non-cooperative.

Buyer power Given the significant role of the big supermarket chains as buyers, buyer power is potentially a key issue in this case. We have already touched upon this above (under 'Vertical structure'), and now provide our own judgement. First, it should be recalled that the Commission itself did not expect that the supermarkets would be able to exert any significant restraining power on the market behaviour of the parties for three reasons:

(i) their dependence on the parties for essential brands;
(ii) their dependence on the parties for private label supplies, due to the inadequacy of supply alternatives, particularly for the growing supersoft segment of the market;
(iii) even if retailers could secure valid long-term alternative supply for private label products, the combined strength of the parties in the branded sector would allow them to pursue a tied branded/private label sales policy.

On point (i), we agree: the leading brands have a clear 'must stock' status, and it is unlikely that buyer power could constrain the parties in their pricing. Indeed, one might even argue that a high price for the leading brands provides the supermarkets with a very convenient reference point in the pricing of their own labels. On point (ii), we disagree, siding instead with the Commission's revised view in the S/M case (see above): the parties' shares of the private label sector were relatively small (see above), and there was a significant number of other suppliers. Moreover, the bidding process described under 'Spot markets or contracts' points strongly to an outcome in which manufacturers, keen to maintain high capacity usage, will ultimately be prepared to offer a wholesale price much nearer to their marginal costs (given that there is no evidence of collusion amongst the manufacturers). As a corollary of rejecting (ii), we also reject point (iii). In short, then, we believe that buyer power was non-existent for branded products, but applies for private labels. We believe that this is also the implication of the Commission's judgement in S/M.

Merger and remedy

Claimed efficiency enhancements pre-remedy We are unaware of any quantified claims by the parties in the European context; however, in the corresponding US investigation, KC estimated that the merger would lead to reductions in marginal cost of 2.4 per cent for Kleenex and Cottonelle and 4 per cent for ScotTissue (see Hausman and Leonard, 1997). Out of interest, we will experiment with these estimates in our own simulations.

Nature of remedy Remedies were required and agreed. The parties committed to divest/license, to a single purchaser, the brands of one or the other partner in each of the three sub-markets. Moreover, KC was required to divest a major production facility, the TAD Prudhoe plant. In other words, the aim of the remedy was to retain the same number of independent suppliers of leading brand names in each sub-market as there was before the merger. Moreover, the buyer would have the appropriate production capacity with which to supply.

The rationale for this remedy was the importance of maintaining competition in the branded segment of the market. Notwithstanding the potential competitive constraints that would remain from private labels, the Commission clearly valued interbrand competition as a potential driver for innovation. It also argued (contrary to the parties) that the removal of one major player from the market might seriously constrain the potential manufacturing supply for private labels.

In terms of our taxonomy, the divestment of production facilities is clearly a structural 'clean break'. However, to classify the divestment of brands, we need to delve deeper into the undertakings. The main provisions were that KC/S should:

1. not use the Kleenex (in toilet paper and towels), or Scottex and Andrex (in facials) trademarks for 15 years;[7]

2. within the 15 years, license the Kleenex (in toilet paper and towels) trademark for up to the first ten years, of which:
   (a) the first three years would be a royalty-free exclusive licence
   (b) for the following seven years, the purchaser would have the option to renew the licence annually with royalties payable.

Basically, these undertakings related to the weaker brands in each sector (that is, Kleenex in toilet tissues and kitchen towels, and the Scott brands in facials).

Strictly speaking, these licences do not constitute a 'clean break' or a complete transfer of property rights, because they imply an ongoing relationship between the merged party and the buyer: in particular, during years 4–10, KC/S might have the right to influence the buyer's costs. Of course, the buyer had the ability to avoid this, by not renewing the licence beyond year three. (In the event, the buyer did not renew the licence.) Therefore our classification would be a mixed structural/behavioural remedy, but with a predominant clear-cut dimension.

Competitive strength or weakness of buyer of divested asset SCA was the buyer of the divested assets. This was one of the largest European paper firms. Although it is now a very major player in the world's tissue sector, at the time of the divestment it only had very minor converting facilities in the UK.

6.1.2 Supplementary Note: Elasticities and Prices

In a case such as this, where much depends on how well we can model inter-brand competition, reliable information on elasticities is of paramount importance. Unfortunately, as explained above, the only information we have from the Commission's own documents is at an aggregate level ('all branded' and 'all private labels'). What is more relevant for our purposes is information on brand own-price and cross-price elasticities, for example, the own-price elasticity for Kleenex, and the cross-price elasticity with respect to the price of Andrex. Moreover, the estimates differ significantly from those in a comparable study for the US market by leading US econometricians (Hausman and Leonard, 1997).

In the absence of appropriate/reliable estimates, we must search for a second-best solution. The most obvious alternative is to estimate price–cost margins at the brand level: as is well known, any profit-maximizing firm will set its price such that this margin is equal to the reciprocal of its own-price elasticity.

Unfortunately, there also appears to be no direct information on typical manufacturers' margins, or even price levels, for the different brands. Therefore we are forced to look for alternative routes.

Table 6.5 Derivation of relative prices in the three segments

(a) Toilet tissue	Vol. share	Value share	'Unit price'
KC (Kleenex)	12.0	13.7	1.142
Scott brands	23.1	29.1	1.260
Jamont	4.6	4.2	0.913
Fort Sterling	4.7	3.4	0.723
Private labels*	55.6	49.6	0.892
(b) Kitchen towels			
KC (Kleenex)	5.2	7.3	1.404
Scott brands	6.8	12.4	1.824
Jamont	4.9	4.5	0.918
Fort Sterling	2.0	2.6	1.3
Private labels*	81.1	73.2	0.903
(c) Facials			
KC (Kleenex)	17	27.7	1.629
Scott brands	6.2	6.3	1.016
Jamont	8.4	6.1	0.726
Fort Sterling	1.3	0.7	0.538
Private labels*	67.1	59.2	0.874

Note: * Strictly speaking, in the raw data provided to us, this category is shown as 'others, including private labels'; however, comparison with the shares for private labels in Table 5.3 confirms that 'private labels' accounts for virtually all of this category.

We believe that the best available alternative open to us is to exploit the fact that we have access to market share data by both volume and value. This was provided by the parties,[8] and the first two numerical columns of Table 6.5 reproduce the available information on market shares by volume and value. In the third column, we divide the latter by the former to derive the 'unit price' for each firm. The precise definition is average price, relative to the average price in the sector. Thus, in toilet tissues, on average, Kleenex products are 14.2 per cent more expensive than the (weighted) average of all toilet tissues.

In themselves, these derived prices are revealing in a number of respects:

1. In all three cases, KC and Scott brands were much higher priced than the average.
2. With the sole exception of Fort Sterling in kitchen towels (in which it has a tiny market share), both of the other, much smaller, sellers of 'branded' products record prices more or less equal to, or lower than, those of the private labels.

3. The relationship between price and the advertising spends reported earlier is very close – the highly advertised brands attract the higher prices, confirming that advertising succeeds in its aim of increasing consumer willingness to pay.

But, to return to the main purpose, what, if anything, can we deduce from these data about likely price–cost margins? We believe that the most promising approach is to treat 'private labels' as a sort of 'numeraire', or base product, and in the second column of Table 6.6, KC and Scott's prices are re-expressed relative to the unit price for private labels.[9]

To see how these relative prices might be employed, consider the following simple model.

Notation

For firm i (KC or Scott), denote the marginal manufacturing costs of producing its branded product and the product supplied to supermarkets to be sold as a private label as, respectively, C_B and C_{PL}. Likewise, the wholesale prices are, respectively, PW_B and PW_{PL}. Suppose retailers add mark-ups to the wholesale prices of M_B and M_{PL}.

Assumptions

I Retailers' buyer power enables them to negotiate a wholesale price for private labels equal to the manufacturers' marginal costs, but the 'must

Table 6.6 Imputing the own-price elasticities

(a) Toilet tissue

	'Unit price'	Price relative to private labels	Implied own-price elasticity	Counterpart US elasticity
KC (Kleenex)	1.142	1.280	−4.571	−3.14
Scott brands	1.260	1.412	−3.427	−2.94
Private labels	0.892			

(b) Kitchen towels

	'Unit price'	Price relative to private labels	Implied own-price elasticity	Counterpart US elasticity
KC (Kleenex)	1.404	1.554	−2.805	
Scott brands	1.824	2.020	−1.980	
Private labels	0.903			

(c) Facials

	'Unit price'	Price relative to private labels	Implied own-price elasticity	Counterpart US elasticity
KC (Kleenex)	1.629	1.864	−2.157	
Scott brands	1.016	1.162	−7.173	
Private labels	0.874			

stock' nature of branded products enables manufacturers to charge the unconstrained profit-maximizing price. Thus:

$$(PW_B - C_B)/PW_B = e_B^{-1} \tag{6.1}$$

but

$$PW_{PL} = C_{PL} \tag{6.2}$$

and

$$PR_B = M_B{}^*PW_B \tag{6.3}$$
$$PR_{PL} = M_{PL}{}^*PW_{PL} \tag{6.4}$$

Substituting (6.1) and (6.2) into (6.3) and (6.4) respectively, after simple rearrangement, the ratio of retail prices is:

$$PR_B/PR_{PL} = (MR_B/MR_{PL})^*(C_B/C_{PL})^*(1 - e_B{}^{-1})^{-1} \tag{6.5}$$

II Retailers use the same retail mark-up on branded and private labels ($MR_B = MR_{PL}$).
III The marginal costs of branded and private labels are identical ($C_B = C_{PL}$).

Substituting into (6.5):

$$PR_B/PR_{PL} = (1 - e_B{}^{-1})^{-1} \tag{6.6}$$

In other words, the ratio (branded to private labels) of relative retail prices depends only on the own-price elasticity of the branded product. Formula (6.6) is used to derive the 'extreme' estimates shown in the third numerical column of Table 6.6.

Of course, both assumptions II and III are questionable. Fortunately, however, any errors are likely to be self-cancelling. On II, for example, the Commission reports (EC, 188), based on information made available, that retailer margins on private labels are 1.35 as opposed to 'just below 1.20' on Andrex, and 'around 1.25' for Kleenex. It is unclear how typical these estimates are, but they suggest that a more reasonable assumption than II might be $M_{PL} = 1.1{}^*M_B$. On III, we have no hard evidence about the relative costs of branded and private labels, but it would be reasonable to assume that the former are typically (if by no means always) of higher quality, with consequent higher marginal costs. If so, supposing a cost differential of 10 per cent ($C_B = 1.1 * C_{PL}$), the error implied by assumption III would exactly cancel the error implicit in II, leaving (6.6) as a reasonably accurate approximation.

Because of the paucity of data on price and elasticities in this case, it is difficult to assess how 'reasonable' are our elasticity estimates derived in this way. However, as a sensitivity test in our simulations, we will also use the estimated elasticities for the counterpart US market, taken from Hausman and Leonard (1997), for toilet tissues: −3.14 for KC and −2.94 for Scott.

6.1.3 Simulations: the General Conceptual Framework

Before moving on to the specifics of simulating this case, we need to explain some features of the framework to be used.

Ex ante and *ex post*

As explained in Chapter 4, the core comparison for our methodology is between the actual outcome (that is, with the remedies imposed) and the simulated outcome – what would have happened had the remedies not been imposed. This comparison can be made either *ex ante* (at the time of the merger)[10] or *ex post* (using all information subsequently available).

In general, the *ex ante* exercise entails comparing two simulations: both with and without remedies. On the other hand, *ex post* compares a simulated (without remedies) and an *actual* (with remedies).

In this particular case, however, the effect of remedies was to maintain the structure of the industry, in each of the three subsectors, exactly as it was before the merger. More correctly, it maintained the same number of independent players, with exactly the same brands, and at least initially the same market shares. The only difference was that the smaller of the two main players, in each sub-market, changed ownership. However, in modelling terms, we do not believe this change was significant. The buyer, SCA, was another large manufacturer in its own right (albeit not in this sector in the UK), and it was able to purchase manufacturing capacity capable of producing the purchased brands on the same terms as the merged firm, and no royalty payments were involved for the first three years. In these special circumstances, then, there is no reason to expect the with-remedies outcome to be any different from the pre-merger *status quo*. Table 6.7 summarizes.

What do we simulate?

The checklist suggests that price is the obvious candidate for simulation. In addition, however, a major competitive weapon used by Scott in the UK was its substantial and sustained advertising of the Andrex brand in particular. On the other hand, product development by KC of its Kleenex

Table 6.7 The required comparisons

	Merger without remedy	Merger with remedy
Ex ante assessment	Simulated outcome	*Status quo*
Ex post assessment	Observed outcome	*Status quo**

Note: * Arguably, this might be adjusted in the light of any known subsequent exogenous changes to the market (see below).

brands has undoubtedly underpinned its strong market position. This suggests that competition might be modelled as a stage game. In the first stage, the two main players compete in differentiating their brands with advertising or product development (that is, R&D broadly defined); in the second, they compete on price with the private labels and lesser branded products. For present purposes we shall abstract from the longer-run competition implied by stage 1. However, had the remedy not been imposed, the market would have seen effectively no stage 1 competition (there being only one major). The incentive to innovate/advertise may thus have been reduced.

The timescale

The essence of nearly all mergers simulations is that they are timeless, in the comparative static sense: one equilibrium is compared with another, with no real explanation of how long it will take for the new equilibrium to be reached. In the present context, we make the pragmatic judgement that the simulations should be compared *ex post* with actual outcomes over the two to three years following the merger.

Nature of the remedy

Over a two- to three-year period, it is reasonable to characterize the remedies in this case as clear-cut and structural: they amount to a once-for-all change (compared to the merger without remedies) to the structure of the industry, but thereafter, there is no significant ongoing relationship between the merged firm and either the buyer or the regulatory body.[11]

Alternative remedies

One attraction of the simulation methodology is that it allows us, in principle, to explore the hypothetical outcomes of alternative remedies. In this case, however, there are no obvious, particularly interesting, alternatives. Of course, KC/S may have sold to a different buyer: (1) perhaps the buyer might have had less experience of, and size in, this industry; (2) perhaps the buyer might have been one of the smaller existing sellers in the UK market (for example, Jamont); (3) perhaps the buyer might have chosen to switch production from branded to private labels.[12] For (1) we could model this as a loss in efficiency for the number 2 firm in each part of the market; for (2) this would be equivalent to a merger between, say, Jamont and the bought brands; and for (3) this would be modelled by the exit of one of the two leading sellers in the branded part of the market. Each of these alternatives could be simulated, but in each case, the outcome is qualitatively predictable: a decline in competition in the branded segment of the market. None of these alternatives would lead to an outcome as favourable as the remedy actually chosen. Potentially, more behavioural remedies might have been imposed, but no such alternatives are obvious to us.

6.1.4 Choosing a Relevant Model of Product Differentiation

The key decision in this case is the choice of model for product differentiation. It should include both branded and private labels, allowing for the possibility that the two types of product may not be very close substitutes.

To help explain the implications of our subsequent choice of simulation models (that is, for pedagogical purposes only), we first write down a fairly general model.

$$q_1 = a_{10} + a_{11}\,p_1 + a_{12}p_2 + a_{13}\,p_3 \tag{6.7}$$
$$q_2 = a_{20} + a_{21}\,p_1 + a_{22}p_2 + a_{23}\,p_3 \tag{6.8}$$
$$q_3 = a_{30} + a_{31}\,p_1 + a_{32}p_2 + a_{33}\,p_3 \tag{6.9}$$

where q_i and p_i are the logarithms of quantity and price respectively of brand i. Thus we posit a series of three demand equations, one for each brand in the market, in which the demand for that brand depends upon its own price and, in principle, the prices of all of the other brands. In this context, 1 and 2 might refer to KC and Scott, while 3 might refer to all other unbranded offerings. Note that this simplifies by assuming that (1) KC and Scott are single-brand firms within each part of the tissue market, (2) all private labels can be grouped together into a single entity, and (3) all elasticities are constant parameters (the a_{ij}).[13]

On the supply side, we assume one-shot Bertrand behaviour (that is, non-cooperative): in this case, there is no mention, in any of the documents we have seen, of cooperative pricing behaviour between firms.

Given these assumptions, we would simulate the effect of the merger on prices by assuming that, post-merger (without remedies), the prices of all brands under common ownership (here 1 and 2) would be set cooperatively (to maximize joint profits of the newly merged firms), but that independent firms (here 1&2 and 3) would still compete with each other non-cooperatively.

Table 6.8 Theoretical mark-ups pre- and post-merger

	Pre-merger	Post-merger
Brand 1	$-1/a_{11}$	$\{a_{21}(R_2/R_1)-a_{22}\}/\{a_{22}a_{11}-a_{21}a_{12}\}$
Brand 2	$-1/a_{22}$	$\{a_{12}(R_1/R_2)-a_{11}\}/\{a_{22}a_{11}-a_{21}a_{12}\}$

Note: R_i denotes revenue of brand *i*.

It can be easily shown that, under these circumstances, the optimizing mark-ups are as in Table 6.8. When firms 1 and 2 are independent (the case both before the merger and after the merger with remedy) each brand has a mark-up equal to the reciprocal of its own-price elasticity. After the merger, and without remedy, the prices of 1 and 2 are set collaboratively, and the mark-ups are higher because each brand is priced taking into account its effect on the demand for the other.

So, if we were to simulate using this model, we would require estimates of the two cross-price elasticities (a_{21} and a_{12}) as well as the two own-price elasticities (a_{11} and a_{22}). We have seen how the own-price elasticities might be estimated, but have insufficient information to compute the cross-price elasticities. Although this is frustrating, it is quite useful for present purposes since it highlights a problem that would often be faced in practice. We use it as an opportunity to describe how two 'simple' options for differentiated products might be used to circumvent the problem.

Option 1: The simple diversion ratio

As shown earlier in Chapter 3, Shapiro's well-known rule of thumb, using the 'diversion ratio', provides one very easy-to-use alternative. Recalling equation (4.7), (assuming no cost savings, and under certain simplifying assumptions) the proportionate growth in the price of brand 1, following a merger with 2, is given by:

$$(p_1{}^*-p_1)/p_1 = D_{12}m_1/(1-D_{12}-m_1) \tag{6.10}$$

where p^* and p are post- and pre-merger prices respectively, m_1 is the initial price cost margin of 1, and D_{12} is the 'diversion ratio', the proportion of the custom lost by brand 1 to brand 2 if the price of 1 is raised.

How does this compare with the more general expressions for the pre- and post-merger mark-ups for 1 in Table 6.8? In fact, it is a special case, where $a_{11}=a_{22}$; $a_{12}=a_{21}$, and $R_2=R_1$, that is, it is the special case in which there is perfect symmetry between brands 1 and 2.[14]

Option 2: PCAIDS

Although the PCAIDS model is also demanding in its assumptions (see Section 4.3), it does take into account all competitors in the market (and not just the merging parties), and with the nesting option (explained below), it can provide the scope for more flexibility on the substitutability between branded and private labels.

The data requirements for basic PCAIDS are: (1) market shares on all players, (2) an estimate of the aggregate demand elasticity, and (3) an estimate of the own-price elasticity of one of the brands. In the nested version, we will need also to specify how closely the groups of products (here, branded and private labels) are substitutable.

In other words, the additional information from (1) and (2) is sufficient to generate estimates of all four elasticities in Table 6.8, albeit conditional on the proportionality assumption.

6.1.5 *Ex ante* Simulation

As already explained, the *ex ante* comparison, given the nature of the remedy in this case, is between a simulation of what would have happened without the remedy, and the *status quo* (the pre-merger position). This is because the remedy, in our judgement, would have led to a market structure in each of the three segments that was no different from the pre-merger structure, and therefore no change in price.

Additional assumptions

Apart from the assumptions, already discussed, implicit in the two alternative demand options, we assume (1) non-cooperative Bertrand behaviour, and (2) no buyer power on branded labels, but buyer power on private labels (see above). Since we are simulating retail price, this allows us to treat private labels as independent sellers.

Option 1: The diversion ratio Table 6.9 shows the arithmetic of calibrating equation (6.10) by using the estimates from Tables 6.6 and 6.3 to derive the pre-merger margins[15] and the diversion ratios respectively. Out of interest, these allow us, in turn, to deduce the cross-price elasticities.[16]

We comment on these results below, and give the PCAIDS results.

Option 2: PCAIDS In order to calibrate a standard version of PCAIDS, we require estimates of two key parameters and market shares. We shall also want to experiment with different assumptions about the nest structure (to allow for weaker substitution between branded and private labels). The assumptions we use are as follows:

Table 6.9 Simulated price increases according to diversion ratio

	Own-price elasticity	Margin	*D*	Implied cross-price elasticity	Predicted price increase
(a) Toilet tissue					
KC	−4.571	0.219	0.263	1.200	11.1
Scott	−3.427	0.292	0.156	0.535	8.2
(b) Kitchen towels					
KC	−2.805	0.357	0.072	0.201	4.5
Scott	−1.980	0.505	0.056	0.110	6.4
(c) Facials					
KC	−2.157	0.464	0.075	0.161	7.5
Scott	−7.173	0.139	0.181	1.300	3.7

The aggregate market demand elasticity

Base case: −1.0

Sensitivity variations: −1.17 (Hausman and Leonard, 1997 for USA)
−0.67 (Cambridge Economics)

Discussion: As explained in the checklist, we have only two extraneous estimates of the aggregate elasticity, and even these are only for toilet tissues. We therefore use −1.0 as a default for all three parts of the market, but undertake a sensitivity analysis for illustrative purposes on toilet tissues, using the two alternative estimates mentioned in the checklist.

Own-price elasticity

Base case: −4.571 for KC (see Table 6.9)

Sensitivity variations: −3.427 for Scott (see Table 6.9)
−3.0 for KC (US study)

Discussion: In PCAIDS, we need to know only one of the own-price elasticities: in this case we arbitrarily choose KC, but alternative simulations for Scott provide a consistency check – if all the PCAIDS assumptions were correct, both would give the same results. We also experiment with −3, a value typical of those found by Hausman et al. for the US (−2.94 for ScotTissue and −3.38 for Kleenex). For towels and facials, we use the elasticities shown in Table 6.6.

Market shares

Table 6.3 reports the market shares of the named brands and aggregate share of private labels. We disaggregate the latter to generate individual

Table 6.10 Imputed market shares for individual private labels

	Toilet tissue	Kitchen towels	Facials
Sainsbury	11	15	13
Tesco	10	14	12
Asda	7	9	8
Safeway	6	8	7
Somerfield	6	8	7

estimates for the five main private labels, assuming that (1) between them, they account for 90 per cent of the private label aggregate, and (2) their individual shares of the 90 per cent correspond to their relative sizes in the overall supermarket market in 1993 (see checklist). Applying these assumptions to the aggregate private label shares in each of the three parts to the market gives the values shown in Table 6.10.

Nests

Base case: No nests

Sensitivity variations: Two nests, one for KC and Scott and one for private labels and the minor brands; we experiment with nesting proportions of 75 per cent, 50 per cent and 25 per cent.

Discussion: Nests play the same role in PCAIDS as in the nested logit model. They allow for deviations from the basic proportionality assumption. In this case, by placing private labels in a separate nest from KC and Scott, we explore the implications where private labels capture a smaller proportion of the sales lost by KC (for example) were KC to increase price, than would be suggested by the simple arithmetic of the private labels' share of the non-KC part of the market. For example, a nest of 50 per cent can be interpreted as meaning that private labels are only half as desirable, compared to Scott, as a substitute for KC.[17]

Epstein and Rubinfeld (2002, p. 898) suggest that 'A coarse grid (for example, 75 per cent, 50 per cent and 25 per cent) covering a range of odds ratio factors is adequate to assess sensitivity.'

Efficiency savings

Base case: None

Sensitivity variations: −3 per cent for KC and Scott

Discussion: As mentioned earlier, we could find no explicit claims of efficiency savings in any of the papers we have seen, but we experiment with the claimed savings for the merger in the USA (see checklist).

Comment

Taking the results of Tables 6.11 and 6.12 at face value, it can be seen that they both suggest that the remedies were extremely effective: they simulate by how much price would have risen without the remedies, as opposed to no change with the remedies. This is particularly true for toilet tissue, for which both the diversion ratio and most of the PCAIDS simulations point to a double-digit increase in the KC price. More generally, the main message appears to be that, without remedies, the merger would have led to significant increases in all prices in both the toilet tissues and facials markets.

Although there is a wealth of detail in these results, we prefer not to highlight the fine differences between different calibrations – this would imply greater confidence in the numbers than the underlying assumptions deserve. Instead, we pick out some generalizations:

1. Results for toilet tissues are not particularly sensitive to which estimate of the industry elasticity is used.
2. There is a worrying divergence between the simulations based on the KC, as opposed to the Scott, own-price elasticities. This is a sort of robustness check, which suggests that the PCAIDS model is not altogether satisfactory as a description of the demand system in this particular market.
3. When we allow for nests (that is, less demand substitutability between branded and private labels) the simulated price increases for KC/S become even larger. This suggests that the key proportionality assumption of

Table 6.11 Simulation results for toilet tissues

	I	II	III	IV	V	VI	VII	VIII
Calibration values								
Aggregate elasticity	−1.0	−1.17	−0.67	−1.0	−1.0	−1.0	−1.0	−1.0
Own price	KC −4.57	KC −4.57	KC −4.57	Scott −3.43	KC −3.0	KC −4.57	KC −4.57	KC −4.57
Nests	None	None	None	None	None	75%	50%	75%
Efficiency savings	None	None	None	None	None	None	None	3%
Predicted price increases								
KC	9.5	9.0	10.5	10.7	12.5	12.6	18.8	10.3
Scott	6.0	5.7	6.7	6.8	7.9	8.3	12.9	6.1
Industry weighted average	4.7	4.4	5.2	5.2	6.0	6.2	9.1	4.8

Table 6.12 Simulation results for kitchen towels and facials

	Kitchen towels				Facials			
Calibration values								
Aggregate elasticity	−1.0	−1.0	−1.0	−1.0	−1.0	−1.0	−1.0	−1.0
Own price	KC	Scott	KC	KC	KC	Scott	KC	KC
	−2.80	−1.98	−2.80	−2.80	−2.16	−7.17	−2.16	−2.16
Nests	None	None	75%	75%	None	None	75%	75%
Efficiency savings	None	None	None	3%	None	None	None	3%
Predicted price increases								
KC	4.6	6.7	**6.1**	**4.0**	4.7	1.7	6.2	3.9
Scott	3.0	**4.3**	4.0	2.0	14.1	4.4	17.6	15.1
Industry weighted average	1.3	1.7	1.6	0.9	3.5	1.3	4.4	3.2

PCAIDS will lead to underestimates of the price-raising effects of the merger.

4. Introducing small efficiency savings makes only a trivial difference.

6.1.6 *Ex post* Assessment

The basis for an *ex post* assessment is a comparison between the actual, rather than the simulated, outcome of the merger with remedy and a simulation of the merger without remedy. However, in any market, there will almost inevitably be exogenous changes – unexpected and unrelated to the merger – and these may sometimes blur the comparison since they will obviously affect the actual outcome, but will have been unanticipated in the simulation.

In this particular case, there were indeed a number of significant changes. Our sources of information on 'what happened next' are (1) our own web searches, and, much more importantly, (2) DG Competition's survey, based on interview/questionnaires, especially with KC and SCA (the buyer).

Prices

In the key toilet tissue market, price actually declined by 5–6 per cent in the three years after the merger (and remedies). The same is true for kitchen towels, but in facials, KC report a major increase in prices – 35 per cent in the following three years (see Table 6.13).

These price outcomes are obviously in contrast to our *status quo* simulation of no price changes,[18] and, in order to discover why, we next look at how market shares changed post-merger.

Table 6.13 Actual price outcomes

(a) Toilet tissues

	1996	1997	1998	1999	2000
KC	100	96	95	n.a.	94
SCA	100	102	98	94	98
(b) Kitchen towels					
KC	100	n.a.	n.a.	n.a.	
SCA	100	102	98	94	
(c) Facials					
KC	100	123	131	135	
SCA-Velvet	100	102	100	98	

Source: Questionnaire returns from KC and SCA.

Market shares

There were two major unexpected exogenous developments:

1. Entry by Procter and Gamble with its 'Charmin' brand (1999/2000). More or less immediately, they captured 7 per cent of the toilet tissue market. P&G is, of course, one of the world's leading tissue products manufacturers, and this particular brand, long established in other countries, competes at the top quality end of the market.
2. The worldwide acquisition of Fort James by Georgia-Pacific Corporation in 2000. This followed an earlier merger, in 1997, between James River and Fort Howard to form Fort James. In terms of the UK market, this brought together 'Jamont' and 'Fort Sterling'. Georgia-Pacific (now selling 'Nouvelle') vies with P&G ('Charmin') for third place in the branded part of toilet tissues; is the largest branded towels seller, but is insignificant in facials.

However, neither of these developments will have significantly affected the market for the relevant three years post-merger: P&G's entry only occurred in 1999, and Jamont and Fort Sterling were relatively minor players.

Turning to the endogenous developments, in toilet tissues and towels, there were no unexpected outcomes. As required, KC licensed (royalty-free) the Kleenex brand to SCA for three years. SCA stopped using the brand before the expiry, having, in the meantime, established 'Double Velvet' and 'Quilted'. 'These are the interesting brands from a commercial point of view and therefore the ones we're focusing on' (interview response, 23

September 2003). Nevertheless, SCA's ability to compete effectively was facilitated by the divestment of the technology embodied in the Prudhoe plant. In toilet tissues, up to 1998, neither KC nor SCA report any major loss in market share (compared to the pre-merger shares of KC and Scott). Georgia-Pacific also remained fairly static; private labels continued their steady growth up to 1997. In kitchen towels, the biggest change has been a large increase in the share of private labels (now accounting for three-quarters of the market). Georgia-Pacific has also grown, and now accounts for half of the branded segment. Both KC (particularly) and SCA have fallen away.

However, in facials, the story is rather different. Again, as required, KC licensed the Scott brands (Scotties and Handy Andies), but apparently these brands 'had very small market shares', and SCA 'never focused on them'. Indeed, it appears to have run them down rapidly, and stopped producing in 1997. Things are complicated by the fact that, thereafter, they explain that they 'purchased from an external supplier', and Handy Andies remains in the market to this day (presumably externally sourced) but now supported by the Velvet brand. This remaining presence does not appear large, however – SCA report their market share three years after merger as 0! It would appear that, to all intents and purposes, this market is now shared almost equally between KC and private labels. There are no other significant players.

SCA's explanation

According to SCA, the reasons why prices (of toilet tissues and towels) fell post-merger were unexpected at the time of its purchase of the divested assets, and in no way connected to the merger or remedies:

> Prices in the UK have decreased about 15 to 20% since we acquired Kimberly-Clark's business. The main reasons for that have been: new entries in the market (there are now more active competitors than before the acquisition); new brands in the market (P&G have introduced American brands); the enlargement of the customers bases to pan-European levels, i.e. we have to negotiate now with bigger and more important customers who require pan-European negotiation's conditions (sic) and therefore lower prices. (Extract from minutes of interview of SCA by Commission, 23 September 2003)

Although the entry of P&G may not have been a cause of the price reductions in 1996–98, this quotation also points to an increase in buyer power and possibly other entry. Neither of these was anticipated by us or the Commission at the time the remedy was imposed.

In principle, both of these developments could be factored into the simulations – how much would price have fallen, without the remedies, but with

Table 6.14 Actual market shares

(a) Toilet tissues

	1994	1996	1997	1998
KC	(29.1)*	25.7	27.1	28.2
SCA	(13.7)*	14.3	12.8	12.5
Private label	44.9	49.1	52.6	52.1
Georgia-Pacific	4.2+3.4*	7	7.8	7.8

Note: * For 1994, the KC figure refers to the Scott brands, which were retained; the SCA figure refers to the KC brands which were divested; Georgia-Pacific refers to Jamont and Fort Sterling respectively.

(b) Kitchen towels

	1994	1996	1997	1998	1999
KC	(12.4)*	11	8	7	6
SCA	(7.3)*	6	6	6	5
Private label	61.3	n.a.	n.a	n.a.	74.6
Georgia-Pacific	4.5+2.6*	6	9	10	11

Note: As for (a).

(c) Facials

	1994	1996	1997	1998	1999
KC	(27.7)*	38	40	43	46
SCA-Velvet	(6.3)*	1	1	0	0
Private label	51.6	53	51	55	49
Georgia-Pacific	6.1+0.7*	3	2	1	1

Note: * For 1994 the figure for KC refers to Kleenex, which was retained; the SCA figure refers to the Scott brands which were divested; Georgia-Pacific refers to Jamont and Fort Sterling respectively.

Source: Questionnaire returns from KC and SCA.

increased buyer power and new entry. In practice, however, we would need more hard information than is provided in this quotation. In the event, our (merger without remedy) simulation has established that, in the absence of these developments, the remedies would have been effective in helping avoid fairly hefty hikes in price. Of course, the increase in buyer power may have been sufficient to achieve the same effect – we cannot be sure, and given the unexpected nature of the event, it would be unreasonable to suggest that the remedy was superfluous – in the context that it was imposed.

For facials, the story is very different. The withdrawal of the previously Scott brands by SCA left the branded part of the market to KC alone. Of course, this was not the Commission's intention, and perhaps it should have sought an assurance from the buyer, that is, that it would *not* phase out the old Scott brands. Equally, our own simulation of the remedy was based on the assumption that there would be no change in market structure. Had we anticipated the withdrawal of SCA from the branded segment, the simulation should have been based on a model in which the Scott brands exited. This would have led to qualitatively similar predictions to the without-remedy simulations already shown in Table 6.12, that is, large price increases, exactly as actually happened. In that sense, we might claim this case as a qualified success for the simulation model – without remedies, it predicts big price increases. The remedy itself, of course, failed because it did not prevent an outcome very similar to what would have happened had the merger been allowed without remedy.

6.2 SCA PACKAGING/METSA CORRUGATED, 2001 – M2032

6.2.1 Applying the Checklist

Decision: Article 6.2 (conditions and obligations) = Phase 1, 25 August 2000

Competition concerns – products and markets that raised concerns Corrugated boxes in Denmark, in which the merger would lead to a dominant firm, with market size in excess of 50 per cent – more than twice the size of its next largest rival.

Product

Nature of product Homogeneous. Although there are different types of corrugated packaging (five types of flute size, according to customers' needs), it is not significantly differentiated within type. The most important difference is between heavy- and light-duty cases, but this is irrelevant in this market because neither of the parties manufactures heavy-duty cases.

Product life cycle: creative destruction or demand changes? This is a mature product, and the market grows by only about 2–3 per cent p.a.

Costs

Overall cost structure Transport costs can be significant – products can only be economically supplied within a radius of 200–300 km: beyond this distance, transport costs exceed 10 per cent.

Capacity constraints There are definite upper limits on the scale of output from any plant in the short to medium run. The only hard numbers we have on capacity usage are that importers from Germany were operating at 80–90 per cent of capacity. Ninety per cent usage of capacity in the paper sector as a whole at this time seems fairly typical (Chapter 5).

Scale economies The minimum efficient scale (MES) of production is large relative to this small market. SCA estimates it to be 10–20 per cent of total market size.

Demand

Elasticity As far as we know, there are no available estimates of the demand elasticity. We suggest one possible way of inferring it from available data in the next subsection.

Who are the buyers? There is a very wide range of industrial users of transport packaging (see below).

Market

Market definition: product and geographic Transport costs dictate that Denmark is the appropriate geographical definition, albeit subject to increasing import competition from adjacent plants in northern Germany. Demand substitution between corrugated board boxes and other forms of transport packaging is constrained by switching costs and time constraints on the buyer's side.

Import competition: actual and potential Before the investigation, imports from (mostly) Germany had risen from 10.5 per cent to 18 per cent in five years (testament to the price differential between the two countries). This rate of growth was expected to decline as the price differential had narrowed, limiting importers' ability to make further inroads into the market. The above-mentioned capacity constraints might also limit the scope for a major increase in the import share.

Vertical structure Basically, there are two production stages: production of sheet from the case materials, and conversion of sheets into case. All significant players in this market are integrated, although there are also a small number of small, relatively inefficient firms who only convert.

Spot market or contracts? By negotiation with individual buyers.

Structure
Table 6.15 shows the number and size distribution of sellers.

Potential for entry Limited by large scale of MES and transport costs (see above).

Number and size distribution of buyers There is a large number, across many buying industries.[19] For instance, SCA has 750 'large' customers and 7000 smaller customers.

Conduct

Main competitive weapons Price, but constrained by fixed capacity. Advertising is presumably trivial, and R&D spends are very small (0.3 per cent of sales for SCA and 0.7 per cent for Metsa).

Table 6.15 Market structure in 2000 (by volume)

	% share, 1999	Post-merger without divestment	Post-merger with divestment**
SCA	40	53	40
Metsa Corrugated	13		
AssiDomän	24	24	24
Importers			
Smurfitt Stone	3		16
Thimm	4		
Klingele	3		
Herzberger (Kappa)	3		
Other small suppliers*	10		

Notes:
* Converters only or, small importers.
** Hypothetical, in that these figures merely add the pre-merger market shares.

Source: EC, p. 6.

Buyer power Bearing in mind the large number of buyers (see above), we would not expect buyer power to be significant, although larger buyers will presumably negotiate some scale-related discounts.

Merger and remedy

Claimed efficiency enhancements pre-remedy None that are likely to be significant in this particular geographical market.

Nature of remedy Structural, that is, clean break: divest to Jefferson Smurfitt: Neopak (the Metsa operations in Denmark) and two sheet plants of SCA's.

Competitive strength or weakness of buyer of divested asset Smurfitt were already large Europe-wide, and selling in the Danish market by importing from plants in Northern Germany.

Impact of remedy on merged firm's efficiency claims None, as far as is known.

6.2.2 Supplementary Note: Estimating the Demand Elasticity

In cases such as this, a 'low-profile' specialized product in a small member state, it is unlikely that there will be previous industry case studies to provide data to calibrate key parameters. As far as we know, there is no previous literature (or information within the confidential documents provided by the Commission) to provide an estimate of the crucial industry elasticity of demand. Thus this case study poses an interesting and challenging problem, which is likely to occur in many real-world cases. For the sake of interest, we suggest a solution that illustrates how one may often have to make use of what data are available, rather than bemoaning the absence of an ideal.

Within the documents received from the Commission are some that give data on the size distribution of firms, and the size of market, both by volume and value, in most member states. We have estimated the HHI index from the former and average price from the latter, for each member state. Figure 6.1 plots average price against HHI.

The linear line of best fit shows a discernible upward-sloping relationship – price tends to be higher in more concentrated markets. However, for three or four member states, price is 'low' in spite of fairly high HHI values, and if these were excluded, the line would be noticeably steeper, albeit curvilinear. The other point to notice from the figure is that there appears

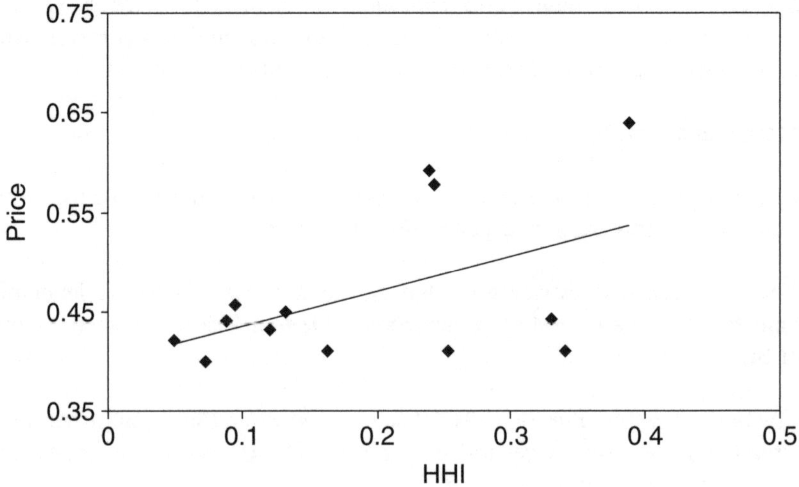

Source: Confidential data from SCA, provided by the Commission.

Figure 6.1 Relationship between price and the HHI index across member states

to be a lower bound on price – it never falls much below a 'floor' of approximately 0.40.

Our reason for examining this relationship is that, under Cournot competition with a homogeneous product (as will be assumed in the simulations below), there is a well-known relationship between the industry's price–cost margin $(P–C)/P$ and its HHI:[20]

$$(P-C)/P = \mathrm{HHI}/e \tag{6.11}$$

where e is the industry demand elasticity. Thus the relationship between P and HHI is:

$$P = C/(1-\mathrm{HHI}/e) \tag{6.12}$$

that is, a non-linear relationship with P, tending to C as HHI tends to zero. This is roughly the relationship we observe in the figure, especially if we ignore the four member states lying well below the line, that is, with low price in spite of higher HHI values.

Turning to the identities of the individual member states, Germany, in particular, deserves close attention. It has the largest market size by some way, coupled with a low HHI (0.05) and price (0.44). Similar values are also

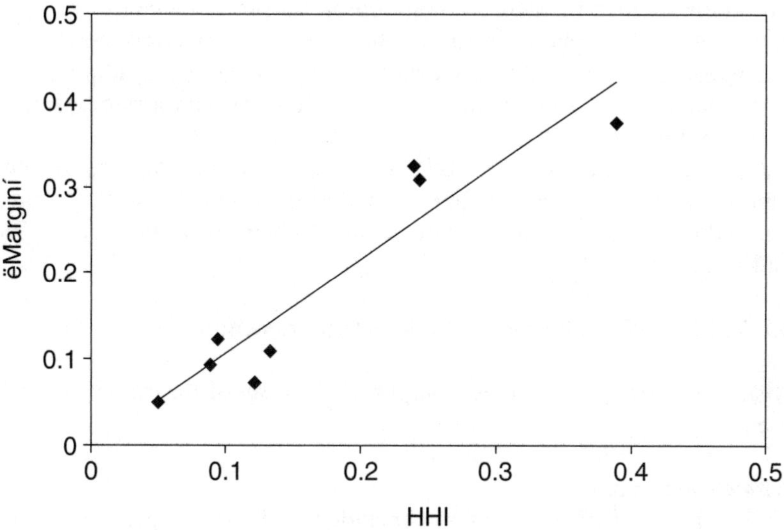

Source: Confidential data from SCA, provided by the Commission.

Figure 6.2 Imputed price–cost margins versus the HHI index (subsample)

observed for the other largest member states (Italy, France and to a lesser extent the UK). For these countries, it could be argued, the size of market is sufficiently large to support relatively unconcentrated industries, and, from (6.12), this leads to a price closer to marginal costs. If we are prepared to accept that the price in Germany (0.421) is fairly close to cost, then it might be reasonable to assume marginal cost in the region of 0.4.

Making this assumption, we can re-express all countries' prices in price–cost margin form. Figure 6.2 shows the subsequent margin data, again, plotted against the HHI, but excluding the four outliers (to which we return presently). The relationship is now quite pronounced, with a slope more or less equal to unity, and intercept equal to zero. This is not inconsistent with equation (6.11) with $e = 1$.

But what of the four outliers, excluded from Figure 6.2? These are Portugal, Ireland, Greece and the Netherlands – all with very small markets and high concentration, but with unexpectedly low prices. If they are to be excluded, we need a justification of why they do not 'fit' the Cournot model. One easy answer is possible errors in the data.[21] A theoretically more interesting possibility is that competition in these countries is described by Bertrand, rather than Cournot, competition: for Bertrand competition, price is forced down to marginal costs, whatever the level of concentration.

Intriguingly, price in each of these four countries is indeed close to the lower bound. To explain why this might be, even more (unverifiable) speculation would be required. Perhaps the market is met largely by imports from larger neighbours, and cut-throat competition from importers results in price close to cost.

In any event, the upshot of this digression is that we shall assume that a typical value of e is about 1. In the simulations below, we take $e = 1.00$ as our middle estimate, with alternative low- and high-value scenarios of 0.75 and 1.25.

6.2.3 Simulations: the General Conceptual Framework

Again, we start by explaining some general features of the framework to be used.

Ex ante and *ex post*

Unfortunately, this case was not included in DG Competition's recent survey, and we have been unable to unearth any publicly available data on prices etc. in the Danish corrugated board market. Therefore only an *ex ante* comparison is possible. This entails comparing two simulations: with and without remedies.

In this case, the effect of the remedy was to produce a market structure that was marginally more concentrated than the pre-merger structure, but much less concentrated than it would have been absent the remedy. The task for simulation is to compare the prices predicted for these two alternative structures (see Table 6.16).

What do we simulate?

The checklist suggests that output, and thus price, are the obvious candidates.

The timescale

As for KC/S, simulations are timeless, and in the present case, we have no real-world post-merger data anyway.

Table 6.16 The required comparisons

	Merger without remedy	Merger with remedy
Ex ante assessment	Simulated outcome	Simulated outcome
Ex post assessment	None possible	None possible

Nature of the remedy

It is reasonable to characterize the remedies in this case as clear-cut and structural: they amount to a once-for-all change (compared to the merger without remedies) to the structure of the industry, but thereafter, no significant ongoing relationship between the merged firm and either the buyer or the regulatory body.

Alternative remedies

The most obvious alternative remedies would have involved different buyers. Basically, there are two options: (1) a third party previously non-existent in the market, or (2) one of the existing players, other than Smurfitt. Potentially, behavioural remedies might have been imposed, but there are no such alternatives obvious to us.

6.2.4 The model: Homogeneous Product, with Potentially Capacity-constrained Cournot Competition

In an extensive modelling of this industry, it would be appropriate to model competition as two-stage: in the first stage, firms set capacity; and in the second, they set price, given their capacities. Essentially, this is a distinction between short-run and long-run competition. In the context of simple simulation modelling, it is reasonable to appeal to the well-known Kreps–Scheinkman result,[22] that such a two-stage game can be approximated by one-stage Cournot competition in quantity. This simplifies the simulation considerably.

From the checklist, the following stylization seems reasonable. The product is homogeneous, and we assume initially that the market demand curve is given by:

$$P=\alpha-\beta X \tag{6.13}$$

where P and X are price and industry output respectively.

Costs

Once MES scale is attained, scale economies are not important. However, in the short run, capacity is limited by the number and size of plants. We assume that firms are unable to produce at output levels in excess of full capacity. Thus, suppose that marginal costs (MC) are constant, but different across firms; so, for firm i:

$$MC_i=c_i. \tag{6.14}$$

For $\text{MES}<X_i<K_i$,

where K_i is capacity of firm i.
Nature of pre-merger conduct: non-cooperative Cournot behaviour.
Allowing also for fixed costs (F), gross profits for firm i are:

$$\pi_i = P.X_i - c_i X_i - F_i \quad (6.15)$$

Option 1: No capacity constraints
Initially, we assume that no firm is capacity constrained, before or after the merger. In that case, we can use the first-order condition (f.o.c.) for a maximum:

$$\delta\pi_i / \delta X_i = P + (dP/dX_i).X_i - c_i = 0 \quad (6.16)$$

Assuming Cournot (zero conjectures), and inserting the slope of the demand curve from (5.13), the f.o.c. can then be rewritten as:

$$P - \beta X_i - c_i = 0 \quad (6.17)$$

[Digression: it will be useful below, although unnecessary at this stage, to rearrange this f.o.c. to read:

$$(P - c_i)/P = \beta X_i / P = (X_i / X).\beta X / P = (s_i / e) \quad (6.17')$$

where s_i is firm i's market share and e is the industry demand elasticity. This is a well-known result which tells us that each firm's mark-up will equal its market share divided by the elasticity.]

Returning to (6.17) and summing across all N firms in the industry:

$$NP - \beta X - \Sigma c_i = 0,$$

that is,

$$P.(N+1) - \alpha - \Sigma c_i = 0. \quad (6.18)$$

From (6.18), pre-merger price is given by:

$$P_0.(N+1) - \alpha - \Sigma c_i = 0,$$

that is,

$$P_0 = \{\alpha + \Sigma c_i\} / (N+1). \quad (6.19)$$

Merger without remedy Simulating the effects of the merger, absent any remedy, firm numbers fall to $N-1$. Assuming that the new configuration of optimal firm outputs involves no firm operating at less than MES or greater than capacity, the industry sum of marginal costs falls by the MC of the 'exiting' firm (denoted by c_x). Thus post-merger price is given by

$$P_1.N-\alpha-(\Sigma c_i-c_x)=0. \tag{6.20}$$

Subtracting (6.19) from (6.20), and rearranging, the proportionate change in price is

$$(P_1-P_0)/P_0=\{(P_0-c_x)/P_0\}/N. \tag{6.21}$$

If the margin of the exiting firm is unknown, we can use the alternative form of the f.o.c (6.17′) for the exiting firm, to re-express (6.21) as

$$(P_1-P_0)/P_0=s_x/(N.e) \tag{6.22}$$

Merger with remedy Assuming, alternatively, that the 'exiting' firm (here Metsä) is sold to a third-party firm not already present in the industry, but with sufficient expertise to operate the purchased plant at the same level as did Metsä, then post-merger structure would be unchanged from pre-merger. If the third party is a firm already existent in the industry, then we assume that the purchaser closes either the Metsä plant (same outcome as merger without remedy) or its own existing operations. The actual remedy was with Smurfitt as the actual buyer. Thus we shall assume that, post-merger, Smurfitt will cease to import from Germany – it exits as an importer. This entails inserting Smurfitt's market share (rather than Metsä's) in (6.22).

As noted above, the most obvious alternative remedies would entail alternative buyers. In this case, there are three alternatives, none of which is of much interest in modelling terms: (1) an 'outside' purchaser, in which case there would be no exit and no price change; (2) AssiDomän, but its large pre-merger market share implies that it would presumably prefer to close the Metsä plants (that is, exactly as would SCA, without remedy); (3) one of the other importers, but each of these has more or less identical pre-merger market shares to Smurfitt, and the outcome will be identical to the sale to Smurfitt. Thus, no further simulations are required.

Option 2: Binding capacity constraints

In deriving the above equilibrium, we have assumed that all firms' post-merger equilibrium outputs are 'feasible', that is, that they have sufficient capacity. As is well known (and established formally by Farrell and Shapiro), the removal of the higher-cost party of the merging firms has the effect of increasing marginal revenue for all surviving firms (including the remaining party to the merger). Thus all find it optimal to increase output beyond pre-merger levels.[23]

But now suppose that all firms are capacity-constrained, so that, with one exception, no post-merger expansion is possible. This means that all non-merging firms will continue to produce at their pre-merger levels. However, we will assume that the merged firm is able to transfer know-how from the previously lower-cost to the previously higher-cost partner.[24] As such, it alone will not be capacity-constrained – rather, it will be able to optimize its output decision – choosing an output that is greater than the pre-merger output of the low-cost party, but still less than the combined pre-merger outputs of the two parties.[25]

Formally, the merged firm faces a post-merger residual demand curve given by

$$P = P_0 - \beta\,(X_m - X_y - X_x), \tag{6.23}$$

where X_m is the post-merger output of the merged firm, and c_y and c_x are the pre-merger outputs of the two parties. Denoting pre-merger marginal costs of the two parties by c_y and c_x ($c_y < c_x$), and substituting for X_x and X_y using the f.o.c. from (6.17), the residual demand curve can be rewritten, after simple rearrangement) as

$$P = 3P_0 - (c_x + c_y) - \beta X_m. \tag{6.24}$$

Substituting this into the merged firm's profit function, and maximizing, the optimal value of output can then be derived as

$$\beta X_m = (3P_0/2) - (c_x + 2c_y). \tag{6.25}$$

Substituting this back into the residual demand curve yields a post-merger industry price:

$$P_1 = (3P_0/2) - (c_x/2), \tag{6.26}$$

and a proportionate increase in price:

$$(P_1 - P_0)/P_0 = \{(P_0 - c_x)/P_0\}/2 \tag{6.27}$$

As before, this can be re-expressed using (6.17′) as

$$(P_1 - P_0)/P_0 = s_x/(2e). \tag{6.28}$$

Of course, both options 1 and 2 are extreme, and, in practice, it is likely that outsiders will be able to expand out, if not necessarily by as much as they would want. Therefore it may be better to specify the post-merger outcome as lying somewhere within the range defined by (6.22) and (6.28):

$$s_x/(2e) > (P_1 - P_0)/P_0 > s_x/(Ne), \tag{6.29}$$

depending on the extent of spare capacity in outside firms.[26]

The intuition of this result might be helped if one thinks of the bounds in (6.29) as two extreme assumptions about the slope of the short-run marginal cost (SRMC) curve – no capacity constraints corresponds to horizontal SRMC, while binding capacity corresponds to vertical SRMC. Given information on the actual slope, we could model more precisely where, within this range, the new equilibrium would be. In this case, however, we do not have this information.

An alternative demand function It is well known that simulations with linear demand generate lower predicted price increases than for constant elasticity demand. As an illustration, consider option 1, but now with a demand function, with a constant elasticity of e:

$$P = \alpha X^{-1/e}. \tag{6.30}$$

In this case, the key f.o.c. becomes

$$P - P/e.(X_i/X) - c_i = 0, \tag{6.31}$$

and summing across all firms:

$$P(N - 1/e) - \Sigma c_i = 0, \tag{6.32}$$

pre-merger and post-merger prices are

$$P_0.(N - 1/e) - \Sigma c_i = 0 \tag{6.33}$$
$$P_1(N - 1 - (1/e)) - \Sigma c_i + c_x = 0 \tag{6.34}$$

and the proportionate change in price is

$$\{(P_1 - P_0)/P_0\} = \{(P_0 - c_x)/P_0\}/\{(N - 1 - (1/e)\}, \tag{6.35}$$

or

$$\{(P_1 - P_0)/P_0\} = s_x/\{Ne - e - 1\}. \tag{6.36}$$

Note that the denominator of the right-hand side of (6.36) is smaller than that for linear demand (6.21), that is, the predicted price increase will be slightly larger.

6.2.5 *Ex ante* Simulation of Merger and Remedy

To simulate the effects of this merger with and without remedy, with and without capacity constraints, from (6.22) and (6.29), we need data on N, e and the market shares of Metsä (without remedy) and Smurfitt (with remedy).[27] We will treat the importers as individual firms,[28] rather than as a single entity (that is, a competitive fringe). This seems most appropriate in the case where there is a small number of identifiable importers – each is assumed to be a separate Cournot player. The results are shown in Table 6.17.

At one extreme (inelastic demand and capacity constraints), the remedy would help soften an 8.67 per cent price increase to only 2 per cent; at the other extreme (more elastic demand, and no capacity constraints), the merger would have led to only a small increase (1.5 per cent), which would be softened to 0.34 per cent by the remedy. In fact, as can be seen, the critical issue is the capacity assumption: with binding capacity (that is, inelastic supply), the merger would have led to serious price increases. But without those constraints, the merger would have raised less concern. The assumptions about the elasticity and the mathematical form of the demand curve are relatively less critical.

Table 6.17 Simulated price increases

	No capacity constraints		Binding capacity constraints	
Elasticity	Without remedy	With remedy	Without remedy	With remedy
0.75	2.48	0.57	8.67	2.0
1.0	1.86	0.43	6.5	1.50
1.25	1.49	0.34	5.2	1.2

Note: All results shown are based on linear demand. Figures tend to be slightly higher assuming a constant elasticity demand function. For example, the comparable figures for the first column are 2.79, 2.6 and 2.5.

6.3 CONCLUSIONS

The paper sector was included in this project as an example of a 'traditional' industry, in which technology is mature and demand fairly steady. This is fairly well-trodden territory for the simulation of mergers (as opposed to the more dynamic pharmaceuticals sector in the next chapter). Within this sector, we selected two specific mergers (and remedies) designed to illustrate how simulation methods might be applied in markets for both homogeneous and differentiated products, and where price is of primary concern.

Since one of the main purposes of the project is to compare and contrast the traditional and dynamic sectors, a full set of conclusions is inappropriate at this stage. Nevertheless, we can highlight some preliminary observations.

As far as the practicability of simulation is concerned, there is a slightly mixed message. On the positive side, in both cases, simple, easy-to-compute simulation of both the merger and the remedy is certainly feasible. This is in spite of only a fairly limited access to data. Moreover, although in these particular cases there was only a restricted range of alternative remedies, the methodology is seen to be sufficiently flexible to simulate and compare whatever alternatives there might be.

On the other hand, we have had to employ a certain degree of ingenuity in order merely to derive estimates of key parameters (for example, demand elasticities). Similarly, in one case, in which capacity and the slope of the short-run marginal cost curve are crucial, we have not found sufficient information in the papers made available to us to draw definitive conclusions. Here, we have compromised by simulating alternative scenarios (using unverifiable assumptions on the extent of spare capacity). If simulation were ever to be used systematically by the Commission – either in formulating an initial decision, or in assessing the efficacy of remedies put into place – it would be desirable to target these variables for accurate data collection. We shall argue in the final chapter that this is desirable anyway, in order to choose appropriate remedies.

Another point, which we believe will prove to be fairly general, is that it will often prove difficult, in *ex post* evaluation, to disentangle the effects of a remedy from other exogenous developments in the marketplace. For example, in the KC/S case, price fell significantly in two parts of the market – apparently because of increased buyer power and new entry. Neither of these developments was anticipated at the time of the remedy, and neither was simulated.

It is not really a major part of this project to make a definitive judgement of the efficacy of the remedies selected in these particular cases. They are only examples, and quite dated examples at that. Nevertheless, it is fair to claim that *ex ante* simulation suggests that the remedies were very effective in one case (KC/S) and possibly also the other (S/M), in helping avoid significant price rises.

However, *ex post* assessment reveals that in one case at least (KC and the facial market), the remedy proved to be ineffective because of an unexpected decision by the buyer of divested assets to subsequently withdraw from the market concerned. Both the remedy and our simulation were premised on the assumption that the firm concerned would not withdraw. Whether this should be judged as a failed remedy is perhaps debatable.

NOTES

1. We have modified the general checklist slightly to reflect the particular features of this case – the ordering of characteristics has been changed slightly, and a few inappropriate characteristics (for example, the potential role of regulation) have been omitted.
2. Hereafter, this is abbreviated to 'facials'. In the UK, there are strong consumer preferences for facial tissues over handkerchiefs (ratio of nearly 20:1). This is in marked contrast with continental Europe (EC, 81–2 and Table 10).
3. Moreover, the Commission believed that there were no competition concerns in AFH, despite market shares in the 50–60 per cent ranges for toilet tissue and paper wipes. This was because there were many potential alternative suppliers of what is essentially a non-differentiated product.
4. According to Datamonitor, the predicted annual growth rates for 1995–2000 were only 1.4 per cent (toilet tissue), 1.5 per cent (facials) and −2.5 per cent (kitchen towels); see EC, 206–10.
5. EC Table 13 shows that 'multiple grocers' account for roughly three-quarters of sales in all three parts of the market; the remainder is sold by independents, chemists, the Co-op and 'others'.
6. The 'through air dried' process, or blow-drying, creates softness in the end product by forcing the paper fibres to protrude vertically from the sheet.
7. In the case of Andrex in facials, it was indefinite.
8. These confidential data were made available to us by the Commission (Attachment 24 to the Form CO). Apparently, the share by value data come from Nielsen and must therefore relate to retail prices.
9. Henceforward, we concentrate only on KC and Scott, since, with the one exception already noted, Fort Sterling and Jamont appear to be priced no higher, and often lower, than private labels. We conclude provisionally that their brands must be of a significantly lower quality.
10. Since we are, of course, writing a decade later, we interpret *ex ante* to mean using only information that was available at the time of the merger.
11. As explained in the checklist, the licences were finite, but royalty-free for three years; moreover, KC/S committed to not using the brand names for 15 years.
12. A fourth possibility is that the merged party could have divested the Andrex brands. In our simulations this would be identical to the actual remedy: divesting Kleenex brands, since, in both cases, this leaves the two main brands in the hands of independent firms, albeit different pairings.
13. The first assumption is often made in simulation for convenience (for example, as here, when there is not separate information on slightly different varieties of the brand on offer. The second assumption is also often made (for example, in Hausman and Leonard (1997)), but can be very misleading when, as here, there are a number of different supermarkets (private labels) – to group them into one entity implicitly assumes away any competition *between* private labels. The third assumption is also often made, either explicitly

or implicitly (for example in PCAIDS; see below). As is well known, constant elasticity demand curves typically tend to lead to higher simulated price increases than do linear demand.

14. *Proof:* (6.10) is derived from the assumption that the post-merger mark-up is given by: $m_1{}^* = 1/(m_1 - m_1\,D_{12})$. And if D_{12} is given by the ratio $-a_{21}/a_{11}$ and m_1 by a_{11}, this implies that $m_1{}^* = -1/(a_{11} + a_{12})$.
15. The implied mark-ups are the reciprocals of the absolute values of the own-price elasticities.
16. Recall that D is equal to the ratio of the cross-price to own-price elasticity.
17. More formally, it means that the odds ratio (OR) is only half as big as it would be under the base proportionality assumption. OR is the ratio of the proportions of the lost custom by firm A which go to firms B and C. So if market shares are: A = 50, B = 30 and C = 20, under proportionality, OR = 30/50 = 0.6, but with a nest of 0.5 (A and C in one nest, B in the other), OR = 0.30.
18. Note that our simulations refer effectively to real price while actual outcomes will be nominal. So the difference between actual and 'simulated' price is slightly greater than implied by the table for toilet tissues and kitchen towels, but slightly smaller for facials.
19. Foodstuffs (accounting for 23 per cent of total sales) is largest, but also important are: agricultural and fresh food, wooden goods, paper goods, beverages, chemicals, cosmetics etc., textiles and clothing, rubber and mineral, tobacco.
20. This is easily derived from the Cournot first-order condition below, (6.17′): since the price–cost margin for firm I is equal to its market share divided by the industry elasticity, then adding mark-ups across all firms in the industry, and weighting by their market shares gives the industry (weighted) price–cost margin as the sum of squared shares (that is, HHI), divided by e.
21. It is clear from the notes to the data tables we have used that all estimates are potentially very imprecise.
22. Kreps and Scheinkman (1983). The intuitive explanation of this result is that firms choose capacity in stage 1, anticipating the Bertrand equilibrium this will imply when they compete on price in stage 2 – for a given equilibrium price, there is an equilibrium capacity. Thus the 'real' decision is the capacity one, which is, in effect, an output decision.
23. In the case of linear demand and costs, it is easily shown that all survivors increase their output by the same amount post-merger (X_x/N, where the subscript x refers to the exiting firm).
24. Thus all plants of the newly merged firms will have marginal costs at the same level as the lower-cost partner.
25. The intuition is clear if one thinks of the merged firm now operating on the residual demand curve (taking the outsiders' outputs as given). Post-merger, it will choose the 'monopoly' output associated with that residual demand curve, which must be smaller than the combined duopoly outputs pre-merger. It is for this reason that it is not capacity-constrained.
26. Two further observations might be made here. First, this way of handling capacity constraints is easily modified to allow for genuine efficiency savings. In this context, we would define this to be a post-merger marginal cost lower than even the marginal cost of the low-cost partner. In that case, it is easily shown that both (6.22) and (6.28) would contain an additional negative term reflecting the magnitude of the efficiency saving relative to the initial price. In this particular case study, there is no mention of any hoped-for efficiency saving. Second, our option 1 encounters the merger paradox, that is, that the merger would not be privately possible. If, as a matter of belief, one feels that firms do not engage in unprofitable mergers, then one might expect that the actual outcome should lie towards the top of the range in (6.29).
27. In other words, we will assume that Smurfitt would use the Metsa plants in Denmark to replace its previous (small) imports from Germany. In that case, the 'exiting firm' is Smurfitt's pre-merger imports.
28. As shown in Table 6.15.

7. Structure and competitive process in pharmaceuticals markets

7.0 INTRODUCTION

The purpose of this chapter is to provide the background for the detailed analysis of individual merger cases and remedies in the pharmaceuticals sector in Chapter 8. It is our view that a deep understanding of an industry is necessary both to identify an appropriate model suitable for estimating potential harm and remedy analysis, and to understand how the results of a necessarily simplified quantitative analysis should be interpreted sensitively. Since pharmaceuticals markets are so complex, this chapter is rather long and the reader may prefer to read it selectively.

There are ten sections. The first three set the scene: Section 7.1 defines the industry/sector; Section 7.2 provides some brief information on broad aggregates and trends, and an assessment of the standing of the European industry in the world as a whole; and Section 7.3 identifies the leading firms, and describes their alternative corporate structures. After these preliminaries, the remainder of the chapter provides a detailed assessment of the nature of the competitive process in pharmaceuticals. This serves three purposes. First, it analyses the main modes of competition in the industry, which is the essential starting point in model selection. Second, it begins to quantify magnitudes that are often available for individual products, and so provides a first step towards calibration. Third, it sets out the very special and important regulatory context of pharmaceuticals, particularly in relation to the buying and remuneration policies of national health insurance authorities in Europe.

7.1 DEFINING THE SECTOR

This case study is defined in the EC's formal industrial classification as NACE 24.4. The intention of choosing pharmaceuticals was to provide a clear contrast with paper: while most parts of the paper sector are 'traditional', competing with largely homogeneous products on the basis of price, pharmaceuticals is a research-intensive sector, in which competition is based on product differentiation and innovation as well as price.

Table 7.1 NACE 24.4 manufacture of pharmaceuticals, medicinal chemicals and botanical products

		EC merger investigations 1990–2003	
		Total	Interventions
24.4	Manufacture of pharmaceuticals, medicinal chemicals and botanical products	39	11
24.41	Manufacture of basic pharmaceutical products	0	0
24.42	Manufacture of pharmaceutical preparations	4	2
Total		43	13
Further disaggregation of 24.42 (not used in EC merger database):			
24.42/1	Manufacture of medicaments		
24.42/2	Manufacture of non-medicaments		

Source: Compiled from EC merger database on http://europa.eu.int/comm/competition/mergers/cases/

Table 7.1 shows the NACE definitions at the 3-, 4- and 5-digit levels. Unlike for paper, this is not particularly helpful for understanding how the sector might be disaggregated into well-defined separate markets. Roughly speaking, 24.41 refers to the basic inputs that go into the products included in 24.42, but the distinction is a little artificial since both activities are often carried out within the same firms. Nearly all the mergers in this sector investigated by the EC can only have been identified with the 3-digit sector as a whole.

A far more helpful and widely accepted disaggregation of pharmaceuticals is the anatomical therapeutic chemical classification system (ATC) devised by the European Pharmaceutical Marketing Research Association. The ATC is hierarchical and has four levels. The first level is reproduced in Table 7.1(a), and the fourth level is the most detailed. The third level (ATC3) groups medicines in terms of their therapeutic uses. It is this level that is typically used by the Commission in its market definitions in merger cases because any products grouped together in a third-level classification can rarely be substituted by products belonging to other ATC3 classes. As far as we know, official economic data are not collected or reported by this classification scheme. However, most of the leading pharmaceutical companies do disaggregate their sales turnover figures along broadly similar lines (see Table 7.1(b) for a stylized example).

Table 7.2 identifies the relevant ATC3 class for the sampling frame of our case study merger interventions (over the period 1990 to date). Following

Table 7.1(a) Anatomical therapeutic chemical classification system

A	Alimentary tract and metabolism
B	Blood and blood-forming organs
C	Cardiovascular system
D	Dermatologicals
G	Genito-urinary system and sex hormones
H	Systemic horomal preparations, excluding sex hormones and insulins
J	Anti-infectives for systemic use
L	Antineoplastic and immuomodulating agents
M	Musculo-skeletal system
N	Nervous system
P	Antiparasitic products, insecticides and repellents
R	Respiratory system
S	Sensory organs
V	Various

2nd level: therapeutic main group (two numeric characters)
3rd level: therapeutic/pharmacological subgroup (one alpha character)
4th level: chemical/therapeutic/pharmacological subgroup (one alpha character)
5th level: subgroup for chemical substance (two numeric characters)

Note: The 3rd level is typically that adopted by the EC as the appropriate market definition.

Table 7.1(b) Typical drug groups as used in the industry (for example, company reports)

Internal medicine
Respiratory
Anti-infective
Cancer
Topical
Pain control
Cardiovascular
Mental health/CNS (central nervous system)
OTC (over-the-counter)

Commission advice, we selected the asterisked mergers and markets for further analysis in Chapter 8. As can be seen, no therapeutic group in particular stands out as most frequently involved. Table 7.2 also illustrates how 'pharmaceuticals' covers a wide range of narrowly defined therapeutic markets. We accept that the ATC3 level is typically appropriate for competition analysis, and use this in our simulations.

Table 7.2 Merger interventions classified by drug type for which remedies were imposed

	Precise market involved		
	ATC3	Product category	Geographical
Glaxo/Wellcome (555) 1995	N2C	Anti-migraine	National
Ciba Geigy/Sandoz (737) 1996	future	Gene therapy tumours	Europe
Hoffmann La Roche/ Boehringer Mannheim (950) 1998*	A5B*	Vitro diagnostics	Europe
Hoechst/Rhône Poulenc (1378) 1999	J1F	Josacine (respiratory and dental applications)	France
	B1B9	Blood and blood-forming organs (Revasc)	Europe
	A11	Active substance (cyanocbalamines)	Europe
Sanofi/Synthelabo (1397) 1999*	n.a.*	Stupefying active substances	France
Astra/Zeneca (1403) 1999*	C7*	Plain betablockers	Sweden, Norway
	C7B	Dual combination betablockers	National
	N1B*	Local anaesthetics	National
Monsanto/Pharmacia and Upjohn (1835) 2000*	N2A*	Narcotic analgesics (painkillers)	Sweden
Glaxo Wellcome/Smithkline Beecham (1846) 2000*	J5B*	Anti-virals	National
	D6D*	Topical anti-virals	National
	A4A	Anti-emetics	National
	J1D	Antibiotics	Spain
	Future	COPD (respiratory)	National
Pfizer/Warner-Lambert (1878) 2000	N7D	Alzheimers	7 member states
	C8A	Calcium antagonists	Austria
	P1B	Antihelmintics	Germany, Austria
Pfizer/Pharmacia (2922) 2003	G4B4	Urinary incontinence	Worldwide
	G4B3	Erectile dysfunction	Worldwide
	C2A	Antihypertensives	Netherlands

Table 7.2 (Continued)

	Precise market involved		
	ATC3	Product category	Geographical
Sanofi-Synthelabo/Aventis (3354) 2004	A11F	Vitamin B12	France
	C1F	Positive inotropic agents	UK, Belgium
	C4A	Cerebral and peripheral vasotherapeutics	Ireland
	C5B	Topical varicose therapy	Italy
	J1F	Macrolides and similar types	France
	J1X1	Glycopeptide antibiotics	France
	M1C	Specific anti-rheumatics	Portugal
	M3B	Muscle relaxants	Portugal
	N5B	Hypnotics and sedatives	4 member states
		Heparins and heparinoids	11 member states
		Treatment of colorectal cancer	7 member states
Others, excluded		**Reason**	
Smith & Nephew/ Beiersdorf (jv54) 2000		Bandages, plasters, that is, not medicine	
American Home PDTS/ Warner-Lambert (1782) 2000		The merger was aborted	
American Home/Monsanto (1299) 1998		In the event, the parties' shareholders opted not to merge	

Note: * Indicates mergers and relevant markets considered in detail in Chapter 8.

7.2 BROAD CONTEXT AND PERFORMANCE OF EU PHARMACEUTICALS INDUSTRY

7.2.1 The 2000 Competitiveness Study of the European Commission

For this sector DG Enterprise has already produced a helpful competitiveness report (Gambardella et al., 2000, updated in Pammolli et al., 2004), and rather than attempt to duplicate or summarize it at length, we shall select some of its most relevant conclusions.

- Pharmaceuticals is a globalized, high-growth, innovation-intensive sector.
- In recent decades there have been major shocks: (1) technological – the life sciences have transformed the process of drug invention and innovation; (2) institutional – faced with the escalating costs of healthcare and prescription drugs, national governments have attempted to contain costs; and (3) more stringent clinical trial requirements – this has raised the costs and risks of development.
- The sector is populated by three broad types of firm: (1) a relatively small number of large multinational firms (MNEs) covers 40–60 per cent of the national market in most advanced countries; (2) a set of smaller companies specializes in the sales of non-R&D-intensive drugs; and (3) more recently, an increasing number of small new biotechnology firms (NBFs) has emerged. Their activities range from the discovery/development of new drug compounds to the development of new drug screening or research tools and technologies in genomics, bioinformatics and so on.
- Value added as a share of production value is lower in Europe than in the USA or Japan, and 'in the European pharmaceutical industry, there is a less pronounced specialization in R&D activities, and there is a larger presence of non R&D intensive firms which conduct fairly mundane activities' (Gambardella et al., 2000).
- More specifically, when confining attention to the large MNEs, the report questions the relative performance of EU MNEs: 'Our data indicate that the sales of major innovative products by the US Multinationals have increased more significantly than those of the European MNEs in the 1990s'[1] (ibid.).
- Europe has limited vertical specialization in the most innovative areas of the sector (that is, the dynamic, initially small, new technology suppliers and innovation specialists – notably in biotechnology).
- 'The national European markets . . . are not competitive enough. We show this by using data on the variation in prices and market shares after patents expire' (ibid., p. 8).

Thorough though this report is, it is insufficient for our present purposes for two reasons. First, some of the data series cited refer to no later than 1998. Second, its main perspective was 'competitiveness on the world stage', rather than 'the state of competition within Europe'. The one significant exception to this remark is the last bullet point. The essence of the argument on this point is that, once patents have expired, in a competitive market one would expect a rapid drop in price and major realignment of market shares. The report claims to find that this effect is typically less significant in European markets than in the USA.

7.2.2 A More Recent Look at the Industry Based on IMS International Databases

As soon becomes apparent from any reading of the 'trade literature', a leading and respected source of databases is the consultancy firm, IMS International. Some of their data are released into the public domain, but much is not. It appears that their primary sources are the sales figures collected from retailers and wholesalers.[2] The next few tables have been constructed by combining IMS data with tables from the Gambardella et al. report. The purpose is, where possible, to update Gambardella or to fill in the gaps.

Table 7.3 summarizes the size and geographical spread of the world market. As can be seen, Europe constitutes roughly a quarter of the world's market for pharmaceuticals, as opposed to roughly one half for North America. Within the EU (see Table 7.3 (a)), the ranking of member states is predictable: the 'big four' account for sales of about $60 billion, and the others for about $20 billion.

European firms occupy 14 (28 per cent) positions in the world's league table of the top 50 pharmaceuticals companies, as opposed to 20 US firms and 11

Table 7.3 Size of the world's market in pharmaceuticals, 1985–2002

		1985	1990	1995	1999	2002
World (US$ bn)		79.1	165.8	280.3	337.2	430
Regional shares (%)						
North America		35.5	32.4	31.2	40.2	51
Europe		27.8	26.5	29.6	26.7	25
of which	EU					22
	Rest of Europe					3
Rest of world		36.7	41.0	39.2	33.0	24
of which	Japan					12
	Asia, Africa, Australia					8
	Latin America					4

Note: While these figures should be directly comparable, we cannot confirm this for certain.

Table 7.3(a) The member states, the USA and Japan

	1999
USA	130.1
Japan	53.5
Germany	18.5
France	17.8
Italy	11.3
UK	11.0
Spain	6.6
Belgium	2.7
Netherlands	2.4
Sweden	2.1
Switzerland	1.8
Austria	1.8
Portugal	1.8
Greece	1.4
Finland	1.0
Denmark	0.9
Norway	0.8

Source: Gambardella et al. (2000), Table 2, updated to 2002.

Japanese (Table 7.4). On average, they are slightly larger than the average top 50 firms, since they account for 33 per cent of the total sales of the top 50. Thus Europe has rather more than its share of very large firms (recall that the European market is about 25 per cent of the world's total). This reflects two factors: (1) like all the largest firms, the Europeans are extensively multinational, with large shares of their activity located outside Europe; and (2) Europe has a positive trade balance with the rest of the world.

As will be seen below, the leading European firms also account for more than their share of the world's R&D,[3] although it should be emphasized that not all is conducted within Europe.

The lower portion of Table 7.4 calculates various concentration indices for the global industry. Thus the top 50 firms account for 75 per cent of world total sales, and the top 5, for 26 per cent. The HHI index of 244 is the same as would be recorded by a hypothetical industry of 40 equal-sized firms. For an individual product market in a single country, these statistics would imply a very unconcentrated structure. However, at the world level, and bearing in mind that 'pharmaceuticals' is actually a consolidation of a very large number of different therapeutic markets, this is consistent with a sector that might include some very concentrated individual product markets.

Table 7.4 The world's 50 largest pharmaceutical firms, 2002

		Origin	Sales, $ bn	R&D, $ bn	R&D/sales, %
1	Pfizer	USA	28.28	5.170	18.3
2	GSK	EU	28.2	4.290	15.2
3	Merck	USA	21.63	2.670	12.3
4	AstraZeneca	EU	17.84	3.060	17.2
5	Aventis	EU	17.25	3.670	21.3
6	Johnson & Johnson	USA	17.20	2.700	15.7
7	Novartis	Switzerland	15.36	2.600	16.9
8	Bristol-Myers Squibb	USA	14.70	2.200	15.0
9	Pharmacia	USA	12.03	2.320	19.3
10	Wyeth	USA	11.70	2.080	17.8
11	Eli Lilly	USA	11.07	2.140	19.3
12	Roche	Switzerland	10.81	2.420	22.4
13	Abbott Labs	USA	9.27	1.500	16.2
14	Schering-Plough	USA	8.70	1.400	16.1
15	Sanofi-Synthélabo	EU	8.01	1.300	16.2
16	Boehringer Ingelheim	EU	7.92	1.400	17.7
17	Takeda	Japan	7.15	0.840	11.7
18	Schering AG	EU	5.40	1.010	18.7
19	Bayer	EU	5.12	1.090	21.3
20	Amgen	USA	4.99	1.100	22.0
21	Sankyo	Japan	3.57	0.720	20.2
22	Akzo Nobel	EU	3.40	0.650	19.1
23	Eisai	Japan	3.39	0.460	13.6
24	Yamanouchi	Japan	3.20	0.546	17.1
25	Merck KgaA	EU	3.19	0.662	20.8
26	Novo Nordisk	EU	3.17	n.a.	n.a.
27	Baxter	USA	3.10	0.501	16.2
28	Shionogi	Japan	3.08	0.256	8.3
29	Daiichi	Japan	2.70	0.386	14.3
30	Teva	Israel	2.51	0.165	6.6
31	Fujisawa	Japan	2.49	0.479	19.2
32	Genetech	USA	2.16	0.623	28.8
33	Solvay	EU	2.00	0.291	14.6
34	Purdue Pharma	USA	1.90	0.306	16.1
35	Altana	EU	1.68	0.361	21.5
36	Otsuka	Japan	1.67	0.325	19.5
37	Tanabe Seiyaku	Japan	1.58	0.174	11.0
38	Forest Labs	USA	1.56	0.157	10.1
39	Serono	Switzerland	1.53	0.386	25.2
40	Allergan	USA	1.38	0.233	16.9
41	Watson	USA	1.22	0.081	6.6

42	Kyowa	Japan	1.18	0.244	20.7
43	King	USA	1.17	0.028	2.4
44	Biogen	USA	1.14	0.367	32.2
45	Ono	Japan	1.11	0.237	21.4
46	Elan	EU	1.11	0.397	35.8
47	Alcon Labs	Switzerland	1.08	0.323	29.9
48	Schwartz Pharma	EU	1.03	0.133	12.9
49	3M	USA	1	n.a.	n.a.
50	Genzyme	USA	0.907	0.23	25.4
	Total for top 50		322.84	54.68	16.9
	World total		430		

Source: IMS International.

World concentration	
CR50 (share of top 50)	75
CR20 (share of top 20)	61
CR10 (share of top 10)	43
C5 (share of top 5)	26
HHI (Hirschman–Herfindahl)	0.0244

Source: Authors' calculations.

Table 7.5 switches the focus from the companies towards the individual products. Two aspects of this table are striking. First, the sales of individual drugs are enormous: these top 20 drugs account for worldwide sales of $65 billion (15 per cent of the entire market), and the two top sellers account for $13.6 billion – 3 per cent of the total world pharmaceuticals market. In turn, they are typically the result of massive R&D outlays, which effectively render this market a 'natural oligopoly'.[4] Second, most of these drugs are not therapeutic substitutes for each other – cholesterol reduction, anaemia therapy, anti-depressants, respiratory drugs, allergy drugs and so on clearly occupy demand-unrelated segments of the aggregate market.

7.3 EUROPE'S LARGEST FIRMS

Returning to Table 7.4, given Europe's prominent position in the world, it is perhaps unsurprising that we found that so many (14) of the world's largest 50 firms in this sector are European. However, we should acknowledge that, precisely because the industry is so genuinely multinational,

Table 7.5 The world's top selling drugs, 2002 ($ bn)

1	Lipitor	7.97	Cholesterol reducer	Pfizer
2	Zocor	5.60	Cholesterol reducer	Merck
3	Prilosec	4.62	Gastrointestinal	AstraZeneca
4	Procrit	4.30	Anaemia therapy	Johnson & Johnson
5	Norvasc	3.84	Antihypertensive	Pfizer
6	Zyprexa	3.69	Antipsychotic	Eli Lilly
7	Paxil	3.22	Antidepressant	GSK
8	Prevacid	3.14	Antiulcerant	Takeda Abbott
9	COX-2	3.05	Anti-inflammatory	Pharmacia
10	Zoloft	2.74	Antidepressant	Pfizer
11	Epogen	2.67	Anemia therapy	Amgen
12	Advair	2.56	Respiratory	GSK
13	Vioxx	2.50	Pain relief	Merck
14	Pravachol	2.26	Cardiovascular	Bristol-Myers Squibb
15	Fosamax	2.2	Osteoporosis	Merck
16	Allegra	2.18	Allergies	Aventis
17	Risperdal	2.10	Antipsychotic	Johnson & Johnson
18	Effexor	2.07	Anti-depressant	Wyeth
19	Nexium	1.97	Gastrointestinal	AstraZeneca
20	Plavix	1.89	Cardiovascular	Bristol-Myers Squibb
Total for top 20 drugs		64.57		

Source: Sellers (2003).

identifying individual countries of origin is a largely vacuous exercise. Examples include GSK (Anglo-American), AstraZeneca (Anglo-Swedish) and Aventis (Franco-German), although some of the smaller firms in Table 7.5 are more likely to have distinct 'home countries', for example, Bayer, Solvay, Boehringer.

As with the paper sector, this listing of the world's largest companies effectively introduces on to the stage all the main players in the rest of the merger story. Thus, in Table 7.6, we find that 27 of the 44 EC merger investigations in this sector involved just ten firms (six European and four US). Even more strikingly, the nine mergers with intervention in our sampling frame involve just a handful of these leaders (Table 7.2): GSK (2), Novartis (1), Aventis (1), AstraZeneca (1) and Pfizer/Pharmacia (3). Indeed, these are typically the mergers that led to the creation of the current giants of EU pharmaceuticals, and, in the case of Pfizer, the sequence that has led to it becoming the world's largest company in the sector.

Table 7.7 illustrates the significance of these mergers. In 1998, Glaxo Wellcome and SmithKline Beecham were ranked numbers 2 and 5 on

Table 7.6 Main mergers by the largest firms

	Date
American home products	
M500 – American Home Products/American Cyanadide	19.9.94
M1229 – American Home Products/Monsanto	*28.9.98*
M1782 – American Home Products/Warner-Lambert	*9.2.00*
AstraZeneca	
M1403 – Astra/Zeneca	***26.2.99***
M1558 – Cinven/Investcorp/Zeneca Chemicals	25.6.99
Aventis	
M426 – Rhône-Poulenc/Cooper	18.4.94
M587 – Hoechst AG/Marion Merrell Dow Inc.	26.6.95
M632 – Rhône-Poulenc/Fisons	21.9.95
M885 – Merck/Rhône-Poulenc – Merial	2.7.97
M954 – Bain/Hoechst – Dade Behring	2.9.97
M1378 – Hoechst/Rhône-Poulenc	*9.8.99*
Bristol-Myers Squibb	
M2517 – Bristol-Myers Squibb/DuPont	9.8.01
GSK	
M555 – Glaxo PLC/Wellcome PLC	*28.2.95*
M1846 – Glaxo Wellcome/SmithKline Beecham	***8.5.00***
Merck	
M285 – Pasteur Merieux/Merck	5.7.93
M1201 – DuPont/Merck	23.6.98
Novartis	
M737 – Ciba-Geigy/Sandoz	*17.7.96*
Pfizer	
M631 – Upjohn/Pharmacia	28.9.95
M1835 – Monsanto/Pharmacia & Upjohn	***3.3.00***
M1878 – Pfizer/Warner-Lambert	*22.5.00*
M2922 – Pfizer/Pharmacia	*27.2.03*
Roche	
M457 – Roche/Syntex	20.6.94
M950 – Hoffmann – La Roche/Boehringer Mannheim	***4.2.98***
Sanofi	
M72 – Sanofi/Sterling Drugs	10.6.91
M480 – Sanofi/Kodak	12.8.94
M1397 – Sanofi/Synthelabo (see also M1542, 21.4.99)	***17.5.99***
Others considered by EC	
M58 – Baxter – Nestlé/Salvia	6.2.91
M323 – Procordia/Erbamont	29.4.93
M328 – Gehe AG/OCP S.A.	5.4.93

Table 7.6 (*continued*)

	Date
M464 – BMSC/UPSA	6.9.94
M495 – Behringwerke AG/Armour Pharma	5.9.94
M572 – Gehe/AAH	3.4.95
M716 – Gehe/Lloyds Chemists	22.3.96
M781 – Schering/Gehe – Jenapharm	13.9.96
M821 – Baxter/Immuno	9.10.96
M1220 – Alliance Unichem/Unifarma	23.7.98
M1366 – Paribas/CDC/Beaufour	9.12.98
M1512 – DuPont/Pioneer Hi-Bred International	21.6.99
M2312 – Abbott/BASF	28.02.01
M2419 – Apax/Schering/Metagen	14.5.01
JV.54 – Smith & Nephew/Beiersdorf	30.1.91
M3015 – Credit Suisse/Blackstone/Nycomed	26.11.02

Note: Mergers shown in bold italics are the merger intervention cases we examine in detail.

the magnitude of European sales, but their merger in 2000 pushed the merged firm into the number 1 spot. Similarly, the Hoechst (no. 7)/Rhône-Poulenc (no. 8) merger in 1999 created Aventis, now ranked at number 3. Even more recently, Pfizer's acquisition of Warner-Lambert (2000) and then Pharmacia (2003) has led to its rise to number 2, the three firms having previously only been ranked number 10, 11 and 18. Finally, the current number 4, AstraZeneca, was formed in 1999 by the merger of Astra and Zeneca.

These leading firms all have extensive cross-border operations, and their core businesses are all human pharmaceuticals. However, they differ slightly in how far they are diversified into adjacent areas such as animal health. Within pharmaceuticals, each is reasonably diversified across therapeutic classes, although their emphases differ. For example, Pfizer has an extremely strong presence in cardiovascular and mental health, GSK in respiratory, anti-infectives and CNS, AstraZeneca in metabolic/gastrointestinal.

7.4 DISTINCTIVE CHARACTERISTICS

We turn now from structure to the nature of the competitive process in pharmaceuticals. Nightingale (2003) identifies four characteristics that distinguish the pharmaceuticals industry from traditional sectors:

Table 7.7 The impact of mega-mergers on Europe's top ten in 2002

	1998		2002 (hypothetical)
	European sales	European rank	European rank
GSK	**6466**		1
Glaxo Wellcome	3588	2	
Smith Beecham	2878	5	
Pfizer	**5032**		2
Pfizer	1936	10	
Pharmacia & Upjohn	1842	11	
Warner-Lambert	1254	18	
Aventis	**4925**		3
Hoechst	2564	7	
Rhône-Poulenc	2361	8	
AstraZeneca	**4140**		4
Astra	2756	6	
Zeneca	1384	16	
Novartis	3764	1	5
Merck	3091	3	6
Roche	2931	4	7
Bristol-Meyer	1991	9	8
Bayer	1834	12	9
Johnson & Johnson	1833	13	10

1. Very large investment in very high-risk R&D.
2. Increasing national and international regulation: healthcare pharmaceutical buyer organizations across the globe often regulate prices and increasingly encourage the use of generics which are now much more rapidly taking a market share.
3. Patent protection is crucial for technical progress because drugs are easy to copy. The actual patent life for a new chemical entity declined to around eight years by the late 1990s (ibid., p. 145). Also, the improved technologies of discovery have reduced the time between first and second products in new markets (the second product might be better, but it might just be an adequate substitute or have slightly different effects and be priced lower).
4. There is a highly skewed distribution of product profitability (half of revenues come from the top 10 per cent, according to Grabowski and Vernon, 1990), and massive sales are necessary to break even (about

$350 million p.a. for a new drug with typical R&D and marketing expenses). This leaves firms highly dependent on one or few blockbusters, and also encourages heavy marketing.

Despite the strong trend towards globalization, American pharmaceutical firms in 1998 earned 63 per cent of their turnover in North America and 25 per cent in Europe, while the Europeans get 36 per cent in North America and 42 per cent in Europe (at the time, North America had 40 per cent overall global sales and Europe 27 per cent) (Nightingale, 2003, p. 149) but there is evidence of convergence (ibid., p. 155; based on Gambardella et al., 2000).

7.5 PRODUCTION SIDE AND NEW PRODUCT DEVELOPMENT

7.5.1 Cost Structure

The broad cost structure is indicated by OECD estimates of the breakdown of revenue in 1989 for R&D-intensive pharmaceutical companies (Jacobzone, 2000, reported in OECD, 2001, p. 31):[5]

- Manufacturing costs (25 per cent)
- Marketing (23 per cent)
- R&D (13 per cent)
- Operating profit (28 per cent)
- Other items (10 per cent).

Compared with ten years earlier, manufacturing costs had fallen as a share, while marketing, R&D and profit had risen. Given the evolving technology of drug development (discussed below), it is likely that the share of R&D has continued to rise. Within these aggregate shares, it is to be expected that newer products account for a higher share of R&D than older products in these companies' portfolios.

R&D and marketing expenditures are complementary, and for new products R&D-intensive pharmaceuticals companies spend roughly equal amounts on each (slightly more on marketing). This is because 'consumers' need informing about new products (for example, face-to-face explanations to individual physicians, known as 'detailing' in the USA). We postpone our analysis of marketing until after the analysis of other costs and of the idiosyncrasies of 'consumers' of pharmaceuticals.

7.5.2 R&D

Two changes during the 1960s fashioned the current setting for research (Nightingale, 2003). The first provided a more systematic method of drug discovery by understanding the biology of receptors in the body and then looking for appropriate drug 'keys' to unlock them. This was followed in the 1970s by advances in genetic research. The second was increasingly strict and costly regulation following the thalidomide tragedy. These costs provide a strong incentive for firms to market their products globally. They also encourage them to target long-term chronic illnesses, which require more treatments than do acute illnesses, but which are often complex and difficult to test for efficacy.

Initial research often involves large-scale screening of numerous molecules. It can take 10 to 20 years from basic research to market, with an average 12 years from initial synthesis to final approval (OECD, 2001). It is estimated that the total R&D costs of bringing a new drug to market were \$350 million in 1995 rising to \$500 million by 2000 (ibid., p. 30).[6]

According to information received from a leading pharmaceuticals company (name withheld on request), there are several 'research platform technologies' that ethical R&D companies need for successful research:

- Genomic nucleotide sequences: human and animal sequences are rapidly entering the public domain, and microbial sequences are largely being developed by specialist firms from which they can be licensed.
- Access to single nucleotide polymorphism (SNP) map: being developed by specialist companies and a consortium of 12 pharmaceuticals companies.
- Ability to read and interpret sequences: also developed by specialist suppliers.
- Large and diverse library of chemicals to screen for therapeutic activity: mathematical modelling suggests 1.5 million compounds is optimal (Pfizer has more than 1 million, Glaxo Wellcome has 5 million), but these are small numbers relative to the size of 'chemical space'.
- High throughput screening (HTS) capability: combines robotic instruments (widely available) and good lab management.
- Skills and facilities in combinatorial chemistry and multiple-parallel synthesis: to enlarge compound collection and to exploit leads found by HTS.[7]

The theme here is that no one pharmaceuticals company can monopolize any of these technologies because either they are too large scale (for example,

SNP), or they are provided to everyone by specialists (for example, instruments), or the potential supply is very large (for example, chemical compounds). However, as Gambardella (1992, cited in Nightingale, 2003) points out, human capital is necessary to apply these technologies, and firms have had to develop costly internal competences to access the external sources of knowledge. The implication is that few firms might have the finance and scale to utilize these technologies efficiently.

Nightingale (2003, pp. 143–4) suggests that many of the mega-mergers of the 1990s involved firms

> attempting to access new sources of knowledge (particularly genetics and HTS technologies which were developing rapidly at the time) and thereby improve their R&D performance. These firms have moved away from an internal focus on 'chemistry and testing' to a more external focus on global biological research networks of academic researchers and biotechnology firms. Today large pharmaceutical firms may spend 25% of their R&D budgets externally. Some large European firms have between 70 and 120 alliances, most commonly with small US-based biotechnology firms.

At the development stage, there are contract research organizations, specialist companies and universities to help out if necessary. Nevertheless, there is a limited supply of academic and hospital clinicians to conduct necessary clinical trials, and they tend to select the most interesting and promising drugs to trial.

Overall, it seems that Schumpeterian competition is a reasonable characterization of long-run new product development in the industry, with high profits both funding new projects and attracting competitors. In Schumpeterian competition, firms compete principally by developing new products that are superior to those currently produced by rivals. The new product may achieve a substantial market share, but this will typically be transient, lasting only until the next technical improvement. Schumpeter refers to this dynamic process as 'creative destruction'. However, it is necessary to be more precise in order to understand the implications for competition and market structure.

Sutton (1998) likens the economic incentives associated with the drug discovery technology to a simple search or lottery. In his terms, it is a 'low-alpha' industry. Alpha is a theoretical 'escalation parameter' which determines the incentive for a single firm, in an initially low-concentration industry, to outspend the R&D of its rivals in order to gain a disproportionate market share. In a high-alpha industry, high-spending achieves a high-quality product that *most* customers prefer, so the industry becomes dominated by one or a few high R&D firms (for example, large commercial jet aircraft, electric generators, colour film before its recent demise).

However, in a low-alpha industry (for example, flow meters, pharmaceuticals), there is no disproportionate gain from high spending – in such industries, if one firm spends twice as much (equivalently buys twice as many lottery tickets), it is likely to discover twice as many new drugs (win twice as many prizes) and achieve twice the market share, but there is no disproportionate advantage.

Sutton shows that this absence of cumulative advantage applies not only within therapeutic categories, but even within chemically related submarkets, where one might have thought that a particular research unit might have developed a specific expertise. Out of 26 new top 50 chemical entities developed in 1960–86, just seven were developed by firms that already had a top 50 drug in the same chemically related category 13 years earlier. Put another way, 'rivals introduced about three-quarters of the later successes' (Sutton, 1998, p. 218). Sutton concludes that there is nothing in the nature of the R&D process in pharmaceuticals that requires substantial economies of scale relative to the pharmaceuticals market.

The reason is that there is a huge potential search set out of which the next new innovation might be found, and firms are thinly spaced across it – no single firm can cover the whole set of possibilities and so cannot expect to lead any particular market for the long term. In such a world, there is no patent race, and rivals are more likely to benefit from another firm's discovery as this throws indirect light on other searches. One potential interpretation of the evidence needs clearing up. Sutton points out that there may be a strategic effect of rivals increasing their R&D efforts in response to a rival's discovery in order to compensate for genuine advantages for the original discoverer in developing the next product. However, Cockburn and Henderson (1994) show empirically that there is no such strategic reaction, either positive or negative. This is consistent with firms each following distinctive research paths, even in quite narrowly defined areas.

Putting this analysis in a wider perspective, a crucial difference between pharmaceuticals and some other R&D-intensive industries (for example, microprocessors, machinery) is that successive products do not build on improvements from the previous generation. There is no design path along which success in one generation confers an advantage on the next. Success is a new chemical entity, not the improvement of an existing one.

Nevertheless, the process of innovation and approval takes a very long time. A survey by CMR (Centre for Medicines Research, www.cmr.org, 'Major challenges for the pharmaceutical industry in the new millennium') shows development times to market of 13 years in 1999, and on a rising trend. According to the OECD, in 1995 the process of obtaining marketing approval absorbed 55 per cent of all R&D expenditure. They report the

Table 7.8 US FDA approval timescale

Regulatory stage	Description	Average time lapse
Investigational new drug application (IND)	Application for approval of human testing	30 days
Phase I	Safety tests	1 year
Phase II	Efficacy tests	2 years
Phase III	Efficacy and long-term reactions	3 years
New drug application (NDA) review	Application for approval	2.5 years
Phase IV	Post-market testing	–

US FDA approval process (see Table 7.8), but the European process is essentially the same.

For 1990–94, adding the clinical stages (phases I–III) of 6.1 years to the NDA review period of 2.6 years and the pre-clinical stages of 6.1 years (averages) gives a total time of 14.8 years. This total compares with 8.1 years in the 1960s and 11.6 years in the 1970s.

7.5.3 Innovation Markets

The US Antitrust Guidelines for the Licensing of Intellectual Property (US Department of Justice, 1995) define an innovation market:

> An innovation market consists of the research and development directed to particular new or improved goods or processes, and the close substitutes for that research and development. The close substitutes are research and development efforts, technologies, and goods that significantly constrain the exercise of market power with respect to the relevant research and development, for example by limiting the ability and incentive of a hypothetical monopolist to retard the pace of research and development. The Agencies will delineate an innovation market only when the capabilities to engage in the relevant research and development can be associated with specialized assets or characteristics of specific firms.

Innovation markets are defined when it is expected that future competition can be harmed by reduced R&D, and competition is more directed at new technologies than at prices. In such cases, competitive rivalry must be preserved, in particular by preserving innovative capability. This is a controversial issue in pharmaceuticals. The FTC seems quite keen on it (DeSanti, 1996). However, the danger of losing diversity in research trajectories is likely to differ across relevant markets.

7.5.4 Pipeline Products

In pursuing a line of research, a pharmaceuticals company will develop a potential product which it hopes will have verifiable efficacy and safety features. These are known as pipeline products, and it is important to understand at what stage they should be included as competitors in a relevant market (sometimes referred to as a 'future market' because the product is not yet in active competition). A confidential submission and the Commission (in Glaxo Wellcome/SKB) provide the estimates of the proportion of pipeline products that ultimately reach the market shown in Table 7.9.

These figures are broadly supported by the CMR survey referred to above.[8] Companies terminated a fifth of their pipeline new active substances in 1999, and nearly a half in the pre-submission stage, by which point over 90 per cent of the total investment in R&D for the compound has already been committed.

Clearly, there is a substantial attrition rate as products progress through the pipeline. Some use this to argue that only exceptionally can an analysis be conducted of 'future markets', because it is so uncertain that any particular product will be brought to that market.[9] In practice, the attrition rate in product development means that the EC has only considered products in the final stage of clinical trials (Phase III).

An example illustrates the potential success of a pipeline or future market remedy. In Glaxo's merger with Wellcome, both were developing non-injectable migraine drugs. Glaxo already had one, but was developing an improvement called Naramig. Wellcome did not have one, but was in Phase III with Zomig, expected to be introduced in two years (that is, 1997).

Table 7.9 Regulatory success rates for pipeline products

Phase	Testing	Time before product marketed (years)	% reaching market	
			Firm	Commission
I	Start of clinical testing on humans	10–12	17.5	10
II	Initial tests of efficiency, safety, dose and applications	5–7	30	30
III	Large group effectiveness	4–6	70	50
Regulatory approval		–2	90	

The FTC required the divestment of Zomig to an approved third party. It was sold to Zeneca. Naramig came to market in March 1997, just eight months before Zomig. Thus competition was successfully preserved. The divestiture required assets relating to: patents, technology, manufacturing information, testing data, research material; customer lists; and inventory needed to complete all trials. Glaxo also had to provide information, technical assistance and advice for the acquirer.[10]

7.5.5 Patents

Patents are a crucial and effective way of protecting intellectual property in pharmaceuticals. Mansfield (quoted in Cohen and Levin, 1989; and DeSanti, 1996, p. 4) found that 65 per cent of pharmaceuticals innovations would not have taken place without patent protection as an inducement, which is a hugely higher figure than for other industries.

Patent protection starts at the time of filing (that is, before start of the process of market approval – before Phase I above). The international standard for patent protection is 20 years.[11] In 1984, the US Hatch–Waxman Act achieved two things. First, it extended pharmaceuticals patent protection by a maximum of five years to take account of the approval process, with a maximum effective patent protection from first marketing of 14 years (which is roughly what is effective for patents subject to simpler approval). Second, it instigated an abbreviated procedure (ANDA) for generics, which can now rely on the research of the branded product as long as they can prove bio-equivalence.

Authorization to market a drug in Europe can be achieved in two ways: from the European Medicines Evaluation Agency (EMEA); or by 'mutual recognition' when applying through an individual member state while declaring in which other states it wants the licence to be valid (OECD, 2001, p. 372).[12] Relevant to when the original patent expires, the EU adopted a Supplementary Protection Certificate which operates in much the same way as the patent extension provisions in the USA. However, there are also data protection rights for ten years on clinical trials. This means that generics have to conduct clinical trials even when the original patent has expired.

Sometimes, patent holders can manipulate the expiry of the patent. Generics need only show bio-equivalence to the marketed reference product in order to gain approval. Anticipating this, a pharmaceuticals firm can take its product off market just before the patent expires, and replace it with a 'new, improved version' so that the generic no longer has a marketed reference product by which to gain approval (for example, AstraZeneca was accused of doing this with Losec). A recent example of how firms try to spin out new versions of drugs due to come off patent is provided by Aventis, who recently filed an application with the US FDA for a new version of Allegra, one of its blockbuster products that was due to face generic competition in 2005 (*Financial Times*, 31 December 2003). It seems that the law in relation to generic entry in Europe is still evolving. Finally, in the USA, the first generic is given six months' exclusivity. There is a danger that this might be used strategically to delay entry, and the FTC charged Aventis and Abbott with paying such generic first movers to delay marketing (OECD, 2001, p. 38).

7.5.6 Manufacture

Once a new product has been approved for sale, the manufacturing process is in three stages. Each stage may take place at different facilities:

- Production of the chemical entity (active ingredient)
- Formulation of the bulk product(s) into useable doses (for example, pills, ampoules)
- Packaging.

There do not appear to be any significant economies of scale or capacity constraints in any of these activities. It seems that existing facilities are readily switched between different pharmaceuticals, though not necessarily between different forms of product (for example, tablet, capsule, etc.). Most large pharmaceuticals companies manufacture most of their needs in house. Some active ingredients may be sold to other firms.

7.5.7 Cooperative Agreements between Producers

There are numerous cooperation agreements in the industry, and a wide range of forms:

- At the development stage, small biotechnology companies or research institutes team up with large ethical drug manufacturers for funding and development expertise, and later for marketing.[13]
- Co-marketing agreements, sometimes between large manufacturers, allow rapid and wide exploitation of drugs subject to patents of limited duration. This may involve using different brand names.
- Co-promotion agreements do not transfer any property rights to the drugs, but 'hire' a complementary sales force in addition to that of the original firm.
- Licensing agreements are typically compensated with a royalty. Arrangements may or may not include manufacture.

A *Financial Times* article (6 January 2004) suggests that licensing deals are becoming more difficult for small biotechnology firms as big pharmaceuticals companies take longer to reach agreement and are offering lower royalties.[14]

7.6 CONSUMPTION SIDE AND BUYER POWER

7.6.1 Separation of Normal Functions of a 'Consumer'

The demand side is much more complex in pharmaceuticals than in most other markets. We normally think of a consumer as a single individual who:

1. derives utility from consuming a product, and
2. chooses which product to consume,
3. subject to their own budget constraint.

In pharmaceuticals, these three functions are often separated into:

1. Patient
2. Prescriber (doctor or hospital)
3. Payer (insurance company or health service).

The divorce between patient and prescriber requires a high degree of professional integrity to ensure the choice is appropriate. Since there is normally no direct conflict of interests, this is often sufficient. The divorce between payer and prescriber, however, is not normally left to professional integrity because interests will often be in conflict. In the absence of any controls, the prescriber would consider only the therapeutic value of a product, and not its cost. Also, even for an agreed product, the payer would like to purchase it at the lowest price possible. If the choice of product is left entirely to the prescriber, the payer is left with no bargaining power with the producer. A credible threat to switch is essential to raise the elasticity of demand and so to reduce the purchase price.

The OECD (2001, p. 70) reports the OECD average share of OTC, as opposed to prescription, drugs at 21 per cent (including 32 per cent in the USA, 35 per cent in Germany, 31 per cent in France, 20 per cent in the UK and 11 per cent in Italy). Put the other way round, roughly 80 per cent of drug sales separate the prescriber from the patient. The separation from the payer will be of a similar order of magnitude.

This incentive problem is addressed by a range of measures by which the payer constrains the choices available to the prescriber, or with this threat negotiates a lower price with the producer. Important examples of this include hospital budgeting, limited lists, reimbursement at generic prices, reference pricing, cost sharing and so on (see below).

7.6.2 Regulation

The need for regulation of the market in pharmaceuticals derives from several well-known economic problems: lack of appropriability of return on R&D investment due to easy copying of drugs (→ patent system); imperfect information (→ health and safety; also, patient–physician professional conduct relationship); third-party payment and reliance on physician as prescriber (→ inelastic demand justifies some form of price control).

These problems can be summarized as three reasons for regulation:

- To provide a suitable return on R&D
- To ensure product efficacy and safety
- To offset the effects of health insurance on demand.

7.6.3 Buyer Power and Pricing

The third of these reasons for regulation (that is, divorce between prescriber and payer) justifies an intervention in pricing. However, an excessive intervention on these grounds reduces the value of patent rights designed to address the first reason for intervention (that is, patent rights to provide appropriate incentives for R&D). Public health and insurance services provide powerful national buying groups, and private health providers in the USA are also beginning to act collectively.

There are various ways in which governments and insurance agencies influence pricing:

- Most countries require patients to contribute either a fixed payment (for example, the UK) or a co-payment (for example, France @ 0/35/65 per cent according to type of drug) for prescription drugs, typically with various waivers. A co-payment may encourage some elasticity into demand (but a fixed payment will have no such effect).
- All OECD countries (health services or insurance companies) list drugs eligible for reimbursement and provide guidelines for physicians. Since prices influence listing, pharmaceuticals companies are constrained by the need to be listed.
- Most countries have some form of policy to encourage the prescription of generics whenever available.

- Some also set indicative budgets, with the UK's early 1990s system of decentralized budgets to GP fund-holders as an extreme example.
- All countries except the USA have some form of price or profitability controls. The UK is the only one with profitability controls, including a 17–21 per cent target rate of return and R&D allowances.
- Many countries invoked price freezes or price cuts at some point during the 1990s.
- Price controls often take account of the
  - therapeutic value and the
  - cost of comparable treatments,

  and most take account of
  - prices charged in other countries – in particular, other European countries often include one or more of Germany, the UK and France as points of reference.

The international context introduces an additional tension in price controls, because individual countries have an incentive to set low prices and free-ride on others to fund R&D. Combined with the free movement of goods within the EU, there can be arbitrage through parallel imports, and this has a tendency to drive down prices across the EU and limit the recovery of sunk R&D costs. It may be fortunate that the world's largest market (the USA) does not have such controls, although buyers are increasingly organized to reduce prices.

7.6.4 Pharmaceuticals Price Regulation in Europe[15]

Each country in the EEA has a different system of regulation, and a different coverage of pharmaceuticals. There are also differences according to whether the product is sold to hospitals (15 per cent pharmaceuticals market in Europe) or via prescription or OTC directly to final consumers. For many countries, hospital purchases are relatively deregulated (an exception is Italy), with hospitals or hospital groups often buying by competitive tender (at least where generics are available). OTC medicine prices are even less regulated (except in Belgium and Greece). The rationale for less price regulation in these sectors is that the buyers are expected to be more price-sensitive because those who choose which product to buy are also responsible for payment. The main focus of price regulation, therefore, applies to out-patient prescribed pharmaceuticals, and the following paragraphs apply to these.[16]

Price controls rarely allow for future price increases, even for inflation, and prices have often been subject to fixed percentage cuts as a way to control spiralling health costs. Germany and Denmark have no direct price controls. The UK indirectly controls prices by allowing a maximum rate of return on capital. All other countries fix prices directly in some way. Launch prices are 'negotiated' with the firms, taking different factors into account in each country. A common input is price comparisons with a selected range of countries, typically including Germany and the UK plus neighbouring countries. In several countries (Italy, the Netherlands, Portugal, Greece and Ireland), there is a strict formula for directly applying these comparator prices. Other inputs are the therapeutic value of the new product, prices of comparable medicines and the volume of expected sales.

Either complementing or substituting for price (or, in the UK case, profitability) regulation are policies on reimbursement. For example, state or insurance reimbursement may be capped at a maximum level (reference price) above which the patient has to pay the difference (the reference price may be set for each molecule with generic substitutes, as originally in Germany;[17] or for the therapeutic class, as in the Netherlands); a positive list (white list) of reimbursable products may be published (all countries except the UK and Germany); or a negative list (black list) of non-reimbursable products may be published (the UK, Germany, Sweden and Spain).

Policy interventions are also applied to encourage price sensitivity by prescribers, dispensers and patients. Some countries have budget limits of various kinds constraining physicians, and most have some form of guidelines with monitoring. Some countries encourage generic prescribing (the UK, Germany, the Netherlands, Denmark), with the exceptions being those with the tightest price regulation (Italy, France, Spain, Greece). Some countries allow pharmacists to substitute generics, but they rarely have incentives to do so, and their discretion is typically constrained by what is written on the prescription. The generic market share in most countries at the end of the 1990s was no higher than 6 per cent, with the exceptions of Germany (41 per cent), Sweden (39 per cent), Denmark (22–44 per cent), the UK (22 per cent) and the Netherlands (12 per cent in 1996). Patient price sensitivity is due to co-payments, which differ greatly across different countries. Most systems involve a fixed payment and/or a percentage of the price. The percentage may depend on the condition being treated (France), therapeutic efficiency of the drug (Italy) or on its price (Sweden). The reference pricing system (Germany, the Netherlands, more recently in Sweden, Denmark)[18] means there is no co-payment for products priced less than the reference, and 100 per cent marginal payment above. The evidence is that either doctors are reluctant to prescribe products priced above the reference level or pharmaceutical companies are unwilling to risk it, so in practice very few products are priced above the reference price. Some of the academic studies discussed below examine the extent to which doctors are sensitive to their patient's ability and willingness to pay their co-payments when writing a prescription.

Overall, the strength and detail of price regulation systems and incredible variety of reimbursement systems mean that it is not possible to apply conventional free market models of the price setting to merger remedies affecting the out-patient prescription sector. One important implication of the existence of price (or profitability) controls for the current merger remedy appraisal is that the controls make it very difficult to raise prices *post*-merger. While it is beyond the scope of this project to model how national pricing committees operate, the recent academic literature provides certain insights (although much relates to the US market). We focus on a selection of recent papers that have attempted to gain insights into competition and pharmaceuticals prices.

7.6.5 Selected Academic Research on Pharmaceuticals Pricing

Over 70 per cent of US pharmaceuticals prescriptions in 1989 were for multi-source drugs (that is, those with both branded and generic versions). Hellerstein (1998) attempts to explain why fewer than 30 per cent of US prescriptions of multi-source drugs were written for the generic versions, despite a potential 30–40 per cent cost saving. Her focus is on the role of prescribing physicians. It seems that even a tiny difference in the effort required by a physician has a major impact, in particular, the design of the prescription form. If the physician has to write three extra words to secure a brand, this is done on only 11 per cent of prescriptions, but if it can be done simply by signing in one place rather than another, it is done for 41 per cent! There is a separate role of dispensing pharmacists who, under some state laws, are able or even required to substitute a generic for a prescribed brand unless the physician explicitly states otherwise (although pharmacists substituted less than 30 per cent of the time they are allowed or required to in 1989, this had risen to 50 per cent by 1995). While Hellerstein is unable to explain in detail why physicians are so reluctant to prescribe generics, she does find that it is quantitatively important. She suspects it may be to do with lack of knowledge about the existence of generics, promotional activities by brand owners, and lack of awareness of price differentials. She applies econometric tests of the hypothesis that there is an agency problem in that the prescriber is not the payer, but her formulation does not support this hypothesis. In particular, she does not find that physicians are more likely to prescribe generics when they expect the patient to have to pay at least a part of the cost (that is, that they are not fully insured). More positively, she does find that Health Maintenance Organization-affiliated physicians are more likely to prescribe generics. We conclude that prescribers are unlikely to be price-sensitive unless there is an institutional constraint on their behaviour, or possibly if they are well aware of generic availability, price differentials and patient exposure to price.

The latter possibility is picked up in an important study by Pavcnik (2002). She investigates a 'natural experiment' in Germany that provides insight into how pharma companies respond to the price exposure of patients (that is, stepping over any intermediate effect on prescriber behaviour and chasing directly to the price response of firms).[19] Over 90 per cent of the German population is covered by statutory health insurance (including for pharmaceuticals). In 1989, Germany introduced reference pricing ('RP'), which set a maximum reimbursement price for a range of products. Denmark and the Netherlands introduced similar systems. Pharma companies can set whatever price they want, but patients have to pay the difference between that and the RP. The RP is set between the price of the most expensive brand and that of generics. Price discrimination is not allowed between pharmacies (although hospitals may negotiate discounts), and pharmacists cannot substitute generics unless prescribed. The scheme has been rolled in, with 75 per cent coverage by 1996. Previous to this, patients would only pay a fixed prescription fee. Physicians are required by law to tell their patients if the prescription exceeds the RP, and they have ready access to price information. Pavcnik's results suggest that there is a significant price response to patient exposure to prices. This is confined to the difference between brands and generics, and not between different drugs for the same therapeutic area. Brand prices fall by around 25 per cent and generics prices by much less, if at all. There is also evidence that an increase in the number of generics makes the branded price response greater. Finally, there was evidence that the introduction of reference pricing cut the branded market share, so the price response was not sufficient to fully defend sales. Overall, the German experience shows that as long as prices are sufficiently visible and the payer is exposed to them, then there is a substantial effect on pharma pricing.

The next paper is interesting in that it estimates the sort of demand system that can be input into a sophisticated simulation model if there are sufficient appropriate data. Ellison et al. (1997) estimate own- and cross-price elasticities between branded and generic versions of four compounds that are close therapeutic substitutes as anti-infectives. Three compounds lost patent protection and experienced generic entry during the period of estimation. They select a two-stage budgeting model and argue that it captures the distinctive prescription and dispensing stages to pharmaceuticals purchasing (recall that pharmacists can substitute generics for branded products in some states, and can be encouraged by Health Maintenance Organizations and insurance plans). As compared with a nested logit model, this approach allows free estimation of elasticities between every pair of products in a group and between every product and every other group. The two-stage model incorporates a second-stage choice (possibly in the hands of the pharmacist) between the branded and generic versions of the drug, and a first-stage choice between the four compounds (decided by the physician). The first stage is modelled by the log of quantity depending on the log of total expenditure on the four drugs and logs of each of the four prices. The second stage has the revenue share of the branded version depending on a measure of quantity, and relative branded and generic prices (this is essentially an AIDS specification). Using monthly data for 1987–89, they find substantial price sensitivity in the choice between generic substitutes and less evidence of price sensitivity in the choice among therapeutic substitutes (ibid., p. 429). One interpretation they put on this is that pharmacists (second-stage choosers) are more price-sensitive than physicians (first-stage choosers). Looking only at the second-stage decision (that is, elasticities conditional on a particular compound having been prescribed), own-price elasticities are between −1.2 and −2 for branded products and between −1.5 and −3 for generics. Conditional cross-price elasticities are between +0.2 and +1.9. The unconditional elasticities take into account the initial prescription decision, and cross-elasticities between compounds can be calculated. These are of a lower order of magnitude and often insignificant.[20] Finally, it should be noted that, as often happens with demand system estimation, there are a number of anomalous results and some implausible estimates in the system.

Caves et al. (1991)[21] examine the effects of patent expiration and subsequent generic entry in the USA. They found a considerable regularity in the price and quantity effects. There was a small (4.5 per cent) decline in the price of the branded product for the mean number of generic entrants (which is typically much higher than in Europe). The first generic reduced branded price by just 2 per cent.[22] During the period between patent expiration and generic entry, the branded product price actually rises. Generic pricing is at a considerable discount to the branded product, and falls with further generic entry, potentially down to below 20 per cent of branded price. Even at less than half the branded price, however, generics capture only 25 per cent of market share. This is much less market penetration that would be expected in non-pharmaceuticals markets with functionally homogeneous products.[23] A major consequence of patent expiry is that marketing expenditure falls considerably (see below for the importance of this). This leads to a reduction of quantity sold, even before generic entry, and it seems that low generic prices cannot recapture this lost market for the drug.[24] There is no evidence in either this pricing or marketing behaviour of any strategic attempt to deter entry.[25] Hospital markets are more susceptible to generic competition, in that they achieve a greater market share despite larger reductions in branded price and lower generic discounts, but it was difficult to quantify how much of the price effects were due to lack of data on discounts. The post-patent expiry advantage of the original innovation brand seems to derive from a first-mover advantage in establishing brand loyalty in conservative prescribers. There is an interesting role for marketing in this: by choosing to reduce marketing spend, the original innovators seem to consider the spillover effects on generic demand to outweigh the advantages of brand consolidation. Overall, Caves et al. pose a dilemma for public policy inasmuch as generic entry reduces both price and quantity because of reduced advertising. Economists do not yet have an agreed methodology to appraise this issue.

Danzon and Chao (2000) examine how different regulatory regimes have an impact on the pricing of pharmaceuticals. A major contribution of their econometric study is that it covers seven countries (Germany, France, Italy, the UK, the USA, Canada, Japan) and 171 single-molecule drugs available in each country in the form of 5690 products. These cover around 20 retail pharmacy therapeutic categories and include data for 1992 on manufacturer price, which they relate to product strength, pack size and so on, number of generic competitors, number of substitute molecules in the same therapeutic group and the number of products per therapeutic substitute molecule. Generic market shares are much higher in countries that allow relatively free pricing (the USA, the UK, Germany, Canada) than where there is strict price or reimbursement regulation (France, Italy, Japan). Since 88 per cent of prescribed drugs in the EU are off-patent, the regulatory effect on generics is very important. The authors find that generic competition is effective in reducing prices only in those countries allowing relatively free pricing, in which case generic prices fall with the number of generic products. This effect offsets much of the savings from price controls. The number of therapeutic substitute molecules does not affect price (except in Italy and Japan). Their suggested explanation is that unregulated markets encourage generics to compete on price, while regulation drives down the innovating brand's price over the life cycle and encourages the owner either to introduce minor 'new' versions of the molecule to squeeze out some extra price or to license and co-market the generics themselves.[26] Successive new molecules in a therapeutic group do not appear to exert competitive pressure on existing product prices, but successive new products are priced lower each time (though not as low as for generics, which is consistent with new molecules having therapeutic advantages at least for some patients or conditions). Some of the structural effects are summarized in Table 7.10.

Table 7.10 Mean number of competitor products per molecule by country

	Generic competitors	Therapeutic substitute molecules TSM	Products per TSM	Age of molecule (years)	Generic entry lag (years)	TSM entry lag (years)
Germany	6.6	10.4	3.0	26	9.5	19.2
UK	2.3	6.8	1.7	24	3.7	12.2
France	2.4	9.2	1.5	22	4.3	15.0
Italy	3.0	9.5	2.1	24	3.8	14.0
USA	11.1	7.3	6.4	20	9.7	13.6
Canada	3.3	6.0	2.2	22	5.6	11.7
Japan	4.5	9.6	2.6	21	5.3	12.9

Lu and Comanor (1998) examine how the prices of patented new drugs are set relative to their existing substitutes and how these prices change after four, six and eight years (that is, essentially before generic competition). Their data cover 144 new introductions in the USA in 1978–87. They find that drugs representing an important therapeutic advance launch at two or three times the price of existing drugs, while those without major advance tend to price at a similar level to existing products. Competitive pressures are also important in that the launch price is lower, the greater the number of branded substitutes on the market. However, by weakening the competitive effect of the out-of-patent brand, generic entry has little net effect on new product prices. A third important factor is that treatments for acute illnesses encourage a 'skimming' strategy of a high initial price followed by a decline, while treatments for a chronic illness have a lower 'penetration' price to hook users before substantially raising price (another possible reason is that chronic illnesses are associated with the elderly, who are more price-sensitive, for example, due to higher co-payment rates, but this does not explain the rising price profile). Drugs that represent an important therapeutic advance follow a price profile consistent with skimming, while more imitative drugs follow a penetration pricing profile. The authors conclude that if regulation discourages penetration pricing by frowning on any price increases, this would ultimately discourage competition by discouraging imitative branded products. The latter are important because they both reduce the introductory price and moderate subsequent price increases.

Ekelund and Persson (2003) apply the same methodology as Lu and Comanor except to a regulated European market. They collected data on all new chemical entities introduced in Sweden in 1987–97. As in the US study, they find that price is directly related to the degree of therapeutic advance (with important advances achieving a price four or five times as much as existing brands, and even twice the price for imitative products), but all prices fall over time because penetration pricing is deterred by regulation (in the Swedish case, a form of price cap). Similarly, there is no difference in price profiles between drugs for acute and chronic conditions. They also find that the number of branded substitutes has no effect on either launch price or the profile over time, suggesting that regulation effectively stifles competition.[27] The main conclusion is that price caps encourage higher launch prices to compensate for a required decline over time. This is consistent with the conclusion reached by Danzon and Chao (2000).

Finally, Berndt et al. (2003) examine product diffusion in a detailed US case study of prices and market share in anti-ulcer treatments.[28] They are particularly interested in investigating whether consumption externalities affect either the value of an established product or the rate at which new drugs can penetrate the market; in other words, does a product with a large initial market establish perceptions of efficacy and safety, and word-of-mouth communication, that give it a long-term advantage (that is, a first-mover advantage leading to persistent dominance and market power)? If this effect is large enough, it can result in 'tipping', by which a large initial market share can prevent the entry of a more efficient product. Berndt et al.'s econometric study found that consumption externalities operated at the brand level only (that is, there was no positive effect on alternative products that had a similar therapeutic effect, in this case H_2-antagonists), but were quantitatively small in explaining price (quality measures, such as low dosage, versatility for multiple indications and lack of known side effects, were more important).[29] However, this consumption externality had a much larger impact in slowing the diffusion of new products. As Tagamet's successful introduction showed, this could be overcome by a product with superior attributes combined with a sufficiently large marketing expenditure on detailing. Nevertheless, the first mover's market share stayed larger for longer because of the consumption externalities.[30]

7.7 MARKETING

While national idiosyncrasies and pricing regulation mean that the geographic extent of markets is national as far as pricing is concerned, it is certainly international as far as R&D is concerned. It is crucial to the return on R&D that successful products are sold globally, and this leads on to the importance of marketing.

Marketing expenditures for prescription drugs are focused on company representatives visiting individual doctors (known as 'detailing'). This accounts for over half of all marketing expenditures.[31] It also creates an economy of scope in being able to discuss several drugs on each visit.[32] This is significant, especially as there is evidence that detailing is necessary in raising sales. Nevertheless, Sutton argues that, as with R&D, pharmaceuticals marketing activities are 'low alpha' in that there is a clear saturation level above which no further sales would be forthcoming. Thus the importance of marketing is that it is equivalent to a fixed overhead that requires a minimum size of firm to attain efficiency. There is no tendency for detailing expenditure to spiral into advertising wars that leaves no room for more than a very few large firms (that is, unlike the situation with, say, cola drinks).

Sutton (1996) uses the case study of stomach ulcer treatments, for which several pharmaceuticals companies were looking for a cure in the 1970s (including SmithKline, Pfizer, Lilly [each US based] and Glaxo [UK]). The basic search was for an anti-histamine to control acid secretions. SmithKline came up with Tagamet, which became the world's leading pharmaceutical within five years. Glaxo followed with Zantac, which performed in a similar way. Early trials suggested it was not obviously better than Tagamet, but each drug might suit particular individuals better. Glaxo's problem was to get doctors to prescribe a drug that was not obviously better than the tried and trusted market leader.

Later evidence suggested that Zantac did have some advantages in that it needed to be taken only half as often, had a 6 per cent higher healing rate, and lower recurrence rate. Glaxo chose to price Zantac close to Tagamet and highlight these advantages, supported by a massive detailing campaign (it had previously adopted the opposite strategy of low price and limited marketing with an asthma drug, Ventolin, which failed to become a top-seller). Glaxo had a similar-sized sales force to SmithKline in the UK, but not elsewhere. Across Europe, Glaxo hired freelance reps and also entered joint marketing agreements with local pharmaceuticals companies who marketed the same drug under a different brand name (in addition to Glaxo's reps selling it as Zantac). The total number of reps significantly exceeded SmithKline's in Europe. In the USA, Glaxo entered a marketing agreement with Roche, who had an extensive network that was underused at the time. Together, they provided 150 000 detailing minutes per month, compared with Tagamet's 100 000. SmithKline responded by matching the 150 000, and both stayed at this level. Zantac was advertised at $600 000 per month, compared with Tagamet's $400 000. By 1987, just over three years after launch, Zantac overtook Tagamet in the USA. Its global share was 42 per cent by 1989, with 52 per cent in the USA. The next new anti-ulcer drug was priced 10 per cent below Zantac and achieved 12 per cent global share, and the third achieved only 2 per cent. Like Zantac, neither had major therapeutic advantages over the existing products.

This simple case study illustrates the crucial influence of marketing decisions on the pricing and market share of a new product.

7.7.1 Competition from Generics

There are two ways in which competition naturally evolves in pharmaceuticals markets. First, new 'second-generation' drugs can be approved while the existing market leader is still on patent. The new drugs may or may not be therapeutically better (see Zantac example above). Second, competition might come from generics once the patent has run out.

Scherer (1993) observes that in the USA, after the 1984 Hatch–Waxman Act, generics were surprisingly slow to penetrate retail prescriptions (17 per cent in 1980 to 30 per cent in 1989), but quicker in hospitals (33 per cent in 1989). His research suggested that price rivalry between branded and generics was not a two-way channel. Essentially, he found that branded prices did not change (and possibly even rose) even when generics were priced between 40 per cent lower (with one generic entrant) and 70 per cent lower (with ten generic entrants). Thus the most common scenario was for the incumbent to maintain price while ceding substantial market share to generics.

Scherer explains this by two 'institutional regularities':[33]

1. 'Individual physicians tend to be risk-averse, insensitive to cost, and creatures of habit, prescribing drugs by brand name even when much less expensive generic substitutes exist' (ibid., p. 101). Committees (set up by payer representatives) tend to be better at containing costs.
2. Non-prescription consumers purchasing direct from pharmacies normally lack the knowledge to be able to switch to generics.

Scherer claims it is 'not too extreme an oversimplification' to identify two distinct groups of consumer: one price-sensitive, and the other not so. With just one branded product, the pricing problem is standard. With a generic competitor, it will often be profit-maximizing for the branded product to abandon the price-sensitive customers.

This might even sound like an optimal price discrimination strategy for a monopolist, but it turns out to be rare for the owner of a branded product to sell a generic of its own product alongside. Scherer says that his talks with US industry executives' suggested fear of arbitrage against the price-insensitive market explained this. However, he also saw evidence that industry practice was changing, with Merck setting up a generics division that would copy one of its analgesics which was off patent. He also says that German firms do it. He expects that if this trend continues, patent expirations will be accompanied by price stability or rises for the original brand, own generic prices will be lower, and rival generics will be sharply lower.

7.8 ADVANTAGES OF SCALE

The above analysis of R&D and marketing can be supplemented by a few observations on financial economies to summarize the overall economies of scale.

7.8.1 R&D

- Sutton argues that economies of scope are very limited. Within therapeutic groups, there is limited demand-side substitution as different drugs often have different effects (and side effects), and are suited to different people. Even within chemically related groups, he shows that there is no tendency for one firm to develop subsequent products.[34]
- This does not mean there are no traditional economies of scale. He estimates development costs in the order of $150 million in 1990. To put this in perspective, this is about 3 per cent of revenues of the largest firm or 0.1 per cent of global industry sales revenue. The US OTA figure reported above is $359 million in the same year. It is not clear whether this latter figure is higher because it makes allowance for failed pipeline products. However, increased safety requirements for drug registrations will have increased these figures.
- This 'unit project' effect is compounded by the huge variance in returns and dependence on a few blockbusters for profits.

7.8.2 Marketing

- The share of revenue devoted to marketing is larger than that allocated to R&D.
- Two firms with similar products may achieve very different results in terms of sales and profitability depending on the size of their sales networks. Sutton illustrates this with a case study of Glaxo's Zantac and SmithKline's Tagamet. Tagamet had a strong first-mover advantage, and Zantac had few clinical advantages, but Glaxo formed a joint venture with Hoffmann–La Roche, marketed it at full price, and achieved similar sales to Tagamet.

- Up to a threshold, there are advantages of having a larger marketing network, but beyond that (large) size, there is no advantage of trying to spend more on marketing.

7.8.3 Financial

- Financial markets could not monitor numerous single-project firms trying to develop speculative new drugs. Without the immediate test of market success, the firm provides an informed internal capital market that reduces the classic problems associated with asymmetric information.
- Bankruptcy costs create an advantage for a diversified portfolio of research and pipeline products to be held by one firm, as distinct from a private portfolio of specialist firms held by a financial investor.
- The stocks and shares of larger firms with a high market capitalization are more liquid than for small firms, and this is particularly valued by insurance companies and mutual funds.

7.8.4 Overall

- Mergers on cost grounds are likely to be most sought when one of the partners is over-reliant on a single drug.
- The success of second-mover drugs without significant therapeutic advantages depends on marketing effort to overcome the first mover's advantage.
- There are also portfolio effects that make independence difficult for small and medium-sized R&D-intensive pharmaceuticals firms.
- There is little first-mover advantage in R&D itself.

7.9 THE COMMISSION'S STANDARD APPROACH TO PHARMACEUTICALS MARKETS

While the Commission's Decisions reveal a broad understanding of the sector, the large number of markets typically involved in any one merger means that its approach is, perhaps inevitably, somewhat stylized. This section provides a background critique and introduction to what simulation might add. Chapter 8 provides further critique based on our detailed work on simulations and *ex post* analysis. The typical approach of the Commission to a pharmaceuticals merger is as detailed below.

7.9.1 Market Definition

Product markets are defined at the 3-digit ATC level, which immediately enables industry data to be used, so competitors can be identified and market shares calculated. In the relatively rare cases in which the main or third parties disagree with this definition, it may be modified.

The geographic market is almost always national. This is justified on the grounds that product approval and registration for particular uses is national, purchasing policies and reimbursement rules are national, and branding, pack size and distribution are national.

There is a broad distinction between selling medicines on prescription versus OTC. However, the Commission invariably shies away from a complex analysis of buyer behaviour (despite this being a justification for defining national markets), presumably because of national differences and complexities. This is a weakness in their analysis. The same approach is applied regardless of which member state market is the cause for concern.

Concerns for future product development only surface in the context of pipeline products. In such cases, they are likely to be considered as being part of a wider geographic market, and possibly a wider product market if the new product might have wider properties.

7.9.2 Assessment of Competition

Market shares

- Simple addition of merging parties: a combined share in excess of 25 per cent merits attention, but 40 per cent is typically treated as a critical threshold. The increment in market share is also important, with very low and stable (or declining) shares considered as *de minimis*.[35]
- Shares of leading competitors: either market share 'distance' (that is, difference between share of merged firms and nearest rival);[36] or absolute share of rival. In BM/Roche (see case study in Chapter 8), the threshold for the 'distance' effect is revealed if combined market share is 'close to 50 per cent' and the next largest competitor is less than half this share (that is, <25 per cent), but not if the combined share of the next two competitors exceeds that of the merging parties.[37] There is no hint of any discussion of what underpins this (for example, no mention of unilateral effects versus coordinated effects). In fact, the emphasis on the competitive benefits of strong third parties in *direct opposition* to the US Guidelines based on the HHI and its conditional change (known as 'delta'). The HHI is *increasing* in *all* market shares, including those of rivals, so a 'strong'

third-party is considered as a competitive *threat*. The true importance of third-party market shares depends on the nature of competition in the market concerned. No doubt strong third parties are helpful for competition in some circumstances, and a hindrance in others. The point we wish to make is that a strong third party is not a self-evident benefit and so this line of argument used by the Commission needs serious justification.

- Attention is given to the trend in market shares, especially of leading competitors – if a potentially strong competitor's share is rising while the merging parties' share is falling, then a combined share >40 per cent may be acceptable.[38]
- The number of competitors is sometimes an additional factor, especially if it is already small (around four) pre-merger. This is also important for future markets (in practice, pipeline products or active development strategies).

Product differentiation

- Different chemical entities: it is recognized that even if products have the same clinical indications, they are differentiated by virtue of different side effects and efficacies for different patients. This may modify the market share analysis, but not in any systematic way.
- Generics: although chemically identical, it is recognized that generics are, in practice, often weak substitutes for the original branded product. Market shares are implicitly used to evaluate substitutability.
- First-mover advantage: this is usually recognized through the existing market share, and is not additional.

Barriers to entry

- Patent protection and remaining patent duration.
- Potential entrants with strong positions (that is, high market share) in other national markets.

Buyers

- Buyer power in the form of customers who account for a large share of purchases is sometimes analysed, with the important and surprising exception of when the buyer (directly or indirectly) is a national health service.
- Buyer incentives: consumers who pay for their own medicines are expected to create more elastic demand than when there is full reimbursement.

Product range

- Bundling possibilities: there is often a vague concern over the ability to sell a broad range of related products, especially if other firms do not have the range to do the same.
- Marketing economies: it is sometimes unclear whether the ability to market a full range of products more efficiently, which is often a major motive for pharma mergers, is treated neutrally or more negatively because it makes life harder for smaller firms.

A typical conclusion from this type of analysis is provided by Hoffmann–La Roche/Boehringer Mannheim (1998, IV/M.950, p. 23 no. 105), where dominance is found 'based not only on the high combined market shares attained by Roche/BM, but also on their advantages in terms of installed base, their unmatched product portfolio, the relative weakness of existing competitors, the insufficient countervailing power of the demand side and the high entry barriers'.

The relevance of this discussion of thresholds for the current analysis is that remedies are currently judged by the same thresholds as for the initial analysis of dominance. We need to ask whether a simulation methodology would provide better outcomes. More specifically, we ask two questions. First, are the thresholds used by the Commission sensible given typical values for own- and cross-price elasticities of demand? Second, to what extent do elasticity estimates add to a simple market share analysis?

As a preliminary analysis, we can use the PCAIDS simulation model to investigate the unilateral price effects of a merger in a market characterized by product differentiation. Our results are summarized in Table 7.11. For example, suppose: the industry elasticity is −1.0 (that is, calculated if all firms raise price a little); the lead merging firm's elasticity is −3.0 (that is, calculated if only one firm raises price); and the merger would reduce marginal costs of the merging firms by 5 per cent each. These parameters are fairly typical for the markets we study below (although they may be very different in other markets). In this case, a merger of firms with existing market shares of 30 per cent and 10 per cent would raise industry average prices by <1 per cent, whereas a merger of firms with shares of 35 per cent and 15 per cent would raise average prices by >3 per cent. This appears to suggest that the combined market share implicit thresholds are quite appropriate.

However, this characterization depends crucially on the assumed elasticities. Table 7.11 examines the sensitivity of the 40 per cent or 50 per cent market share thresholds to the own-price elasticity of demand of the lead merging firm. If the competition authority is willing to accept average price rises of no more than 1 per cent as a *de minimis* level, then a 40 per cent

Table 7.11 Importance of elasticities – market share analysis compared with basic simulation (using PCAIDS)

Market shares of merging firms, %	Own-price elasticity of larger merging firm	Range of market average price increases, %
35 + 15	−2	6.1–6.4
	−3	3.1–3.4
	−4	1.7–1.9
	−5	0.9–1.0
30 + 10	−2	2.3–2.4
	−3	0.8–0.9
	−4	0.1–0.1
	−5	−0.3–−0.3

Notes:
1. *Assumes*: single product firms; industry elasticity of −1; and 5% marginal cost efficiency gain for both merging parties.
2. The range of price increases depends on third-party market shares, with the lower figure applying when none has a market share exceeding 10 per cent and the higher figure applying when one third party has a market share of 45 per cent.

threshold is appropriate only as long as the elasticity is less than three, but a 50 per cent market share should be acceptable if the elasticity is at least five. Of course, this is not a firm rule, because the basic simulation makes other assumptions about efficiencies, industry elasticity, number of brands per firm, incremental market share and third-party market shares. This is why each case requires individual simulation, even when the PCAIDS model is deemed appropriate.

In contrast to the effect of alternative elasticities, average price rises are relatively insensitive to the pattern of market shares of independent rivals, and inasmuch as there is a relationship, prices rise more if there is a 'strong' rival with a large market relative to the merging parties. This raises a serious doubt about the Commission's analysis of 'distance' between market shares, which would be aggravated if coordinated effects were considered a possibility.[39] Of course, there are very good non-price reasons to be concerned about rival market shares in pharma markets, in particular the ability and incentive to invest in R&D and marketing. The latter may be the more important as there could be a threat to a continuing commitment to the market if a firm has only a small share, especially if it does not have other relevant products with which to support an efficient marketing network. The important point is that it is necessary to understand exactly *why* the shares of non-merging parties might be important, or else the 'remedy' may fail to alleviate the problem (for example, is it better to sell divested assets to a firm already operating in the market, or to a new entrant?). Inasmuch as buyers of divested assets may be expected to have different efficiencies to the existing owners, then an additional benefit of basic simulation is that the consequences can be incorporated into the analysis.

7.10 CONCLUSION

Competition for the market is the most important element of long-run pharmaceuticals competition. Large R&D requirements, high risks of failure and long lead times all contribute to the rise of very large firms with diversified portfolios of drugs. However, the existence of so many potentially beneficial drugs yet to be discovered still makes it possible for much smaller firms to compete in the early stages of research. This is an important contrast to industries in which technologies build on proprietary knowledge and tightly held patents, and so where a technological lead is cumulative in the absence of a huge effort by laggards. Nevertheless, the need for even higher expenditures on marketing in order to maximize the revenues of a new product means that small firms cannot usually take new drugs through to market.

Even more distinctive of the pharmaceuticals market is its complex relationship with consumers. The distinction between patient, prescriber and payer means that drug pricing does not fit the standard models of markets, particularly in out-patient prescription markets. For example, the payers have to constrain prescriber behaviour in order to induce a non-zero price elasticity of demand. A very significant consequence in Europe is the way in which pharmaceuticals companies are regulated, directly or indirectly, in their price setting. This means that accurate simulations of various merger remedies would require a very detailed knowledge of the effectiveness of regulation in each member state. For example, where it would be practically impossible to raise price in the future, this will affect introductory pricing. It will also have obvious implications for the pricing consequences of an unremedied merger. Another member-state-specific effect is likely to be felt through different prescribing cultures. For example, the price effect of introducing either a generic or a new branded drug will depend on the response of physicians. The complexities of modelling features specific to individual member states are beyond the remit of this project. However, it is worrying that there is so little evidence in Commission Decisions that features specific to member states have received sufficient attention.

The academic literature has created a substantial body of knowledge about how the peculiar circumstances of the pharmaceuticals industry affect pricing behaviour. This chapter has summarized a small part of this literature with a view to illustrating its importance. Without this background, it is not possible to understand the impact on an existing brand of a generic, or of a new chemical entity with similar therapeutic properties. The interaction of pricing and marketing decisions following new or anticipated entry is another feature of these markets. Perhaps the most important feature to understand, however, is the constraint that regulation puts on the dynamic profile of pricing. It is extremely difficult to implement price rises in a regulated market because most important costs are sunk and production costs are only a small part of the price. Anticipating this constraint, entrants raise launch prices, and one side effect is that they become less effective competitors, hampered by the inability to adopt a penetration pricing strategy to overcome existing product loyalties. Another consequence of very direct interest to merger and remedy analysis is that, under many regulatory regimes, they will be unable to raise post-merger prices.[40]

Nevertheless, in the context of the present study, the detailed econometric estimates of own- and cross-price elasticities for particular products in unregulated US markets provide an important point of comparison with some of the elasticity estimates derived from the questionnaire questions asked of industry experts and used in Chapter 8. These help explain the pricing pressures created by a merger, even if the exact price predictions are unreliable when derived from models that do not incorporate regulation.

Finally, we must acknowledge that a merger between two large pharmaceutical companies with overlapping product portfolios will inevitably provide a serious administrative problem for the Commission. This is because geographic markets are national, so all market overlaps have to be multiplied by a number close to 25. The Commission needs simple rules to decide cases with all due speed and legal certainty. It currently uses a procedure that comes close to a strict 40 per cent market share rule. While this is not necessarily an unreasonable threshold, it is unlikely to be optimal. One purpose of the following simulations is to see whether there are any simple alternatives, even ignoring national idiosyncrasies. However, we suggest that there are two more things that the Commission can do. First, the Commission should develop a greater background understanding of national markets in relation to pricing. This expertise could then be drawn on rapidly as required. Second, the Commission should impose very strict requirements before even considering a clearance in Phase I when so many relevant markets are at issue. There will inevitably be more errors of analysis in Phase I than in Phase II, and even if type 2 errors (that is, allowing a merger that is harmful) can be squeezed down by a sufficiently tight standard of referral, type 1 errors (that is, preventing a merger that is beneficial) can still arise due to a hastily agreed 'remedy' (for example, a divestiture to a buyer who does not operate it in such a way as to restore competition). For a given resource constraint on the part of the competition authority, the greater the number of markets under investigation, the more likely simple rules of thumb are to be followed, and the greater is the likelihood of error. A suitable compromise might be to use Phase I to rule out markets that definitely cause no concern, and allow the merging firms to proceed in integrating their activities in these areas. At the same time, all contentious markets could be investigated in detail in Phase II, where remedies could be more carefully crafted.

NOTES

1. This is in spite of the fact that the Europeans are apparently just as successful at developing new chemical entities (NCEs) – the implication is that European MNEs find it harder to sell those drugs, once invented. The authors attribute this to less restricted demand in the US (ibid., p. 6).
2. Quoting from their web page: 'Data is sourced from MIDAS, the world's largest pharmaceutical information system. This data is used by all of the world's leading pharmaceutical, biotech and financial companies. In order to give as complete a picture as possible, estimated sales through all distribution channels in all countries are presented.' See also the description of IMS Health in the European Court of First Instance President order of 26 October 2001, Case T-184/01 R, and the European Commission's decision of 3 July 2001, NDC Health/IMS Health (2001/165/EC).
3. While the term 'R&D' has a fairly unambiguous meaning for economic theorists, in practice it will typically be imprecise. Most published data will be taken from company accounts and the precise definition may vary between companies, albeit within the constraints imposed by national accounting and tax practices. There is inevitably an ambiguous dividing line between R&D and marketing. We are advised by Commission industry experts that regulatory expenses relating to product authorization are typically labelled R&D expenses because they also involve clinical trials. In our opinion, this is theoretically correct as these are capital expenses associated with the pre-market development of the product. On the other hand, GP training on how to prescribe new drugs straddles R&D and marketing.
4. We use this term following Sutton (1991). It is analogous to the 'natural monopoly', in that the nature of the cost curve renders the 'most efficient' market structure one on which only a small number of firms are able to exist profitably. However, what makes it different from the natural monopoly is that it is the escalating endogenous sunk costs (usually R&D and/or advertising) chosen by those leading firms that render the market inaccessible to smaller potential competitors.
5. Unfortunately, no more recent data have been found.
6. According to the US Office of Technology Assessment (US Congress), the average cost of bringing a new drug to market rose from $116 million in 1976 to $359 million in 1990 (constant 1990 dollars). Leading pharmaceuticals companies now typically spend $1–2 billion p.a.
7. However, it appears that combinatorial chemistry may not have brought about the advantages the industry had hoped for, and the synthesis of natural or slightly optimized compounds from nature has become increasingly attractive again.
8. The same survey shows that the majors invest a third of their R&D online extensions.
9. Ben-Asher (1999) argues that no products under development should be considered, because it is not clear that a loss of R&D competition leads to less R&D, or even that less R&D leads to a welfare loss.

10. See FTC submission to the OECD (OECD, 2001, pp. 320, 381). However, note that the characteristics of pharmaceuticals R&D can create problems with divestiture of an R&D programme (Levy [at FTC], 1999): R&D assets must be readily identified; there should not be a loss of efficiency in complementary R&D assets; and a strong buyer needs to be able to compete in the product market.
11. In 1995, the USA raised its standard duration of patent from 17 to 20 years to bring it into international conformity.
12. It is not clear what the relative merits of these alternatives are.
13. This has implications for Schumpeterian creative destruction. As Gans et al. (2002) show, the characteristics of biotech, including pharmaceuticals, mean that new start-ups rarely if ever grow to take up a position of leadership. This is because the high costs of commercialization and strength of patent protection combine to make cooperation a more attractive strategy for a young firm with a good potential product.
14. One reason is that, following an insider trading scandal at ImClone, due diligence is more intense.
15. The following section is largely based on a 2000 study commissioned by DG Enterprise; see especially the summary paper by P. Kanavos (2000), 'Overview of pharmaceutical pricing and reimbursement regulation in Europe'.
16. Accompanying price controls on pharmaceuticals companies, many countries also control wholesale and sometimes retail margins.
17. Germany has extended reference pricing to include patented drugs.
18. See Hellerstein (1998).
19. Pavcnik also points to another US study which finds a very large effect of free-care plans versus 95 per cent co-insurance. The former results in 78 per cent higher expenditure on pharmaceuticals as compared with the latter.
20. Bearing in mind the likelihood that price visibility and pressure from generics appears to have risen in recent years, elasticities may now be higher than those estimated on this sample.
21. Caves et al. (1991) and following 'Comment' by P. Temin (pp. 57–62).
22. Frank and Salkever (1992), and especially Frank and Salkever (1997), provide evidence that branded prices rise on patent expiry.
23. Similar results apply to therapeutic substitutes in the UK. A study by the Department of Health and the Association of the British Pharmaceutical Industry, 'PPRS: the study into the extent of competition in the supply of branded medicines to the NHS', studied 11 new submarkets and found an average time lag for second product entry to be three years (ranging from nought to nine years), with a third product likely within a year. Later entrants set a lower price, and despite the fact that the original product does not typically respond by changing price, it still maintains a high market share.
24. Temin observes that this might be due to the natural product cycle of drugs, which appears to peak at 14 years and so more or less coincides with effective patent duration (10–12 years).
25. However, there are numerous instances of firms trying to buy off generic entrants (for example, paying them to delay entry). These are not mentioned by Caves et al.
26. An implication is that tight price regulation diverts R&D away from innovative new products towards minor 'tweaks' to existing molecules.
27. Another consequence is that generics have little market share in Sweden; in 1991, it was 30 per cent by volume and only 12 per cent by value.
28. This is the same market as analysed by Sutton (see below), who was more concerned with the technology of new product development (R&D). Also, Berndt et al. go beyond the introduction of Zantac in 1983 (to take on Tagamet), to include Pepcid (in 1986) and Axid (in 1988).
29. They found that Zantac had a \$0.72 quality advantage, and a \$0.12 consumer base disadvantage, so its launch price premium of \$0.61 was almost exactly explained by these factors.
30. Berndt et al. estimate that, had this effect been 50 per cent smaller, Zantac would have earned \$882 million less in gross profits, roughly equivalent to three months of 1992 sales.

31. The OECD quote a US Senate figure that more than $8000 is spent on marketing for each physician. Around 1990, the US pharmaceutical industry spent around $5 billion p.a. on marketing and $4 billion on R&D.
32. An unnamed pharmaceuticals company (confidential submission) claims that an ethical manufacturer may wish to be a licensee in co-marketing or co-promotion to fill a gap in their product portfolio. Presumably this has to do with the way in which their sales reps present treatments to doctors.
33. Another explanation of the persistence or elevation of the price of branded products post-entry is offered in our model for the Chirocaine remedy for the Astra/Zeneca merger.
34. This is important in relation to the possibility that mergers might lead to collusion, for example in implicitly segmenting R&D efforts according to therapeutic areas. This would require economies of scope if it were to be effective; otherwise specialist firms could enter into competition to undermine the tacit collusion.
35. For example, in PU/Monsanto (M1835, no. 69), plain corticosteroids (H2A) in Belgium gave the merging parties a combined market share of 75.4 per cent, but Monsanto's contribution was only 0.2 per cent points, and this was considered too small to be a concern.
36. For example '>40% indicates that no competitor is able to challenge' the leader (HLR/BM, p. 15, no. 64).
37. Where most national markets have small combined market shares, but one is high, the analysis tends to be more lenient (for example, in immunochemistry diagnostics, BM/Roche had a combined share of 62.1 per cent, but two rivals, one with <20 per cent and the other with <10 per cent, were found to exert a sufficient constraint). This is justified on several grounds, including that market shares elsewhere suggest the possibility of entry.
38. For instance, Sanofi-Synthélabo (M1397, 1999, no. 54) for myorelaxants (M3B) in France with a combined share of 42.5 per cent by value and 46.2 per cent by volume. The rise of a branded product by AHP and a generics market share of 25 per cent are both mentioned, as well as a small increment (1.9 per cent).
39. Coordinated effects are most likely to become a problem if market shares are more balanced, because it is usually the smallest firms that have the greatest incentive to cut price – they have much more potential market share to gain.
40. Unfortunately, within the limited time we had available for this study, we have not come across any studies of how the post-merger consolidation may or may not affect bargaining power with the regulators.

8. Assessment of remedies adopted by the EC in pharmaceuticals mergers[1]

8.0 INTRODUCTION AND OVERVIEW

This chapter considers the choice and impact of remedies required by the European Commission. It uses the benchmarking methodology outlined in Chapter 3 to investigate the *ex ante* choice of remedy whenever this might be relevant. However, given the extensive review of pharmaceuticals competition set out in Chapter 7, simple simulation techniques are not always appropriate in this industry. The equivalent task in the presence of buyers who have such an influence on prices should be a complementary analysis of how the direct and indirect effects of the price regulation process would be affected by the merger and its proposed remedy. Unfortunately, the documents at our disposal did not allow us to do this.

In this chapter, we also introduce an experimental new model which aims to explain the incentives and price consequences of a merger involving a pipeline product. Unlike standard models reviewed in Chapter 3, it is consistent with the pricing results in an unregulated market (see Chapter 7) and it draws out the incentive to suppress or introduce the pipeline product under different ownerships. However, it is currently insufficiently developed to be able to rely on it as a practical simulation model.

The range of cases, markets and simulation techniques applied is summarized in Table 8.1. Sections 8.1–8.5 review these cases in detail. Section 8.6 draws some conclusions for merger appraisal and remedy in pharmaceuticals markets. Some more general conclusions on the simulation methodology are reserved for Chapter 9. Finally, Section 8.7 contains an appendix setting out the formal theory of our experimental simulation model. The technique is applied in Section 8.4.4.

8.1 HOFFMANN–LA ROCHE/BOEHRINGER MANNHEIM (1998) – M950

Decision: Article 8(2) with conditions and obligations = Phase II clearance subject to remedies. This is the only Phase II decision out of the five large-scale mergers we examine in pharmaceuticals.

Table 8.1 Pharmaceuticals mergers, markets and simulations

Merger	Product market	Geographic market	Simulation technique	Year	Estimated price effect of merger without remedy (%)
Hoffmann–La Roche/ Boehringer Mannheim	Clinical chemistry systems	Germany, Austria EEA	PCAIDS	1998	−0.1–2.0 3.8–9.2
	DNA probes		–		Not simulated
Monsanto/Pharmacia & Upjohn	Immediate release analgesics	Sweden	PCAIDS	2000	10–80
Sanofi/Synthélabo	Stupefying active substances	France	–	1999	Not simulated (no data available)
Astra/Zeneca	Plain betablockers	Sweden, Norway	–	1999	Not simulated (particular market circumstances)
	Long-acting local anaesthetics	Germany, UK, Netherlands	Vertical product differentiation with new product		Merger would have prevented entry of new-product which would have caused a price fall of Astra's products by 17–45% for the base product and −11–18% for the 'premium' product
Glaxo Wellcome/ SmithKline Beecham	Anti-virals	Germany, UK, Netherlands	PCAIDS	2000	−2.7–0.4 13.3–20.6 Not simulated
	Topical anti-virals	Germany, UK, Netherlands	PCAIDS		−3.1–0.1 −1.4–2.8 Not simulated (no data available)
	Anti-migraine compounds	Germany, UK, Netherlands	–		Not simulated (pipeline product)
	Chronic obstructive pulmonary disease	Germany, UK, Netherlands	–		Not simulated (pipeline product)

8.1.1 Competition Concerns

Products and markets that raised concerns

There were two broad areas of overlap: pharmaceutical products, and in vitro diagnostics (IVD). For pharmaceuticals, there were eight 3-digit ATC markets (for each member state national market) with some degree of overlap. Most markets had combined market shares of <25 per cent and all but one was <30 per cent. The one worrying market was for vitamin B1 compounds (A11D) in Italy, where BM's share of 18 per cent would be added to Roche's share of 49 per cent to achieve a combined 67 per cent. The increasing penetration of a new Pfizer product, the lack of patent protection for Roche/BM products, low barriers to entry, and non-reimbursement by the Italian National Health Service (so consumers would be price-sensitive) combined to lead the Commission to conclude that there would be no creation or strengthening of dominance in this remaining market. This is a relatively rare breach of 'the 40 per cent rule', but the decision seems justified on these grounds. It may be significant that this was a Phase II clearance and so gave the Commission time for a comprehensive assessment.

Greater concerns were found in IVD, which is a technology that conducts tests outside the body (*in vitro* = 'in glass', compared with *in vivo* = 'in body') to measure substances in a patient's tissue, blood or urine samples. This enables a physician to diagnose, treat and monitor a patient. The concern was with multi-use IVD for use on site. These diagnostics products generally form a system composed of an automatic measuring instrument that can quickly perform several tests, and 'reagents' which are the compounds used to perform the tests. Most major suppliers offer a bundled product with the instrument, a test kit of reagents and so on, and servicing (including quality control), but reagents can be purchased separately. The diagnostics industry spends around 10 per cent revenue on R&D. Only up to 20 per cent of turnover is achieved through instrument sale, so reagent sales are the focus of competition, with instruments often subsidized if a long-term reagent contract is signed. For budgetary reasons, laboratories seem to prefer current expenditures to large capital expenditures, so they will sign such contracts. Also, switching reagent supplier requires customer know-how, time and effort.

IVD markets were considered national on the basis that there are divergences in national health policies, social security regulations and technology used in laboratories. Consequently, there exist very substantial price differences (up to 200 per cent) and these seem to reflect reimbursement policies in different member states.

A major motive for the merger (p. 30, no. 128)[2] was to get 'access to a larger sales force to maximise the marketing for PCR products, and to create possibilities to successfully bundle sales of clinical chemistry, immunochemistry (for which no serious product overlaps were found) and DNA probe products'. Thus, as claimed for most pharma mergers, it seems that it was marketing-driven. The Commission was concerned that Roche could then 'offer its customers volume discounts or special rebates if a package deal is concluded . . . but no other company has a position approaching that of the combined Roche/BM . . . It must therefore be concluded that . . . this effect of the proposed transaction would significantly consolidate and strengthen its dominant position on the DNA Probe market' (p. 31, no. 130). This represents a familiar Commission concern about the potential anticompetitive effects of product bundling.

While this might sound speculative, there was evidence of a practice already used by Roche. 'Several customers have referred to Roche's unique system of charging its customers (the laboratories) a fixed percentage of their turnover on PCR tests as a "royalty"' (p. 31, no. 132). This is reminiscent of an early Microsoft case in the USA relating to PC manufacturers being charged for Windows whether or not they loaded the software on a PC before delivery, which was found to be an anticompetitive practice to preserve dominance.

Finally, note that this is not strictly a pharmaceuticals market, and as such it does not face the price controls that affect the analysis of the other markets we consider. This means that it provides a useful point of departure for simulation analysis.

Products and markets for which remedy was required

Two separate IVD markets were identified as creating dominance problems: classical clinical chemistry diagnostics comprising clinical chemistry reagents and instruments (CCR and CCI, which are collectively known as systems CCS); and DNA probes.

CCS are used to test for glucose, cholesterol, sodium and other substances found in large concentrations in the body. All major CCR suppliers also provide CCI. The main overlap was in automated CCI and associated CCR. BM was the market leader and Roche had only a small business called 'Cobas Mira' (which was not even operated as a separate business internally). Roche was required to divest in eight European countries (including customer lists, supply agreements, service agreements, stock of spares, and service software and tools). Roche would also be 'ready to sell to the buyer new Mira instruments, the necessary spare parts, and, if needed, reagents, all at a favourable transfer price'. There is no mention of how 'favourable' was to be defined. Roche also undertook to sell to a single purchaser who would be a viable competitor, and within six months. With the Commission's permission, the business in different countries might be sold to different purchasers. In the event, the whole European business was sold to a single purchaser (ABX), who also purchased the CCI business because they understood it to be essential to develop a customer base for the CCRs. According to the purchaser, Roche interpreted this as only 'routine reagents' and not 'specific reagents' which were consequently provided on unfavourable terms. The Cobas Mira business accounted for 65 per cent of Roche's total installed base of instruments, including all its smaller instruments. The remaining Roche instruments would add only a small amount to BM's market share.

DNA probes detect infectious diseases, genetic disorders and cancer cells with much greater speed and accuracy than any other technology. The market was growing rapidly. Roche held the patents for the world-leading polymerase chain reaction (PCR) technology. It agreed to offer 'worldwide licences for all in vitro diagnostic applications to all interested market participants'. These were to include future as well as current technologies. There were to be two types of licence: option A covered the fundamental PCR patents; option B covered additional applications patents. Option B could be either for the full range 'broad licence' or a 'targeted licence' for a specific disease. The idea was to allow competition to develop with both large competitors and more specialist firms. Before this, firms using a research licence could only market any tests they developed in conjunction with Roche or a firm with a commercial licence. Licences were to be offered on 'non-discriminatory terms . . . which are favourable compared to recently negotiated similar licences . . . For the purpose of ensuring the non-discriminatory treatment of all licensees Roche will grant each licensee a "most-favoured-customer" clause.' A trustee would be appointed to ensure compliance. At least one general and one targeted licence should be sold within three months. Anticipating licence fees related to sales, and 'to reduce information exchanges between Roche and the licensees' (presumably either because of collusion possibilities, or because knowledge of a competitor's business secret might give Roche an unfair advantage), an independent auditor would delay the feedback of sales figures for 12 months.

The Commission has not asked us to examine the DNA probe market in detail, but it has some interesting features in relation to remedies. This is because BM was not active in this market at the time and had no actual pipeline products. However, it had 'invested substantial efforts in positioning itself in this market'. It had acquired a substantial portfolio of patents relating to the DNA probe market and concluded collaboration agreements with ten independent parties who were developing DNA probe products for BM. BM also had an instrument distribution agreement with a US company, and had an in-house development programme to produce such instruments. The latter would be stopped post-merger. Thus BM was well positioned to enter this high-growth market, and it had already agreed in principle to a commercial licence for the use of Roche's PCR technology. The combination of Roche's existing 60 per cent market share with the removal of BM as a potential competitor and access to BM marketing organization and bundling possibilities provided the grounds for enhanced dominance requiring remedy.

There must be a concern about the MFC (most favoured customer) clause in the remedy imposed by the Commission, because it very much reduces the incentive for a licensor to cut price to new customers – this would be very expensive because rebates would have to be given to the existing customer base. The problem is enhanced by the likelihood that those who have already purchased a licence are those who value it most and so who will have paid the highest price. This makes the time limit for the granting of a specified number of licences crucial, but it still raises a concern about how many future licences will, in practice, be granted.

Unsurprisingly, it turns out that there have been problems. The following is an extract from correspondence with the Commission.

> Recently, Roche came to see the Commission to discuss the possibility of (i) a complete waiver or (ii) review of the commitments. Indeed it has become increasingly difficult for Roche to find licensees under the strict provisions of the commitments regarding downpayments, royalty rates and the MFC clause. The commitments provide for fixed downpayments and royalty rates, depending on the type of licence concerned. However, many foundational PCR patents will expire in 2006 in Europe. New licensees are less willing to pay high sums in view of the approaching expiration.

In the light of the above *ex ante* analysis, the appropriate response to achieve the required level of competition should have been to require Roche to improve the terms, even though this might imply a rebate to existing customers.

8.1.2 *Ex ante* Simulations

For all but one national CCS market, the threshold for dominance was 40 per cent.[3] The exception was Norway (combined share 49.5 per cent = 41.4 per cent + 8.1 per cent, with the next firm having a market share <30 per cent and two others <20 per cent). It is instructive to compare this with the finding of dominance in Italy (combined share 47 per cent = 40.8 per cent + 6.2 per cent, with the next firm having a market share <30 per cent, another <20 per cent and two more with <10 per cent) and Denmark (combined share 43.1 per cent = 28.9 per cent + 14.2 per cent, with two others <20 per cent). The reasoning provided is that in Norway, the next two firms have a market share claimed to be higher than BM/Roche (though this seems unlikely from the reported market shares), whereas in Italy the combined shares of the next two firms would be less than BM/Roche and in Denmark BM/Roche would be more than double the next biggest competitor. For our critique of this approach by the Commission, the reader is referred back to our discussion in Chapter 7.

Given the large number of national markets (30, that is, two product markets in each of 15 countries) we set out to provide simulations for CCS in three countries: Germany, Austria and Sweden (see Table 8.2 for market

Table 8.2 Market shares for selected CCR markets

Country	Firm	1996 market share %	Firm	1998 market share %	2001 market share %
EEA	BM	39			
	Roche	4			
	Combined	43			
Germany	BM	52.8	BM		
	Roche	2.5	Roche		
	Combined	55.3	Combined	55.3	57.6
	J&J	<10	Beckman	<10	<10
	Beckman	<10	Ortho	<10	<10
	Merck	<10	Dade	<10	<10
	Dade	<10			
Austria	BM	72.5	Combined	65	68
	Roche	5.5	J&J	<10	<10
	Combined	78.0	Behring	<10	10
	J&J	<10	Beckman	<10	
			Abbott		<10
Sweden	BM	39.1			
	Roche	8.9			
	Combined	48.0			
	J&J	<20			
	Bayer	<20			
	Beckman	<10			
	Merck	<10			

Notes:

1. Other firms included if market share >5 per cent.
2. 1996 market shares formed the basis of the Decision; 1998 provided by the parties for the time of the merger (they claim these shares are overstated for Austria because some firms do not report to EDMD, which is the data source referenced in the Decision); there is no explanation provided for the apparent fall in BM/Roche share in Austria 1996–8.

shares). As it turns out, no data could be provided for Sweden, so we examine only the German and Austrian markets.

As part of the follow-up questionnaires, Roche were asked to provide estimates of the *market* elasticity (more precisely, we asked: how much would sales volumes decrease if *all firms* raised their prices by 5 per cent?) and the unilateral *own-price* elasticity for retained businesses at the time of acquisition (that is, we asked: how much would sales volumes decrease if *you* raised your prices by 5 per cent while competitors sales prices remained the same?). In principle, questions can be asked in relation to either sales volumes or sales values, but complex pricing and discounts mean that businesses often think in terms of values. These can straightforwardly be translated into volume elasticities. For questions asked in terms of sales values, the elasticity, η, is derived from the following formula:

$$\frac{d(pq)}{dp} = p\frac{dq}{dp} + q \Rightarrow \frac{d(pq)}{dp}\cdot\frac{p}{(pq)} = \frac{dq}{dp}\cdot\frac{p}{q} + \frac{q}{q} = \eta + 1,$$

where η is the price elasticity.

Thus, $\eta = \frac{d(pq)}{dp}\cdot\frac{p}{(pq)} - 1$. For example, if the response to the question 'how would the *value* of sales change if price were to increase by 5 per cent?' is given by x per cent, then $\eta = \frac{x}{5} - 1$.

For the German market, Roche's replies implied market and own-price elasticities of zero and −4.0 respectively, and for the Austrian market they implied −0.6 and −2.6 respectively. Marketing efficiencies were not quantified, but they would presumably have been greater for the partner with the smaller market share and relatively small for the dominant partner. According to the parties, marketing and distribution account for just over a third of CCS costs, so if these are treated as marginal costs and subject to merger synergies as systems are integrated, a 30 per cent reduction in these costs would be necessary to reduce overall marginal costs by 10 per cent. Market shares of the four named firms <10 per cent were assumed to be 9 per cent, 8 per cent, 7 per cent and 6 per cent, with three other firms assumed to have shares of 5 per cent, 5 per cent and 4.7 per cent to complete the market. The largest customer in Germany accounted for 6 per cent of sales (3.3 per cent in Austria), so buyer power is unlikely to be strong.

In the simulations, we assume that the divestiture of the Cobas Mira business accounted for all of Roche's CCS business, since the residual business share could not be identified but would anyway be very small. Thus our simulations ask: 'What would have been the price effect of not requiring the disposal of the Cobas Mira business?'

Table 8.3 Simulated effect of allowing merger of BM/Roche CCS businesses

1. Germany						
Assumptions				*Results*		
Industry elasticity	BM own elasticity	BM cost efficiency, %	Roche efficiency, %	BM/Roche price rise, %	Market-weighted price rise	BM/Roche change in joint share
−0.5	−4.0	2	10	−0.1	0.0	+0.1
−0.5	−4.0	0	5	1.3	0.9	−1.4
−0.5	−3.0	0	5	1.9	1.3	−1.5
−0.5	−4.0	0	10	1.1	0.8	−1.3
−0.5	−3.0	0	10	1.7	1.2	−1.4
−0.1	−4.0	0	5	1.3	0.9	−1.6
−0.1	−3.0	0	5	2.0	1.4	−1.6
2. Austria						
−0.6	−2.6	2	10	7.6	6.6	−5.0
−0.6	−2.6	0	5	9.2	8.0	−6.0
−0.6	−4.0	2	10	3.8	3.3	−4.3
−0.6	−4.0	0	5	5.3	4.6	−6.0

The first part of Table 8.3 relates to Germany. The first row shows that for sufficiently large marginal cost efficiencies, if the merger had been allowed there would have been no significant effect on prices or market shares. Unfortunately, we do not have *ex ante* estimates of these efficiencies because the Commission did not report them. The next three pairs of rows examine the sensitivity of this result to changes in assumptions relating to own and industry elasticities, and more modest cost efficiencies. In each case, both BM/Roche and industry average prices rise by about 1–2 per cent, and because BM/Roche prices rise by a little more than the remainder of the industry, its joint market share falls by about 1.5 per cent. Comparing lines 1 and 4 shows that efficiencies have a much greater impact if they apply even modestly to the larger of the merging businesses. Closer examination of Table 8.3 shows that own-price elasticity has a much greater effect than the industry elasticity in the range of values examined.[4] Overall, it appears that the merger would have had little impact on average prices in Germany. The desirability or otherwise of the divestiture remedy therefore has to be judged on other grounds.

In contrast, the second part of Table 8.3 reveals that the Austrian market would have suffered much more. Prices could have been expected to rise about 4–9 per cent, and BM/Roche would have sacrificed about 5 per cent of their initial joint market share as a result of pushing up their prices more than the industry average. In part, this more negative effect as compared with Germany is due to both BM and Roche starting with a larger market share, but it is also due to the lower estimated own-price elasticity in Austria. The simulations confirm the desirability, at least on price grounds, of requiring the divestiture of Cobas Mira.

8.1.3 *Ex post* Analysis[5]

Divestiture of Cobas Mira in CCS

In the event, the greater part of Roche's European CCS business was sold to ABX (a subsidiary of a Japanese firm). There is a severe danger of splitting operations in technologically progressive industries as the incentive to invent is, as a first approximation, proportional to the size of the market. In practice, it seems that Roche had already made a strategic decision not to invest further in Cobas Mira, even before the Commission's own Decision.

There was also a problem with some parts of what might form a coherent business being left out of commitments. ABX had to negotiate separately both for the proteins part of the business, because clients want both products together, and for the manufacture of CCI, because an established base of instruments was crucial for selling CCR. Problems should have been anticipated because Cobas Mira was not a stand-alone business within Roche. Nevertheless, because ABX should have been able to negotiate for all its requirements at the same time, it should have been able to buy these ancillary parts of the business for an all-in-one price. Since there was effectively no other viable buyer, ABX was indeed able to negotiate a reasonable price.

However, this does not mean there were no problems. There were inevitably problems in transferring people, inaccurate information was provided in relation to the number of machines installed, and some assets were disposed of before transfer. Furthermore, knowledge of the divested client list allowed Roche to target major clients of Mira (for example, in relation to its Coba Integra 400 instruments) as soon as the deal was closed. Consequently, some important customers were lost. This may have been exacerbated by the increasing needs of many clients, who upgraded to larger machines supplied by BM but not Mira. Cobas Mira sales of CCR fell from €16 million in 1999 to €14 million in 2000 and just €11 million in 2001. More positively, ABX is planning to introduce a bigger machine with the ambition to double revenues, so it is possible that the divestiture will have encouraged a viable competitor in the long term. This is more than

Roche were planning at the time of the merger. However, even six years after the remedy was imposed, this was still speculative.

According to Roche/BM, three years after the merger, the market share of its retained CCS business in Germany had risen by 2.3 percentage points (3 percentage points in Austria), and its prices had fallen by 3 per cent (also in Austria). In each market, there was some minor entry but no major moves in rival market share. They were both improving their reagents and introduced three new systems in 2000. They also claimed that their clients were under increasing pressure to cut costs.

Overall, it seems that the divestiture remedy may have had a very marginal effect on long-term competition in CCS, and probably had a useful short-term effect in preventing price rises in Austria. However, these are not major impacts, and the divestiture would probably have had greater impact if more thought had been given to establishing a coherent business to be sold.

Licensing of PCR technology

It appears that requiring the PCR technology to be licensed helped establish it as the industry standard. It is not clear whether Roche would have appreciated this in the absence of the remedy – from the outside, it is not possible to say whether compulsory licensing was a concession or just good business advice. By the time of the interviews in 2003/04, six years after the remedy was agreed, 15 targeted and three broad licences had been sold. Licences were normally for the duration of the patent.

One aspect of the remedy was a 12-month delay before handing Roche information on sales by the licensee. This delayed the payment of rebates, and caused problems for licensees. It is not clear from the interview reports why Roche appears to have been allowed to require large up-front payments, which could be rebated in the event of low sales, as opposed to low up-front payment, which could be supplemented in the event of high sales. This rebate system does not encourage entry. At least one licensee bemoaned the lack of flexibility in Roche's approach to licensing.

Furthermore, the royalty rate was very high at 20 per cent of the end-user price. Combined with a high up-front fee, this seems to have effectively squeezed all profits out of licensees. Overall, the Commission should have paid much greater attention to licensing terms (although it is possible that we have not been given the complete details).

8.1.4 Main Lessons

***Ex ante* analysis**

There is circumstantial evidence that a Phase II investigation permits a more sophisticated analysis of the competitive conditions in each market, and so limits the number of markets requiring unnecessary remedy. In terms of good practice in quantifying competitive effects, we find that:

- Useful information on industry and own-brand elasticities for simulation analysis can be gathered from simple questions asked of industry experts. In practice, a number of experts from different perspectives (for example, main parties, rivals, customers) should be asked, and challenged with each other's estimates, in order to gain a consensus and range for sensitivity analysis. Large quantities of data and sophisticated econometric techniques are not a prerequisite for basic simulation.
- Alongside combined and incremental market share, own-price elasticities and marginal cost efficiencies are particularly important for the expected competitive impact of a merger and remedy.[6]

Ex post analysis

Lessons for remedy design include that:

- Licensing remedies need very careful specification if they are to restore competition. Particular attention is necessary for the terms of payment. For example, 'most favoured customer' clauses can deter price cuts and high up-front royalty payments can deter entry.
- Effective licensing remedies need diligent monitoring. For example, delay in selling an appropriate number of non-exclusive licences can render a remedy ineffective, especially if the delay gets close to the end of a patent's life.

8.2 MONSANTO/PHARMACIA & UPJOHN (2000) – M1835

Decision: 6(1)b with conditions and obligations; Phase I clearance for two US firms subject to a single remedy. Note that Monsanto agrichemicals were spun off, and the remaining Pharmacia Corp was sold to Pfizer in 2003.

8.2.1 Competition Concerns

The parties would have combined ATC3 shares at the member state level of 25 per cent or over in eight markets, but only one was found to cause concern: narcotic analgesics.

Narcotic analgesics (N2A): this is an example where the Commission accepted the parties' opinion that the ATC3 classification is not relevant, and should be divided into immediate- and slow-release analgesics, even though the same active ingredients are used in each segment.[7] Sometimes, the immediate-release version of the molecule is used to treat breakthrough pain while the patient is under treatment for chronic pain, so there are some complementarities.

The dominance problem identified by the Commission applied only in Sweden, where 'immediate-release' shares of 40–50 per cent (declining) for PU and 35–45 per cent (rising) for Monsanto would be combined to give 80–90 per cent of the market (no. 81).[8] The parties argued that PU's products were generic (Morfin and Pethidin being effectively the names of the relevant active ingredients) and that the market was highly contestable by any generic producer who wished to promote their generic equivalent. However, the market evolution in Sweden was not showing any evolution in favour of generics.

The required remedy was for the exclusive licensing of PU's full product range in the immediate release segment in Sweden (Morfin, Morfin Skopolamin, Morfin Epidural and Pethidin). According to the decision, the key components of the sale were the marketing authorizations (including trademarks), and manufacturing and supply agreements.

8.2.2 *Ex ante* Simulations[9]

We begin by observing that, unlike the previous case study of Roche/BM, the present pharmaceuticals market includes firms with multiple brands. Unfortunately, there is no discussion of the degree of product differentiation and within-market substitutability for immediate-release analgesics. Furthermore, there was no useful elasticity information available from the follow-up questionnaires (see note 12). For these reasons, we have used elasticity values that are highly speculative, being based on academic estimates for the USA and our own findings for other markets.[10] These are -1.0 for the industry elasticity and -4.0 for the lead brand (Ketogan Norum owned by Monsanto). Better information on the true elasticities would obviously change the quantitative results (see other cases for examples of sensitivity), but as will be seen would have less effect on the qualitative results.

Brand market shares are given in Table 8.4. The modelling is conducted for 1999, which is the date relied on in the Commission Decision. However, the trend from 1997 to 2001 is revealing because it shows how unstable this market was. In particular, Morfin was losing share fast, and Ketogan Norum was rising at the same rate, so combined share was fairly stable. This suggests that a successful, relatively new product was having a major impact on the market. This should be a warning against relying on

Table 8.4 Market shares in immediate-release analgesics in Sweden

Firm	Brand	Market share, %		
		1997	1999	2001 (est.)
PU	Morfin Morfin-Sko Morfin Epidural Pethidin	50–60	40–50	40–50
Monsanto	Ketogan Norum Ketogan	20–30	35–45	35–45
AstraZeneca	Morfin Special	<10	<10	<10
Abigo	Spasmofer	<5	<5	<5
Knoll	Dilaudid-Atro	<5	<5	<5
Mundipharma	Oxynorm	0	<5	<10
Boeringer-Ing	Oramorph	0	0	<5
Other		<10	<5	0

equilibrium simulation models (or, indeed, any sort of market share analysis). Two new entrants launched products in 1999 (although one of the entrants, Mundipharma, had an exclusive licensing agreement with PU in the slow-release segment). PU's product portfolio was of generics with relatively low prices and margins, and often sold to hospitals. The parties claimed that any significant price rises would be met by entry from producers who were already well established in other national markets.

Nevertheless, we focus on two variations to the PCAIDS basic simulation technique compared with what we conducted for Roche/BM. First, this market gives us the opportunity to provide an illustrative example of the use of nests. Second, we simulate the actual divestiture, which involved (at PU/Monsanto's request) the break-up of PU's portfolio of products in this market. In neither case do we model any changes in efficiencies. This is because efficiencies in marketing these mature generic products were not an issue in the documents available to us. Once again, we highlight our warning that neither combined market shares nor simulation models can be relied on to determine competitive effects in the presence of strongly changing market shares, as in this case.

The first part of Table 8.5 investigates what might have happened if the merger had been allowed to go ahead without remedy. All three simulations result in unacceptably high predicted price rises. These range from: 10–20 per cent, when the nesting parameters are set to indicate that there is very low substitutability between Pethidin, the set of four Morfin products (including one owned by AstraZeneca) and the Ketogan products, and

Table 8.5 Simulated effect of allowing merger and accepted remedies for PU/Monsanto in immediate-release analgesics in Sweden

1. Effects of unremedied merger (compared with pre-merger position)						
Assumptions				*Results*		
Industry elasticity	Ketogan Norum own elasticity	Nests?	Own/rival nesting parameter, %	PU/M price rise, %	Market-weighted price rise	PU/M change in joint share
−1.0	−4.0	No	n.a.	70–80	60–70	−10 to −20
−1.0	−4.0	Yes	50/50	50–60	50–60	−10 to −20
−1.0	−4.0	Yes	10/50	10–20	10–20	−10 to −20
2. Effects of actual remedy (compared with pre-merger position)						
Industry elasticity	Ketogan Norum own elasticity	Nests?	Own/rival nesting parameter, %	Monsanto price rise, %	Market-weighted price rise	Monsanto (and ex-PU) change in share
−1.0	−4.0	No	n.a.	0 to −5	0 to −5	Negligible
−1.0	−4.0	Yes	50/50	0 to −5	0 to −5	Negligible
−1.0	−4.0	Yes	10/50	0 to −5	0 to −5	Negligible

intermediate substitutability between each of these and all other products; and up to 70–80 per cent when all brands are considered equally good substitutes for each other. The former are extreme and fairly implausible assumptions, chosen to be the most favourable possible for the merger. The latter undoubtedly imposes too much symmetry. This range of price rises would have led to a substantial loss of market share (between 10 per cent and 20 per cent), but the potential price rises would none the less have been profitable. The main conclusion is that for a wide range of assumptions, the PCAIDS model predicts a very powerful price-raising effect of the unremedied merger, and on this basis the Commission was right to be concerned.

Before moving on, it is important to introduce another strong note of caution about this modelling technique. As explained in detail in Chapter 7, buyers have an enormous influence on pricing in regulated pharmaceuticals markets, such as in Sweden. Even if the underlying elasticity and nesting assumptions made in the previous paragraph were correct, there is no way that a merged PU/Monsanto could possibly raise prices post-merger by 10–20 per cent, let alone 70–80 per cent. This would simply not be allowed.

It would be more realistic to look at this analysis as a guide to the resistance to price falls. And even on this interpretation, a more complete assessment would have to take account of the potential for entry in a market with strong (even if declining) generic market shares.

We next turn to the predicted effect of the remedy. If PU had sold all its product range to a single buyer from outside the market, with the merged entity retaining Monsanto brands, then the present modelling approach would predict no change from the *status quo*. There would simply have been a change of ownership. Only if we had reason to expect efficiency changes (for example, sale to a more/less efficient buyer) would there be any effects. However, the PU portfolio was not sold as a single business. PU had four products in its range of immediate-release analgesics, and it sold its three morphine-based products to Bioglan, and its Pethidin to Recip. Thus, as long as there were no efficiencies destroyed by fragmentation, an extra competitor was created as two firms replaced one for coordinating brand pricing decisions. The predicted effects of this remedy are set out in the second part of Table 8.5. Under none of our elasticity and nesting assumptions do industry prices fall by more than 0–5 per cent. Bearing in mind that this modelling technique makes a small price fall inevitable,[11] this means that there was no significant increase in competition as a result of the remedy. Put another way, the question of potential loss of efficiencies by splitting up the product portfolio should have been a greater issue than enhanced competition as even quite modest losses would have led to a predicted price rise.

This case study serves to highlight some important reservations about using simple techniques of merger and remedy appraisal – notably, a dynamic market with changing market shares, and a powerful buying body which regulates price. However, the simulations still serve as helpful indicators of the magnitude of market forces in relation to incentives for firms to raise price. In the context of remedy analysis, where the required divestiture was split between buyers, it shows that greater concern in this market should have been paid to potential efficiency losses rather than competition gains. For example, the market-weighted price falls in part 2 of Table 8.5 would disappear, and be reversed if the buying firms had marginal costs any more than a figure less than 5 per cent higher than PU. This serves as a warning that divestiture to a weak buyer can result in a lessening of competition even if the market structure appears more competitive.

Finally, we observe that this remedy will have had no impact on the incentive to invent. This is because the divested products were mature generics, and in any case Sweden was a tiny part of the aggregate global market (which is relevant for R&D incentives).

8.2.3 *Ex post* Analysis[12]

The Commission's original intention had been that the divestiture package would be to a single buyer. In the end, PU was allowed to make separate sales for Pethidin (to Recip) and the Morfin range (to Bioglan). As it happens, Recip sold the Pethidin product the day after it bought it from PU, because it did not fit its business strategy of only buying products it could manufacture! Recip only bought Pethidin because it was part of a package of 13 products being sold by PU as part of its Nordic rationalization. Recip kept nine products and had already lined up a buyer (a small Swedish company, IPEX) for the other four. Neither PU nor Recip appear to have had any interest in the ultimate fate of the product. Even more worrying, no one had even told Recip that the purpose was to restore competition, let alone got any assurances of a vigorous business plan. Clearly, PU did not see Pethidin as a competitive concern in relation to its other products. The morphine products were not in this list, and were sold to Bioglan, which already had an interest in analgesics.[13] Bioglan reported that PU was very cooperative with the sale, and they had every assistance they wanted. Both sales were clean breaks.[14]

Both Recip and Bioglan were small local companies, and it appears that the ability to buy individual or small bundles of products no longer wanted by the large MNEs is important for them to build a portfolio of products sufficient to justify marketing or production capacity. This suggests a delicate trade-off between selling an independently viable business (which the divested bundle was not) and selling individual products that fit appropriately into the portfolios of smaller firms. In the latter case, the appropriate divestiture bundle will be very sensitive to the needs of existing firms in the market or related markets in a particular country. We should also note that we are talking about a tiny market: the Recip interviewee pointed out that the sales of Pethidin in Sweden were roughly the same as the salary of a single sales representative!

We have only very limited indicators of the success of the remedy. First, we note that both sets of products are still operating. However, at the time of the sale Bioglan had been a subsidiary of Paraglan Pharma (UK), which went bankrupt in February 2002. Although Wilhelm Solason (Sweden) bought Bioglan and kept it going, it is noticeable that neither product bundle stayed with the original buyer, and their continued presence in the market seems more due to luck than judgement. Second, it seems that sales have been very stable for Bioglan (at around €1.5 million).[15] This is due to the conservative prescribing habits of older doctors, the low price of generics, and a change in social attitudes that has encouraged more prescribing for pain control. Third, Bioglan felt they were very fortunate in being able to secure the services of PU's previous sales officer. This was not part of PU's commitment. Fourth, the buyers did not see themselves in serious competition with PU/Monsanto's retained portfolio of brands.

8.2.4 Main Lessons

Ex ante analysis

- Markets in which market shares are changing rapidly are not suitable for simulation based on equilibrium analysis.
- Basic simulations which do not model the regulator and predict large price increases cannot be realistic in a heavily regulated market. If the regulator might feasibly allow price increases, then at best the simulations illustrate the incentive for the firms to bargain harder with the regulator. And if the regulator cannot be expected to allow a price rise, the best such simulations can do is suggest a strong resistance to price decreases should there be pressure from the regulator or a change in the conditions of entry.
- Another role for simulations can be to test for the effectiveness of a divestiture that might appear to restore competition, but which would be compromised by selling to a weaker (less efficient) buyer. The simulations can show the effect of cost increases on customer prices. This might be a useful way of quantifying the concern the Commission should have with finding a strong buyer for any particular divestiture.

Ex post analysis

- Smaller buyers have very specific needs in creating a viable product portfolio. In the absence of a divestiture of a stand-alone business, this suggests that the required divestiture may have to be tailored to the individual needs of the buyer (as much as to the interests of the seller/merging parties). If such needs are not recognized, the divested assets may simply be sold on without any control by the Commission, and so with no concern for the competitive consequences.
- While smaller buyers may value the opportunity to buy small bundles of possibly declining assets that would not interest the large multinationals, given the previous point, it is not obvious that divestiture is the most appropriate remedy when sales are very small. For example, when there is only one small national market involved and that market has a regulator to monitor prices, a tight price cap and guarantee to continue production may be more effective and incur much lower transaction costs.

- Divestiture trustees do not automatically see themselves as representing the Commission. While they might do a good job in preserving the business during transition, they lack instruction in the motivation to restore competition. The Commission should be proactive in briefing trustees.

8.3 SANOFI/SYNTHÉLABO (1999) – M1397

Decision: 6(1)b with conditions and obligations; Phase I clearance subject to one remedy. Unusually, this was not picked up in the original unconditional clearance, but followed the reopening of the case after complaints that the parties had not declared an overlap in an apparently significant market in France.

8.3.1 Competition Concern

The only concern related to the market for 'stupefying active substances' in France. There are two categories involved: upstream morphine (derived from poppy or opium) and downstream derivatives (especially codeine, chlorhydrate and sulphate morphines, and pholcodeine). In particular, codeine and pholcodeine are both used further downstream in cough medicines (ATC3: R5D). The broad linkages within France are shown in Figure 8.1.

Because of the extreme sensitivity of morphine and its derivatives, many countries (including France) control who has access by designating a single supplier. This is the case for Sanofi with morphine and codeine, and Synthélabo for pholcodeine. Surprisingly, none of these products is subject to price control, although the main parties claimed that there is an indirect constraint because health insurance reimbursement policies result in effective regulation of downstream cough medicine prices, which feed back into what the suppliers of active substances can charge. However, this still seems to allow considerable pricing discretion as a monopolist of one element in a mixture can appropriate a disproportionate share of any given revenues.

Sanofi also commercializes morphine in Germany, Belgium, Spain and the UK, and codeine in five other member states (see Figure 8.2). Perhaps more importantly, it has two very significant minority stakes in the Belgian (Belgopia) and Spanish firms, which are both in monopoly situations with respect to morphine derivatives in their own countries.

The Commission was concerned that the merger of Sanofi and Synthélabo would allow them to exploit their vertical linkages in France. In particular, they might withhold supplies of pholcodeine from other firms

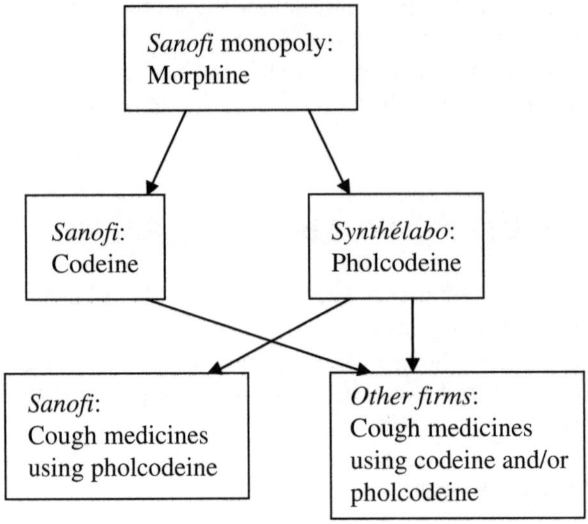

Figure 8.1 Linkages in market for 'stupefying active substances' in France

who use this in their cough mixtures, or raise price to these firms to the benefit of Sanofi's own medicines. To the extent that codeine and pholcodeine are substitutes in these medicines, there would also be a direct increase in horizontal market power.

The remedy

Divestiture of Synthélabo's pholcodeine business was required. It was acknowledged that the buyer would need to be approved by the French health and interior ministries, as well as by the Commission. A potential flaw in the remedy was a very weak commitment by Sanofi to provide the buyer with morphine 'at normal and non-discriminatory commercial conditions'. Of course, such an assurance was not available to Synthélabo before the merger, so this may potentially be more than restoring pre-merger competition. However, if the buyer were to have less buyer power than the independent Synthélabo, then there would be a potential deterioration of competition.

8.3.2 *Ex ante* Simulation

Simulations were not possible due to the lack of available data in the Decision. This followed from the unusual way in which the competitive concern was revealed only after the merger was initially cleared.

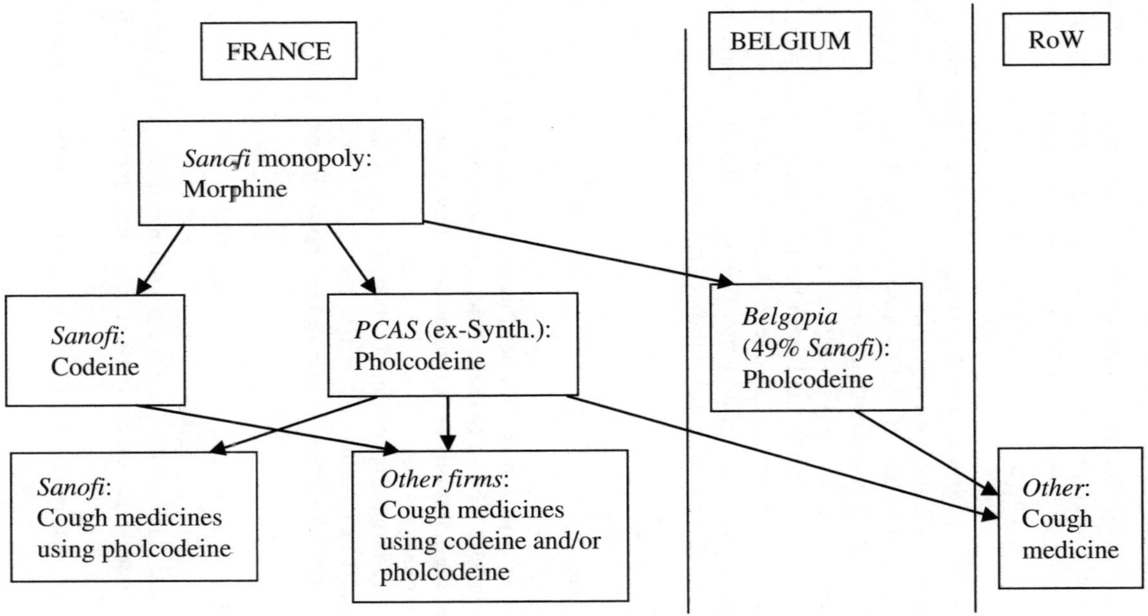

Figure 8.2 *Linkages in market for 'stupefying active substances' in France, Belgium and the rest of the world*

8.3.3 *Ex post* Analysis

This was an extremely small business, with sales of €3.5 million p.a. and declining. It was never self-standing. It consisted of five people, a crushing machine, stocks and very high-security premises. The premises at Synthélabo were integrated into other operations and so the workshop had to be moved when PCAS bought it. PCAS had to invest heavily to meet the security needs. The transfer costs were high relative to the size of the business.

The trustee did not ensure that there was a suitable arbitration clause to ensure non-discriminatory pricing, and there is a suspicion that this may have been exploited by Sanofi. PCAS saw its extra-EEA export market fall away sharply, while it appears that Sanofi's joint venture Belgopia's sales rose at the same time. There is no explicit evidence, but it is possible that Belgopia was getting a better deal from Sanofi for its morphine than was PCAS. Once again, however, this does not explain why Sanofi would not have been doing this before the merger (unless PCAS did have less buyer power with Sanofi than did Synthélabo).

8.3.4 Main Lessons

Ex post analysis

- Non-discrimination clauses need careful monitoring. The questionnaire evidence shows that the price of morphine to PCAS did not change at all, but this does not mean there was not a price reduction to Belgopia.
- Given the large relative cost of transferring a small and declining business, a behavioural remedy in the form of price controls might have been both more effective and less costly in this case.

8.4 ASTRA/ZENECA (1999) – M1403

Decision: Article 6(1)(b) with conditions and obligations; Phase I clearance subject to a remedy package for three products, including one pipeline product.

This chapter focuses on two of the identified problem products, plain betablockers and long-acting local anaesthetics in selected national markets.

Betablockers

Betablockers are a particular class of anti-hypertension drug. Plain betablockers are a single chemical entity that performs this function. Combined betablockers are mixed with a diuretic, which is necessary for some patients. The diuretic could be prescribed separately, but patient compliance is enhanced by the combined product. Once on a combined betablocker, patients rarely return to the plain version, especially as a switch in medication can be dangerous. By far the largest market is for plain versions and the total EEA market for plain betablockers was €875 million in 1997.

There are many different chemical entities that act as betablockers. Most are off patent, except for some special formulations. Plain betablockers have generic competitors, but generics have not entered the combined market, probably because it is too small – there are no blocking patents for either component. Thus, for most member states, there is considerable competition in plain, but much less in combined. Generics make up around 15 per cent of the plain market in the EEA.

Betablockers are prescribed by clinicians in general practice and hospitals. Price negotiations are typically national. Prices of plain and combined products have been able to drift apart, even though the combination can be mimicked with clinical equivalence by taking just two pills instead of one. This reflects a convenience and compliance premium resulting from the ability to take just one pill instead of two or more.

For plain betablockers, Astra (metoprolol, alprenolol) and Zeneca (anenolol, propranolol) were among the first to enter this market, and these substances remain market leaders. Astra's 13 brand names include Seloken and Seloken-Zok (branded Beloc and Beloc-Zok in Austria and Germany). Zeneca has eight brands, the best selling being Tenormin and Inderal. For combination products, Astra's brands include Seloken-Comp/Beloc-Comp/Selozide-Dur. Zeneca's brands include Tenoretic and Inderex. Further entry is possible, but probably depends on a distinctly superior product, or one with distinctively different properties.

The merging parties claimed there would be efficiency enhancements: 'Greater global reach in sales and marketing, combined with greater financial resources and operational efficiencies will enable the merged AstraZeneca to compete more effectively with competitors than either Astra or Zeneca can do on its own' (p. 125). It was also claimed that in-house R&D would be strengthened, 'as will its ability to provide partnership to academic institutions, biotech companies and others seeking to out-license their R&D activities'.

Long-acting local anaesthetics

Long-acting local anaesthetics are effective for six to seven hours, allowing a patient to be awake during a medical procedure. They relieve pain by blocking pain impulses from the central nervous system. Each drug has slightly different properties, so there is some horizontal differentiation. However, the main dimension is vertical differentiation from two sources: the first-mover drug has the advantage that its properties are known and understood. Also, prescribers are conservative and not particularly price-sensitive. Consequently, for the same drug, the original version has a continuing advantage of brand loyalty over generics, the importance of which depends on price incentives for the prescriber. Core anaesthetic properties do not differ much, but newer products (for example, ropivacaine and levobupivacaine) have some advantages over the well-established baseline drug bupivacaine in terms of safety and onset.

Sales of the leading local anaesthetics (lidocaine, bupivicaine and mepivicaine), all owned by Astra and with 56 per cent EEA sales in 1997, were long off patent and subject to generic competition (as were many other competitors). Astra claims (p. 97) that 30 per cent of the value of its three leading drugs was made by third parties (generics). The figure would be higher in volume terms. Note that lidocaine is a surface short-acting anaesthetic and mepivacaine is used in dentistry, so bupivicaine is the crucial drug for the long-acting market.

The long-acting therapeutic class includes several long-off-patent drugs, including the market leader (bipuvacaine, marketed by Astra as Marcain, but also available as a generic). Astra's newer drug (ropivicaine, marketed as Naropin) is on patent. Zeneca's near-end-of-pipeline product (levobupivacaine, to be marketed as Chirocaine) was considered to have the potential to take market from bupivacaine probably at the expense of Naropin. These products can also be used for pain management, but this requires further development costs to ensure suitable doses in slow release. A particular issue for Chirocaine was the need to develop a 'polybag' for this purpose and to achieve its full commercial potential.

Total EEA market in 1997 (p. 97) was worth only some €200 million. The main buyers are hospitals, though price negotiations are typically national. Only in Italy (for this particular market) are firms free to set their own prices without negotiation. No specific figures are available, but it is likely that much is spent on marketing/detailing activities by on-patent branded products. Further entry into this small market is highly unlikely.

8.4.1 Competition Concerns

Products and markets for which the merger was found to impede competition

1. *Long-acting local anaesthetics (N1B)*: Zeneca had no actual or potential presence in the market until it bought a licence for Chirocaine (worldwide exclusive except Japan) in March 1998. Chirocaine gained regulatory approval, in Sweden only, a day after the Astra bid was announced in December 1998. Astra was 'by far the market leader' with >50 per cent in at least Germany, Italy and the UK. Other firms, such as Baxter, had no more than 5 per cent. Astra might have gained some marketing/contracting advantage with hospitals by being able to sell alongside Zeneca's market leading general anaesthetics, but there were no significant substitution or leverage possibilities between local and general anaesthetics. The Commission concluded in its Decision: 'Given Astra's high market share, the lack of introduction of new products and the absence of strong competitors, it can be concluded that the exclusive license for Chirocaine would . . . remov[e] the only likely source of competition, as it is doubtful whether the parties would be willing to launch and to support a product that will compete strongly with their own products'. Thus the expected harm was the loss of a potential rival product.
2. *Plain betablockers (C7A)*: in Sweden and Norway (joint market shares 78 per cent and 61 per cent respectively) Astra and Zeneca were each other's main competitors, and they could not demonstrate that generics or imports would sufficiently restrain their behaviour. Note that market shares by value (as used by the Commission) are higher for branded goods and lower for generics than are market shares by volume. For betablockers, not surprisingly, the parties argued that market shares should have been calculated by volume.
3. *Combined betablockers (C7B)*: the Commission was concerned by 'market shares indicative of dominance in most Member States, and in particular in Austria, Belgium, Germany, Greece, Ireland, Portugal and the UK . . . the concerns are aggravated by figures provided by the parties, showing a considerably lower downward pressure on prices by national authorities for the products where they have historically had high market shares . . .'

Remedies agreed

1. *Long-acting local anaesthetics*: remedy was required by reversing the Chirocaine licensing arrangements. Meanwhile, Zeneca was required

to provide all help and financial assistance in its development and launch. The same remedy was required by the US FTC, which was simultaneously investigating this merger.

2. *Plain betablockers*: the remedy was to grant 'exclusive arm's length' distribution rights for Zeneca's leading plain betablocker, Tenormin, in Sweden and Norway for at least ten years. AstraZeneca retained rights outside these countries. Tenormin represented >70 per cent of Zeneca's sales in those countries. The agreed remedy states only that 'AstraZeneca will supply the product at a price which will ensure that the third party distributor can compete effectively in the market. The third party distributor will be responsible for any price negotiations with the authorities.'
3. *Combined betablockers*: the remedy was to divest Astra's entire EEA interests in dual combination betablockers (but not triple combination) by granting an indefinite and exclusive trademark licence, with associated patent rights and supply agreement. The essential element was metoprolol sold in fixed combination with a diuretic product. The arrangements were to be for at least six years, which would coincide with the expiry of the patent period for the metoprolol Zoc form included in the product in most countries. The main brands were Selokomb, Beloc Comp and Seloken Retard Plus. AstraZeneca retained rights outside these countries. 'Pricing will be at a level designed to ensure that the purchaser will be a viable competitor in the market.'

8.4.2 *Ex ante* Analysis: Plain Betablockers

We focus on plain betablockers in Sweden and Norway, not least because AstraZeneca was willing to provide data for this remedy. The remedy required AstraZeneca to grant an exclusive marketing licence for Zeneca's leading product, Tenormin. This represents more than 70 per cent of Zeneca's sales in these countries. The licences should be for ten years, but automatically renewable unless the Commission grants permission otherwise. AstraZeneca is required (see Annex 2, no. 1) to 'supply the product at a price which will ensure that the third party distributor can compete effectively in the market. The third party distributor will be responsible for any price negotiations with the authorities.' It is left to 'a Trustee to report to the Commission on the suitability of the transfer price arrangements . . . and on the identity and characteristics of the potential distributors identified by AstraZeneca' (Annex 2, no. 2).

Unfortunately, there is no follow-up interview on this case. However, given the role of the trustee in other cases, this seems to be a very unsatisfactory arrangement. Trustees often have little understanding of the competitive issues underlying the remedy, and have somewhat divided loyalties having been appointed and paid by the parties. There is clearly a serious possibility that royalty arrangements could be used to manipulate final prices.

There are three constraints on such a strategy: competition from other ethical and generic manufacturers; parallel imports; and national regulation of pricing. The first and second of these are little extra constraint beyond what would exist in the absence of the remedy.[16] The third might even be weakened if the licensee could point to its costs (imposed by AstraZeneca) and require a mark-up that allows it to survive in the market. This does not mean it would be an 'effective competitor'.

Further analysis requires an understanding of how prices are regulated. In Sweden, firms can, in principle, set any price they want, but they will only be reimbursed from the national health insurance system at a price reached by negotiation. A new product price, therefore, tends to be at around the average for the relevant therapeutic class unless it represents a significant clinical advance. It is then difficult to justify real price increases. Furthermore, the loss of patent protection and the consequent introduction of generics adds competitive pressure (without necessarily lowering prices – see Chapter 7). For example, the merging parties report that the price of Astra's Seloken ZOC increased by just 19 per cent eight years after launch in 1990 despite 24 per cent CPI inflation. In Norway, reimbursement prices take into account clinical value, R&D costs and the prices of similar products. As in Sweden, it is difficult to make price increases. For example, the merging parties report that the price of Astra's Seloken ZOC increased by just 1 per cent, despite inflation, in 1992–98.

In these circumstances, it is unlikely that a free-pricing model like PCAIDS would be very helpful in predicting prices in an *ex ante* study, though it might provide some insight into the relative bargaining power of the firms. We do not pursue this in the present study because there are some more important facts buried in the available data.[17]

The plain betablockers covered by the remedy were launched in 1976 and were long off patent, facing generic competition. Furthermore, there are numerous other leading firms active in Sweden and Norway or elsewhere in Europe that could relatively easily enter the market if prices were to rise significantly. However, an important set of facts taken from the Commission's file and main party submissions relates to the prices of the retained products (mainly, but not exclusively, Astra) and the price of Zeneca's products (mainly Tenormin). First, consider international price comparisons. In 1998, Astra's Seloken and Seloken ZOC were priced higher (€ per tablet/capsule) in Sweden and Norway than in any of the five other European countries for which data are available (for example,

Seloken ZOC 100 mg was €0.31 in Sweden, €0.33 in Norway and between €0.14 and €0.28 in four other countries). The divested Tenormin was priced much lower in Sweden than in any other European country, and Norway was not far behind. For example, 50 mg tablets were priced at €0.07 in Sweden, €0.11 in Norway and €0.24 in the relatively unregulated UK. Second, consider price comparisons within the relevant countries. In 1998, using value shares divided by volume shares to calculate a measure of each firm's average prices relative to the quantity weighted average for the whole plain betablocker market, in both Sweden and Norway, Astra had the most expensive prices of any firm with a volume share ≥5 per cent (relative prices 160 per cent and 147 per cent respectively), while Zeneca had the cheapest prices of any firm with a non-negligible market share (relative prices 41 per cent and 55 per cent respectively). Thus, both in terms of international and within-market comparisons, the divested Tenormin products were very low priced in Sweden and Norway, and the retained AstraZeneca products were very high priced in these markets. It seems implausible to expect the third-party licensees to drive Tenormin prices even lower, especially when they have to pay AstraZeneca to buy the product. It is far more likely that the price will rise because of double marginalization.

The remaining consideration is whether, had AstraZeneca been allowed to retain Tenormin in these countries, they would have raised its price because they would be less concerned about demand diversion towards the Astra products. An appropriate answer would require more information about the cross-elasticity between Tenormin and Seloken-ZOC, further examination of the way in which prices are negotiated with the health authorities, and any restrictions on entry. However, it seems clear that a behavioural remedy in the form of a price guarantee would probably have satisfied most parties, and most importantly guaranteed against significant price rises. This form of remedy can be recommended in particular when there are just one or two member state markets that create a concern over combined market shares. Monitoring should not be a problem given the national regulation of prices.

8.4.3 *Ex post* Analysis: Plain Betablockers[18]

The remedy applied to a small and declining market that was very marginal to the merger. The merging parties expressed concerns about the transaction costs of divesting products with relatively small sales (£20 million and declining). They disagreed with this part of the Commission's Decision (for example, market definition), and would have challenged the need for this divestiture much more vehemently had the merger control process gone into Phase II. In particular, the prescription and health insurance systems in most European countries effectively eliminate the potential for post-merger price increases. This reinforces our concern that the choice of remedy may have done more harm than good.

Finland and Denmark were added to the divested Tenormin (atenolol) business for Sweden and Norway during negotiations with Searle, who purchased the distribution rights. The agreement included a substantial royalty payment. At the same time, Searle also bought exclusive EEA rights for Seloken Comp, the divested combination betablocker business. Searle was the pharmaceuticals division of Monsanto.[19] The transaction was announced in October 1999. AstraZeneca retained Astra's Seloken (metoprolol and alprenolol). They were, however, concerned about the split of ownership of Tenormin across geographic areas because of the potential loss of product reputation (if the licensee was less established than Searle) and the monitoring of health and safety issues, such as any adverse effects reported by doctors nationally.

In Sweden, AstraZeneca agreed an exclusive distribution agreement with Tamro for several products including its retained plain betablocker (Seloken ZOC). Tamro is the leading pharmaceutical wholesaler and distributor in Northern Europe. AstraZeneca's value market share in Sweden at the time of the merger (excluding Tenormin) was 64.2 per cent, and eroded slowly to 61.3 per cent after three years. During this period, Seloken ZOC received a new indication (for heart failure) and a new 25 mg strength was introduced. Meanwhile, Tenormin maintained its 7.9 per cent share over the same period, but lost its second place marginally to Kredex (rising from 7.8 per cent to 8.1 per cent). Third-placed Sotanol NM lost share from 4.7 per cent to 4.2 per cent. During this period, there were three new entrants (IPEX, Biochemie and GEA), each with generic versions of Metoprolol Retard. Two of these soon exited (IPEX and Biochemie), which was possibly due to problems with their product approval documentation. Other events to affect the market were the expiry of the patent on carvedilol and the new Swedish pricing authority.

In Norway, AstraZeneca's major customer was NMD (a wholesaler, especially to hospitals), with 41 per cent. AZ's value market share in Norway at the time of the merger (excluding Tenormin) was 57.4 per cent, and eroded to 53.9 per cent after three years. As for Sweden, Seloken ZOC received a new indication (for heart failure) and a new 25 mg strength was introduced. Meanwhile, Tenormin's share slid significantly from 9.7 per cent to 5.9 per cent, losing its second place very substantially to Kredex (rising from 7.9 per cent to 17.7 per cent). Third-placed Sotacor lost its share from 6.7 per cent to 3.2 per cent. During this period, there were three new entrants (Merck, Biochemie and GEA), one of which soon exited

(Biochemie). Other events to affect the market were the expiry of the patent on carvedilol and increased price focus from the authorities.

Unfortunately, we could not obtain relative price trend information for either Sweden or Norway, so it was not possible directly to confirm our fears of post-remedy price rises. Although both AZ's retained products and Tenormin lost some market share, we are unable to attribute this to the details of the divestment as distinct from wider market trends.

8.4.4 *Ex ante* Simulations: Long-acting Local Anaesthetics

Recall that the agreed remedy was for Zeneca to reverse its Chirocaine licensing arrangements so that this new product could be developed and launched by an independent competitor. Zeneca was required to provide all help and financial assistance in its development and launch. This market presents at least two major new issues, even if we assume that costs are unaffected by the change of ownership of the licence.

Previous simulations we have used in this book look simply at the transfer of ownership of existing products that compete horizontally with each other. The issue is then to use evidence on elasticities and cross-elasticities to estimate the price effects of a change of ownership. As we have seen, this is difficult enough. The first new issue we must address is that a pipeline product has no history on which to find evidence on these elasticities. Second, the case notes suggest that the products in question were not so much horizontally differentiated (that is, neither better nor worse than each other, but meeting overlapping preferences for different users) as vertically differentiated (that is, in a hierarchy such that most users would prefer to use the 'best' product were it not for price differences).

This is new territory for simple simulations, so we decided to experiment with the simplest possible model in order to see what could be done. The formal assumptions and derivation of our model of vertical product differentiation are developed in the Appendix to this chapter. In this section, we show how such a model can be calibrated. It should be seen very much as an illustration that this kind of market can be simulated.

Table 8.6 provides a matching of commercial and scientific names of products in this market in order to help the reader through this section. Products are labelled such that higher numbers represent higher qualities. Astra already owned the bottom- and top-ranked products, and Zeneca's pipeline product would be ranked in between. The baseline 'product 0' (that is, minimum sustainable quality) is bupivacaine, which is long off patent and is available as a generic.[20] It is also available in its original branded form, Marcain (made by Astra), but we assume this is tightly constrained in its pricing by the mature generic. In this context, the generic is

Table 8.6 Commercial and scientific names of main products

Commercial brand (owner)	Scientific name
Marcain (Astra)	Bupivacaine
Also generic	Bupivacaine
Naropin (Astra)	Ropivacaine
Chirocaine (licensed from Chiroscience to Zeneca)	Levobupivacaine

the strategic price setter, with Marcain being able to sustain a fixed mark-up on the generic. This mark-up represents a dimension of horizontal differentiation due to loyalty to a chemically identical but branded product. Ropivacaine (marketed as Naropin by Astra) remains on patent and has advantages for certain purposes (for example, speed of onset, safety, packaging). These advantages identify it as 'product 2' (that is, the highest-quality product). The original two-product market is calibrated on the basis of Marcain's equilibrium pricing with generic bupivacaine. Levobupivacaine is the on-patent entrant to be marketed (originally by Zeneca) as Chirocaine. This is 'product 1' (that is, of intermediate quality), which has yet to establish the perceived quality of ropivacaine, but which can claim similar advantages over bupivacaine.

It is likely that Chirocaine would not have been taken through to final development by AstraZeneca. There are suggestions to that effect in the background evidence provided to the Commission and this provides the rationale for their chosen remedy. It is also in line with the model's predictions. Chirocaine would largely cannibalize market from Naropin. Alternatively, if it was brought to market, the optimal pricing strategy for a firm owning both would be to price Chirocaine very close to Naropin in order to minimize the loss to its higher-priced, higher-margin product. This would leave Chirocaine with very low sales, which would be unlikely to justify the overheads. Thus the expectation without the remedy is that Chirocaine would either not enter the market at all or it would be brought to market as a niche product with no significant impact on the prices of other products. The choice would probably depend on the details of the original licensing agreement with Chiroscience.

It remains to predict the pricing impact of an independently owned Chirocaine.

Calibration of our Pipeline Product Model

A major attraction of our simulation model is that, by assuming optimal pre-merger pricing behaviour by the firms, implicit quality differentials for the original products can be retrieved with minimal information requirements: marginal costs and pre-merger price differentials (see equations (8A.6) and (8A.7) in the Appendix).

Marginal costs

Costs are not generally available for individual pharmaceuticals, but marginal costs are likely to be low. There are two possibilities. First, we could assume identical costs. Second, we can use the standard distribution of revenues for branded products (see OECD figures at the start of Chapter 7) to impute marginal costs by allocating certain cost categories to marginal or fixed components. This is our preferred method. For an upper bound on marginal costs, we assume generic bupivicaine (product 0) has marginal costs of 72 per cent of initial price (that is, everything except the typical pharmaceuticals profit margin); and product 2 has 52 per cent of marginal costs (that is, also subtracts marketing costs). These costs feed into simulations A–C below. However, we expect simulations D–I below to have more realistic costs: for generic bupivicaine, the marginal cost share is 55 per cent, which is manufacturing plus marketing cost shares relative to all other cost shares except R&D (R&D costs are assumed irrelevant for established generics); and for ropivicaine, the marginal cost share is 43 per cent (the numerator is manufacturing plus marketing cost shares but it is assumed that there is a 26 per cent R&D cost share to be added to the denominator). We used pre-merger prices to convert these percentages into absolute levels of costs.

Pre-merger (and pre-Chirocaine) prices

These are taken from confidential marketing assessments provided by Zeneca. Combined with the above initial marginal cost shares of revenue, this fixes marginal cost levels. These costs are assumed to be unchanged post-merger, and the same absolute marginal costs are attributed to Chirocaine as to ropivacaine. In the simulations, we use prices calibrated on the German market (simulations A–F) and UK prices (G–I). Note that although we calibrated this model *ex ante* for Germany, at the time of writing it was not yet marketed there.

Post-remedy (and post-entry of Chirocaine) prices are predicted by equations (8A.3), (8A.4) and (8A.5) in the Appendix. The one additional parameter that requires calibration is Chirocaine's relative quality.

Relative quality of new product

We need an estimate or assumption about δ, which calibrates how near Chirocaine is to the top-quality product (Naropin). Consistent with the natural therapeutic qualities that any chemical entity has, this is taken to be exogenous. In particular, Chirocaine has certain properties as a result of the claims justified for labelling under the regulatory procedure.[21] Bearing in mind its similarity to ropivacaine in its claims and indications, $\delta \in [0.5, 0.65]$ might be appropriate (that is, nearer to levobupivacaine than to bupivacaine, but still some way short at least in initial perception). As is clear from the model, price competition gets fierce if product 1 is too close to one of the existing products. In particular, if δ is too large, the pricing battle between Chirocaine and Naropin would drive prices down and the low-quality bupivacaine would be forced out of those uses for which the new drugs exhibit specific advantages (see earlier discussion). On the assumption that bupivacaine remains an active competitor for these uses, this sets an upper limit on δ, set by the requirement that the generic must have a non-negative market share. This upper limit value of δ is used in simulations A, D and G. Our preferred value of δ is 0.6.

The simulation results are presented in Table 8.7. Nine simulations in columns labelled A–I are reported in order to demonstrate the sensitivity of price predictions to alternative calibrations. The first three rows show marginal costs, which are higher for branded than generic products. The quality parameters have been calibrated from pre-Chirocaine prices, which are given lower down the table. The lower half of the table presents the predicted prices once Chirocaine has been established by an independent firm (that is, post-divestiture). The remainder of the table uses these predictions to calculate some relative prices, price changes post-entry, and gross margins. For expositional purposes, we will focus on the highlighted simulation E, which arguably combines the most plausible calibrations.

The simulations show that the existence of an independently owned Chirocaine has relatively little effect on the price of its closest competitor, Naropin, but it has a greater impact on the generic, whose price falls considerably. The price premium of Naropin over Chirocaine is predicted to be approximately 40 per cent, and Chirocaine is expected to be priced at around two and a half times generic bupivacaine. Note that this price impact on the market leader is exactly as was found empirically for a range of other pharmaceuticals in the USA by Scherer (see Chapter 7). Overall, this suggests that a successful divestiture should be a very good remedy.

We do not believe that such a simple model is yet ready to be used other than to illustrate the potential for developing a simulation methodology for product introductions in vertically differentiated markets. However, we do believe that even the current level of development demonstrates that such models are feasible, in particular, in using existing price differentials to imply quality differentials.

Table 8.7 AstraZeneca: chirocaine simulations

	Simulation								
Parameters	A	B	C	D	E	F	G	H	I
Marginal costs									
C_0	0.65	0.65	0.65	0.50	**0.50**	0.50	0.39	0.39	0.39
C_1	1.30	1.30	1.30	1.07	**1.07**	1.07	0.94	0.94	0.94
C_2	1.30	1.30	1.30	1.07	**1.07**	1.07	0.94	0.94	0.94
Quality parameters									
$\Delta\underline{\theta}$	1.35	1.35	1.35	1.20	**1.20**	1.20	1.19	1.19	1.19
$\Delta\overline{\overline{\theta}}$	5.40	5.40	5.40	5.17	**5.17**	5.17	4.64	4.64	4.64
Δ	*0.65*	*0.60*	*0.50*	*0.67*	***0.6***	*0.5*	*0.63*	*0.6*	*0.5*
Pre-Chirocaine prices									
p_0*	*0.90*	*0.90*	*0.90*	*0.90*	***0.90***	*0.90*	*0.70*	*0.70*	*0.70*
p_2*	*2.50*	*2.50*	*2.50*	*2.50*	***2.50***	*2.50*	*2.20*	*2.20*	*2.20*
Predicted prices									
p_0**	0.65	0.69	0.75	0.50	**0.55**	0.60	0.39	0.41	0.47
p_1**	1.53	1.54	1.53	1.30	**1.31**	1.31	1.14	1.15	1.14
p_2**	2.36	2.50	2.76	2.04	**2.23**	2.48	1.90	1.97	2.20
p_1**/p_2**	0.65	0.62	0.55	0.64	**0.59**	0.53	0.60	0.58	0.52
Post-entry price fall, %									
p_0*	28	24	17	45	**39**	33	44	41	33
p_2*	6	0	−11	18	**11**	1	14	10	0
Gross margins									
m_0%**	1	6	14	0	**9**	18	1	6	17
m_1%**	15	15	15	18	**18**	18	17	18	17
m_2%**	45	48	53	47	**52**	57	50	52	57
m_0%*	28	28	28	45	**45**	45	45	45	45
m_2%*	48	48	48	57	**57**	57	57	57	57

Note: * pre-merger estimate; ** post-merger prediction.

8.4.5 *Ex post* Analysis: Long-acting Local Anaesthetics

As for betablockers, the required divestiture was a small business that was very marginal to the merger. In contrast, however, far from being a declining business, Chirocaine had not yet reached the market. AZ retained Marcain (bupivacaine) and Naropin (ropivacaine). In the UK, AZ's main customers for long-acting local anaesthetics were regional health authorities and hospital trusts, but even the largest accounted for only a small percentage of sales so there was no buyer power. AZ were explicit that there would have been no potential synergies in retaining Chirocaine.

Zeneca's Chirocaine license was divested to Abbott, who launched the product in the UK market in 2000. During the following three years, its share grew to 6 per cent. It entered the Dutch market at the same time and its market share grew to only 2 per cent over the next three years. Chirocaine was not launched in Germany until 2004.

Even before the AZ merger, there was an unfortunate split between US, Japan and rest of the world licences 'for competition and business reasons'. It seems the merger, including remedy process, probably delayed Chirocaine by six to nine months before getting to market. It may also have contributed to delays in designing the polybag which would have greatly enhanced Chirocaine's potential.

Overall, at the time of writing, it is clear that Chirocaine has been a fairly marginal product in the Netherlands, and has had no competitive effect in Germany, but its impact on the UK can be considered as significant, even though not quantitatively large. It seems that early results of animal tests were difficult to replicate in humans, and the quality of Chirocaine has not been easy to prove. Nevertheless, the product would almost certainly have been withdrawn if it had been retained by AZ so divestiture was better than leaving it with the merged firms.

8.4.6 Main Lessons

Ex ante analysis

- Where the merging parties have very different pricing strategies pre-merger (as for plain betablockers), and the remedy applies to a single national market so that the buying licensee is reliant on the merged parties for its supplies, then a remedy requiring sale of the pre-merger low-priced product is unlikely to restore competition and may well lead to price rises.
- The betablocker licence allowed for royalty payments which further encourage upward pricing pressure. It would have been better to have

a 'clean break' licence, without continuing royalties, though this was probably not feasible given the limited geographic market and need to purchase supplies from the merged parties.

- Once again, the presence of a regulator facilitates consideration of an alternative behavioural remedy, especially when only one or few national markets within Europe are at issue. Behavioural remedies in such circumstances are likely to be better than structural ones.
- For product introductions in the presence of actual or perceived product quality differences, new simulation models need to be developed. Our experimental model is currently too simplified, and a desirable model would include an element of horizontal as well as vertical differentiation. In contrast to their complaint that the betablocker remedy was too harsh, the parties agreed that divestiture was inevitable for Chirocaine. This view is consistent with results from our experimental model.

Ex post analysis

- Entry into the betablocker market suggests that this might have provided a long-run constraint.
- Divestiture of a pipeline product can result in it coming to market when development effort would have been discontinued in the absence of a remedy.
- At the same time, and even with the most cooperative seller, the transfer of ownership is likely to result in significant delays in product development. In this sense, a divestiture remedy cannot be said to have succeeded in fully restoring competition.

8.5 GLAXO WELLCOME/SMITHKLINE BEECHAM (2000) – M1846

Decision: Article 6(2) = Phase I clearance subject to undertakings.

This merger created the largest pharmaceutical company in the world as measured by global sales (7.3 per cent of all pharmaceuticals). At the time, next in rank were Pfizer/Warner-Lambert, AstraZeneca and Aventis. Six 3-digit ATC markets had sufficient market shares and overlaps to warrant deeper investigation and remedies. With some 17 national markets in the EEA, this meant that over 100 markets were examined and decided upon within the six weeks allowed for a Phase I investigation. There were also eight 'future markets' considered, though these tend to have a geographic market defined as 'at least the EEA'. Clearly, the Commission has to use shortcuts if it is to reach such a complex decision in such a tight time constraint. Whether it is wise to even attempt to address such complexity in Phase I is a question to which we shall have to return. The alternative would be automatic referral to Phase II.

8.5.1 Competition Concerns

The merging parties had combined market shares exceeding 15 per cent in 12 ATC3 product areas, and these were investigated further. Six products were found to present competition problems. Following the usual practice for pharmaceuticals, the geographic markets were defined as national due to the administration procedures of national health services, price regulations, and differences in branding, pack-size strategies and distribution. The only exception is for 'future products', for which the market is 'at least' at the Community level 'because R&D is normally global' (no. 75). The investigation focused on no. 82: 18 national markets for which combined market share 15–40 per cent; seven for which combined share >40 per cent but with accretion <1 per cent; and 40 national markets for which combined market share >40 per cent and with accretion >1 per cent. We start with an overview of the six product markets before looking at the first two in depth.

Anti-virals excluding anti-HIV (J5B)

These are principally used for treatment of herpes simplex and varicella zoster. Aciclovir (marketed by GW as Zovirax) has been the 'gold standard' since the early 1980s. Patent production had lapsed and there was competition from generic acyclovir. Both parties had developed second-generation products for herpes. GW marketed valaciclovir (which metabolizes to acyclovir in the body) as Valtrex. SKB marketed famciclovir (which metabolizes to penciclovir in the body) as Famvir. These second generation drugs have greater oral bio-availability, allowing reduced frequency of oral daily doses but, unlike acyclovir, they are available only as tablets.

In 11 national markets, combined shares exceeded 52 per cent;[22] although in five of these accretion was <5 per cent, the combined shares were considered sufficiently high to cause concern. In four of these, the largest competitor had 20–23 per cent of the market but this was only a third of the merging parties' share and others had <10 per cent, so the Commission concluded they would not provide a competitive constraint. In two further markets, the parties account for <37 per cent and competitors were considered 'strong' (this was not quantified), so there was adjudged to be no concern. Thus, although there was a consideration of third-party shares, the conclusions are consistent with the application of a strict 40 per cent rule for defining dominance.

Since Zovirax had come off patent in 1995, its market share had halved from 70 per cent to 36 per cent in the face of generic competition. However, Famvir and Valtrex increased their shares by 21 per cent over the same period, and the increment in the overall share of generics was only 3 per cent. The evidence was that generic aciclovir brought about some reduction in the price of Zovirax, but had little effect on second generation products. Moreover, Zovirax maintained a very strong market share.

GW's marketing strategy for Valtrex was to market it at comparable or lower prices than Zovirax, despite the former's advantages as a dosing regime. The intention was to migrate customers from the off-patent to the on-patent molecule. Third-party evidence confirmed this, and suggested at the time of the inquiry that the first generation products may 'become obsolete within the next 3–5 years' (no. 93). The main parties also claimed that national pricing regimes did not allow it to price Valtrex at a premium. SKB claimed it was less concerned with 'migrating' consumers from Zovirax, but the pricing of Famvir was severely constrained by national price controls. The Commission concluded that since the merger would eliminate competition in second-generation drugs, this was a serious competitive concern.

Its inability to obtain a satisfactory price with the relevant authorities meant that SKB had not introduced Famvir in Italy, Portugal or Norway. Ironically, this meant that there could be no competition concern in those national markets. It also provides evidence that global pharmaceuticals firms have a credible threat of non-introduction when negotiating prices. This option may not be credible for smaller firms.

Less obvious was a claim (no. 96) by competitors that they would be discouraged from developing anti-virals if the merger in this market were unremedied. The theory behind this claim was not explained (one possibility might be that they feared a 'fighting brand' whereby one of the existing products could be priced low against entry – however, there is no mention of this in the report, and no assessment of whether that would be a credible strategy).

The agreed remedy was to outlicense Famvir (famciclovir), but only for use as a treatment for herpes simplex and herpes zoster in the EEA (no. 217). This eliminated any overlap created by the merger in this market.

Topical anti-virals (D6D)

These are principally used for treatment of herpes labialis (cold sores). GW had Zovirax (acyclovir) and SKB had Vectavir (penciclovir). Ninety-eight per cent of cold sores were self-medicated OTC and only 2 per cent on prescription. OTC and prescription prices can vary except where regulated to be the same (that is, in Belgium, Austria, Denmark and Germany). GW had a similar market share in each segment.

In three countries (Portugal, Ireland and Sweden), one or other company had no registered products. In all other national markets, combined shares exceeded 45 per cent, despite Zovirax having lost patent protection between 1990 and 1997 in the relevant member states.[23]

Heavy advertising and brand awareness have limited the extent of customer switching from Zovirax to generic acyclovir. Much of the switching appears to have been in favour of SKB's product: 'almost half of the market share lost by Zovirax in value terms and some third in volume terms on an EU level migrated to SKB's Vectavir between 1997 and 1999' (no. 108). This is despite the fact that Vectovir had only recently been launched in several member states (for example, launched in France, Italy, Netherlands and Spain only in 1999).

The agreed remedy was to outlicense *either* Vectavir (penciclovir) *or* Zovirax (acyclovir) for use in topical treatment of herpes simplex in the EEA. In the event, Vectavir was sold to Novartis. This eliminated any overlap created by the merger in this market.

Anti-emetics/anti-nauseants (A4A)

These are used principally to control the side effects of chemotherapy, where 5HT3-antagonists are the gold standard and used prophylactically. Leading products were GW's Zofran (ondansetron) and SKB's Kytril (granisetron) with alternatives of Novartis's Navoban (tropisetron) and Aventis's Anzemet (dolasetron).

Combined market shares ranged from 55 per cent to 90 per cent (no. 115).

The main parties claimed that 'competition is intensified by the buying power and tendering practices of the major customers' (no. 121). Third parties confirm that hospitals try to obtain lower prices by: tenders; buying consortia; and offering exclusivity in a particular category if a quantity discount is offered. However, Anzemet was available only in a few member states, so in practice this would be a merger from three to two, and between the two market leaders. Third parties considered neither Anzemet nor Navoban brought substantial medical benefits over Zofran and Kytril, and would not replace them. Post-merger would give the parties some 80 per cent, leaving Novartis and Aventis with 20 per cent, thus creating a dominant position in 5HT3-antagonists. The Commission concluded that the merger would reduce the possibility for major customers to negotiate discounts. 'Moreover, the combination of the parties' products would give them the possibility to set up barriers for market entry by granting quantity discounts for hospitals' (no. 123). This is consistent if the implied threat to offer discounts would deter entry and so obviate the need for them to concede discounts in practice. Without going so far as to dispute this finding, it does seem that there is too little distinction made between the application of market share analysis when there are many dispersed buyers (for example, OTC customers), as compared with when there are larger buyers who can create competitive tendering conditions (for example, hospitals when there are close substitutes available).

The agreed remedy was to outlicense Kytril and Kevatril (granisetron) for anti-emetic use in the EEA. This eliminated any overlap created by the merger in this market.

Antibiotics – cephalosporins (J1D)[24]

The only serious concern was raised for Spain, where the merger would lead to a combined share of 42.3 per cent. The main overlap was SB's Monocid (contributing 15 per cent incremental share), which was frequently used in rural Spain for elderly patients undergoing minor surgery. The parties claimed considerable substitutability, yet the 40 per cent rule seems to have been applied rigorously (see nos 132–6). This provides an example of a complex Phase I investigation necessarily having to use simple rules, but possibly requiring an inefficient remedy.

Asthma/COPD

SKB did not have any COPD products on the market, but GW had a long-established position (including Seretide and Ventolin/salbutamol) with an aggregate EEA share of between 43 per cent and 100 per cent in ten member states. This led to a focus on SKB's two pipeline asthma products (one in Phase I of development and another, Ariflo, in Phase III), even though they were not planned to be marketed for COPD. There were three other Phase III compounds in development by other companies (including AstraZeneca's Symbicourt, which was expected to compete closely with Seretide).

The Commission accepted an undertaking 'under the very special circumstances of the case' that 'SB's Ariflo will be outlicensed but only in the event that competing Phase III pipeline compounds for second line treatment fail' (no. 194; see also no. 221). These four 'competing pipeline products' are named in the decision (Annex no. 32, p. 51 and Annex no.46, p. 53; they included AZ's Symbicourt). This is a rare conditional remedy which is underpinned by the thought that the probability of success in Phase III is only 50 per cent.[25]

Anti-migraine (N2C)

GW had two leading products, including the 'gold standard' Imigran (sumatriptan), and a potential product in Phase II development. SKB had no active products, but one that had completed Phase II trials, though they had suspended development with the intention of out-licensing it. Nevertheless, this was included in the decision as a commitment relating only to migraine use within the EEA.

Some general observations on the GWSB remedies

Overall, the merger required three European licences, one Spanish licence, and two pipeline licences in order to gain the Commission approval. Each of these essentially eliminates any overlaps that the unremedied merger could have caused.[26] However, this does not necessarily mean that competition was restored.

Most of the licences apply to the EEA (only), so rest-of-the-world (RoW) rights are retained. Furthermore, the rights for Granisetron (anti-emetic) and the ciclovirs were limited to particular uses (for example, aciclovir for the topical treatment of herpes simplex; and the parties could retain exclusive rights to the Zovirax trade mark for the systemic treatment of herpes simplex and herpes zoster). Such split rights may well cause problems. As it happens, the FTC was raising similar concerns for the USA, so these licences ended up being sold worldwide (except where otherwise already licensed). However, this was due to factors other than the remedy agreed by the Commission.

The general criteria required for a suitable licensee were that they should (1) possess the status and resources necessary to manufacture and develop the product as a viable, active and significant competitor, (2) be independent of the parties, and (3) not have significant and relevant commercial connections with the parties. These are good conditions as long as there is a suitable buyer with these characteristics.

The financial compensation in return for granting the licence for an 'unlimited period of time' should be 'adequate compensation', but there was no mention in the decision of the form this should take (for example, lump sum, staged payments, royalties). As it turns out, the FTC was more directive on its required disposals of the non-pipeline products, and insisted on a clean break. Once again, this was not the design that the Commission would have agreed on its own.

Expected synergies

The merging parties claimed that synergies should be expected in all areas. For example, there were expected to be synergies in R&D due to complementary strengths in different technologies and the elimination of duplication. In the long term, these would be the most important justification for the merger. There would also be savings from administrative rationalisation. However, savings on production and marketing would be potentially most important for the shorter-term competition effects. Marketing would benefit from combining sales and distribution forces (for example, 8000 reps in the USA and 40 000 in sales and distribution worldwide) to enhance 'share of the voice'. SKB's expertise in direct-to-consumer marketing would also benefit GW. The parties' combined cost shares were expected to be: production, 29 per cent; sales and marketing, 39 per cent; admin, 10 per cent; and R&D, 22 per cent. Predicted synergies on production were 3 per cent and sales and marketing 7 per cent. If we take these two as the main components of marginal costs, then the weighted average marginal cost savings would be 5.3 per cent. The parties believe that their expected synergies were conservative compared with announced expectations for other pharmaceutical mergers. If we considered these wider industry expectations as possible, then our calculations of marginal cost savings would be nearer 9 per cent. There is insufficient evidence to disaggregate these cost savings by product or geographic market. Nevertheless, they provide a suitable background for our simulations.

8.5.2 *Ex ante* Simulations

The Commission suggested that we should look at four of the above markets for three selected national markets: Germany, the UK and the Netherlands. The parties were only able to provide necessary data for the former two, so no explicit simulations were possible for the Netherlands. However, as we argue below, the regulatory framework means that this is probably not a drawback. Furthermore, we did not have sufficient information to calibrate our model of new product introductions in COPD and anti-migraine, especially given that the pipeline products were so far from market. Simulations in such cases would be too highly speculative (see Section 8.4.4). We therefore limited our simulations to anti-virals and topical anti-virals.

Anti-virals excluding anti-HIV (J5B)

Market shares by brand are available only for the merging parties. For Table 8.8 we have used Table 6.5 and Appendix 11 from the CO (some small adjustments have been necessary to make the two compatible). Comparable data for other firms dictated the choice of value shares. Some assumptions have had to be made about the minor shares.[27] The total for generic acyclovir is also given. A simple market share analysis would suggest that the unremedied merger would create dominance in the UK and the Netherlands, but it might not be problematic in Germany. Next, we compare this with a simple simulation taking account of information we gathered on elasticities. Once again, we simulated the merger using the PCAIDS model.

Table 8.8 Market shares in anti-virals (excluding HIV)

Firm	Brand	Market share by value		
		Germany	UK	Netherlands
GW	Zovirax	15.5	31.3	21.6
	Valtrex	8.2	7.0	35.3
SB	Famvir	4.3	29.9	11.6
Combined GWSB		37.0	79.0	82.0
Roche		18.5	6.9	10.9
Other 1		16.5	20.4	6.5
Other 2		12.6	2.9	3.3
Other 3		6.6	1.6	2.7
Other 4		6.0		2.7
Other 5		6.0		2.7
Other 6		5.8		2.7
Total generic	*acyclovir*	29.9	22.1	18.1

No evidence on elasticities was provided either in the Decision or CO documentation. Our questionnaire responses suggested very different elasticities for each country. For Germany, the aggregate elasticity was reported as being completely inelastic, as was 'free-priced' Valtrex, while the reference-priced (and off-patent) Zovirax has very elastic demand and would lose 80 per cent sales if it raised price by 5 per cent (own-price elasticity $= -17$). This suggests that Zovirax and generic acyclovir should be in a separate nest. For the purpose of these simulations, we assume that all 'Other' firms in the table of market shares are generics in this nest with Zovirax, and the remaining three brands (including Roche) are in a separate nest. We also assume that the industry elasticity is -0.5. Unfortunately, PCAIDS is insufficiently flexible to allow different elasticities within the Zovirax + generics and other-brands nests, with a 50 per cent nesting parameter. For comparison, we report simulations: without nests, with branded products in separate nests, each with a 50 per cent nesting parameter; and without and with the predicted synergies.

The simulations (Table 8.9) show that, for Germany, even without efficiencies the unremedied merger would have had at most a negligible effect on price, with Famvir being the only product with any noticeable price-raising potential. If the predicted efficiencies were to arise and feed through to prices, then the remedy establishing the structural *status quo* might have denied customers a modest price fall of around 2 per cent (especially for GWSB products, but also for others).

In the relatively unregulated UK market, the aggregate elasticity was estimated as being -1.0, with an own-price elasticity of -2.0. Combined with

Table 8.9 Simulated effects of unremedied GWSB merger in anti-virals (excluding HIV): effects of unremedied merger (compared with pre-merger position)

Assumptions				*Results*		
Industry elasticity/ Zovirax own elasticity	GWSB cost efficiency gain, %	Nests?	Nesting parameter, %	GWSB weighted price rise, %	Market weighted price rise, %	Famvir price rise, %
Germany						
−0.5/−17.0	0	No	n.a.	0.4	0.2	0.9
−0.5/−17.0	0	Yes	50	0.4	0.2	1.1
−0.5/−17.0	5.3	No	n.a.	−2.7	−1.2	−2.2
−0.5/−17.0	5.3	Yes	50	−2.7	−1.2	−2.0
UK						
−1.0/−2.0	0	No	n.a.	20.6	13.0	22.5
−1.0/−2.0	0	Yes	50	18.2	11.2	22.7
−1.0/−2.0	5.3	No	n.a.	15.7	9.9	17.6
−1.0/−2.0	5.3	Yes	50	13.3	8.2	17.5

the higher initial market shares, this suggests a very much higher price-raising impact of the merger. This is moderated only slightly by predicted efficiencies. Thus the simulated effects, in this case for both Germany and the UK, are in accord with a simple market share analysis.

However, in order to check the relative importance of market shares and elasticities, we applied the UK elasticities to the German market and vice versa. Accepting the 5.3 per cent efficiency gains, this has a profound effect on the simulation results. For Germany, price rises of 3.6 per cent for GWSB, 1.3 per cent for the market and 10 per cent for Famvir are now predicted, despite a combined market share of only 37 per cent. Even more dramatically, the high price rises simulated for the UK turn into price falls (−1.3 per cent for GWSB, −0.9 per cent for the market and −1.1 per cent for Famvir) despite a combined market share of 79 per cent. This serves to reinforce a major theme of this book – that basic simulations are an important complement to simple market share analysis. In the absence of information on product elasticities, market share analysis may lead to the wrong conclusion.

Finally, the Netherlands has a relatively straightforward international reference pricing system, based on an average of prices in Belgium, France, Italy and the UK. Thus, on the basis of the predictions for Germany and the UK, the unremedied merger would have had an intermediate price raising impact in the Netherlands.

We conclude that institutional characteristics in different national markets require careful consideration in any simulation study. In this case, the generics reference pricing system in Germany has the effect of very substantially raising elasticities. We provide the above simulations to demonstrate this point. In terms of remedy appraisal, the simulations provide a context for assessing the benefits of country-specific remedies. As argued elsewhere in this report, international brand fragmentation might damage incentives to invest in product development. These simulations provide a benchmark benefit against which to judge such costs, and to explore alternative remedies. For example, if it were only in the UK that there was a problem, then a price control might be considered. However, that is not the situation for the case in hand, where Germany and Finland are the only countries with low combined market shares. In this case, EEA-wide divestiture was probably appropriate.

Topical anti-virals (D6D)

The main contrast with the non-topical anti-virals markets is that the market share of Zovirax is much higher, but the increment due to SKB's product is much smaller. A simple market share analysis might suggest an adverse effect of an unremedied merger, though the small accretion might mitigate this at least for Germany (see Table 8.10).

The parties suggested exactly the same elasticities as for the J5B category. The simulation results in Table 8.11 show a similar pattern to Table 8.9. For Germany, the results and conclusions are much the same for both product markets. For the UK, the model failed to converge in the absence of nests. This is due to the combination of low assumed elasticities and high market

Table 8.10 Market shares in topical anti-virals

Firm	Brand	Market share by value		
		Germany	UK	Netherlands
GW	Zovirax	44.2	81.0	55.7
SKB	Vectavir	1.1	1.6	3.5
Combined GWSB		*48*	*88*	*70*
Other 1		11.2	4.9	7.8
Other 2		9.6	3.4	7.6
Other 3		7.4	2.6	6.7
Other 4		5.6	2.0	5.6
Other 5		5.3	2.2	4.4
Other 6		5.2	2.2	4.4
Total generic	*acyclovir*	32.0	25.5	9.3

Table 8.11 Simulated effects of unremedied GWSB merger in topical anti-virals: effects of unremedied merger (compared with pre-merger position)

Assumptions				*Results*		
Industry elasticity/ Zovirax own elasticity	GWSB cost efficiency gain, %	Nests?	Nesting parameter, %	GWSB weighted price rise, %	Market weighted price rise, %	Vectavir price rise, %
Germany						
−0.5/−17.0	0	No	n.a.	0.1	0.1	1.4
−0.5/−17.0	0	Yes	50	0.1	0.1	1.5
−0.5/−17.0	5.3	No	n.a.	−3.1	−2.0	−1.8
−0.5/−17.0	5.3	Yes	50	−3.1	−2.0	−1.8
UK						
−1.0/−2.0	0	No	n.a.	?	?	?
−1.0/−2.0	0	Yes	50	2.8	2.5	36.1
−1.0/−2.0	5.3	No	n.a.	?	?	?
−1.0/−2.0	5.3	Yes	50	−1.4	−1.3	30.5

Note: ? means that the model did not converge (due to the specified elasticities being too low).

shares, and possibly suggests that the elasticity estimates may be unreliable. It would be much better to have elasticities corroborated by third parties, including customers and competitors. Such an avenue should be open to the Commission during an investigation. With nests, the model converges, and the UK results look much more like the German geographic market than for UK non-topical anti-virals. Thus the very minor increment in market share has no significant impact on price.[28] In other national markets, such as Denmark, Finland and Italy, the incremental share would have been larger, but the absence of elasticity information means we have insufficient information to simulate these markets.

8.5.3 *Ex post* Assessment

The two anti-viral products

Both anti-viral products were bought by Novartis, a very large and strong multinational pharmaceuticals company. Novartis was active in related fields and expected to achieve marketing economies with its other products.[29] This was a clean break, global (except Japan) sale for a very large lump sum ($1.6 billion). The divestiture was for exclusive product rights and involved no personnel at all. Production was soon transferred. The buyer had no real complaints about the transition. They were given all the information they requested. Thus, this is a case of divestiture on the most favourable conditions.

The two pipeline products (COPD and anti-migraine)

We next focus on the pipeline products. As it turns out, the conditional divestiture of Ariflo was not triggered in the COPD market. This was because AstraZeneca's Symbicort completed Phase III clinical trials in autumn 2002. Interestingly, until Symbicort's success, Novartis (that is, the buyer of the anti-virals) was in dispute with GSK and the Commission over whether its own product, Formoterol, was sufficient to discharge the GSK obligation to divest Ariflo. Novartis claimed not, and the dispute was ongoing when Symbicort arrived. Presumably, Novartis thought that a divested Ariflo would be a less effective competitor for its own product. This also illustrates the difficulty of making a remedy conditional on some state of the world. Such states are very difficult to specify in contracts. Symbicort has been very successful and achieved market share of 10 per cent in Germany by 2003. In addition, a product not mentioned in the Decision as having high potential (Spiriva) has been a major success, achieving 7 per cent in Germany and 10 per cent in the Netherlands by 2003. GW's Seretide has successfully evolved from a successful asthma drug, out of Phase III for COPD, to become the market leader with shares of 20 per cent in the UK, 15 per cent in Germany and 27 per cent in the Netherlands. In contrast, SKB's Ariflo has yet to reach market despite being in Phase III at the time of the merger. It is not possible to say whether Ariflo's development would have been speedier or more successful had SKB not merged with GW.

In the anti-migraine market, divestiture was not conditional – it was required to take place. A trustee was appointed late. The parties said it was difficult to find a buyer for the pipeline, Tonabersat, and there was only one serious bidder. It was bought by BioPartners, a small biotech development company which was effectively a spin-off from GSK. The company had only two compounds, both of which came from GSK, and in 2004 they were still looking for a partner to help develop Tonabersat. It was not yet in Phase III, and the most optimistic date for reaching market was 2008, nearly a decade after the merger was proposed. It appears that BioPartners was a small acquirer for a product with a small probability of success (it was still in Phase II and development had already been suspended). While the requirement to divest has yet to provide any competition, it does not seem that the merger has harmed it. This compound might become an inevitable addition to the long list of drugs that turn out to have little or no market value.

Finally, it is possible to compare the detail required by the US FTC, as compared with the European Commission, in specifying remedies. The FTC is very much tighter in its requirements, for example: interim supply agreements are not time-limited; more technical assistance with regulatory filings is required; tighter constraints are set on recruiting personnel from a divested business; and so on.

8.5.4 Main Lessons

Ex ante analysis

- In a regulated price market, large multinationals have a credible threat not to introduce a product in a particular country if an acceptable price cannot be negotiated. A significant, if unsurprising, implication is that multinationals do have bargaining power. This power is enhanced if a merger removes independent alternative therapeutic substitutes. While basic simulations do not provide accurate predictions of the price-raising effects of such a merger, they do provide insight into the incentive for merged firms to use their enhanced bargaining power to negotiate higher prices with the regulator.
- In a complex merger decided in Phase I, the merging parties may agree an inefficient remedy in order to avoid the costs of a Phase II inquiry.
- Aspects of the regulatory impact on prices can sometimes be captured by appropriate elasticities in basic simulations.
- It is undesirable to rely on a single expert for elasticity estimates.
- The Commission accepts more narrowly defined, market-specific remedies than does the FTC in the USA, and this leads to split property rights both geographically and for specific end uses. Such splits are likely to reduce the incentives for product development.
- The Commission is also less specific in its required licensing terms, with the FTC being more likely to require (in our terminology) a 'clean break' licence.

Ex post analysis

- There is a disrupting effect on the development of products during a divestiture, whether the divestiture is enforced by a competition authority or part of standard industry practice in routine acquisitions and disposals. Enforced divestitures can expect no better treatment than unforced ones. Buyers are not necessarily concerned by this because the effects are reflected in the acquisition price. However, this does not mean that the competition authority should not be concerned, because it means that the restoration of market structure does not restore competition, at least in the short run.

- Conditional remedies (for example, the divestiture of a pipeline product conditional on no other effective products reaching the relevant market) are very difficult to specify, because concepts such as 'effective' are difficult to implement.
- It is very difficult to find appropriate buyers for risky niche pipeline products.
- Milestone and royalty payments attached to a pipeline divestiture may reduce the incentive for the rapid development of a pipeline product – such licences are not clean breaks.

8.6 CONCLUSIONS ON THE EC'S APPROACH TO ASSESSING PHARMACEUTICALS MERGERS AND REMEDIES

The Commission's general approach to pharmaceuticals mergers adopts a number of maintained hypotheses, which seem to be based on the opinions they have heard from third parties. There is no apparent distinction made as to whether the third parties are customers or competitors. Some of these maintained hypotheses are backed by academic research, but others are not. In this section, we summarize what appear to be these maintained hypotheses and comment on them. The first six relate to the analysis of merger harm drawing on a wide range of pharmaceuticals mergers, and the next five relate to our more specific detailed analysis of remedies. The text in italics summarizes the Commission's apparent approach, which is followed by our commentary.

General Approach to Pharmaceuticals Mergers

1. *Competition between patented and generic pharmaceuticals is weak.* Although surprising for chemically equivalent products, the persistence of price differentials and other academic research support this lack of competition. The reasons are complex, and include the marketing response of the original brand, the influence of the number of generics, the extent and nature of price control, prescribing habits and substitution rules. We note that these all differ significantly across EEA national markets, so it is likely that the competitive effect of generics also varies across countries.

2. *Price controls and reimbursement schemes are insufficient to restrain market power*. This seems to be taken as an article of faith, but there is never any discussion of this crucial aspect of the pharmaceuticals market. This is a very serious omission that should be addressed by research on the interaction between regulatory systems and the influence of market power.
3. *Relatively small market shares for competitors is an indicator that they are unable to constrain the market power of merged parties with a large market share*. This position is consistent with allowing mergers that create a larger market share that is none the less less than the share of the leading firm or firms.[30] However, this approach is inconsistent with many simulation models, in which larger market shares always tend to raise prices, even if developed by relatively minor firms. This is an important point of difference. Of course, the standard simulation models may be inappropriate when applied to pharmaceuticals markets (even when price is unregulated). This could be because distribution systems and particularly marketing are crucial aspects of competitiveness, and create endogenous economies of scale even once the product is brought to market. Consequently, isolated minor products will not invest sufficiently to be effective competitors, and might benefit from being sold alongside apparent substitutes. Which approach to minor market shares is correct? It is beyond this project to answer this question. However, it is important that the Commission should argue precisely why larger minor shares are better than smaller minor shares. Otherwise, both the analysis of harm and the chosen remedy could be counterproductive.
4. *There is little buyer power*. Almost no practical distinction is drawn between, say, OTC consumers and hospital buyers purchasing by tender. Although the nature of the buyers is mentioned, the 40 per cent market share threshold is applied more or less across the board. In contrast, the economics literature suggests that the competition analysis for bidding markets should be modified as compared with markets where firms set a single price for all buyers. In general, a given market share is likely to be more worrying in the latter case than in a bidding market.[31]
5. *High barriers to entry exist in pharmaceuticals*. This is certainly true, but it does not mean that the argument applies to all product and national markets. R&D and product approval barriers are massive, but these are much reduced once a product has been approved in one country. A competitively structured market in one member state should signal the competitive pressure in another, particularly if the owner of the relevant products is large or has access to a marketing

network in the latter. Nevertheless, it is also true that physicians put great stress on the reliability found in prescribing an existing 'gold standard' product. Beyond this, many physicians are also creatures of habit in their brand loyalty.

6. *Technological and innovation incentives are reduced by a merger that creates a large market share*. This is not often articulated, but there are hints that both existing rivals will be put off investing in R&D if there is a dominant firm in the market, and that the merging parties will reduce their combined investment in R&D. The academic literature suggests that this doubly pessimistic view might need modifying in some cases (though it is always appropriate to remain cautious in relation to such important effects as long-term R&D). For example, there is support for the perception that big multinationals do not conduct research into drugs with only small potential markets (although this does create an opportunity for smaller firms); but there is also evidence that, because of the way that new drugs are developed these days, innovative new drugs do not come disproportionately from firms with existing leading products.

Pharmaceuticals merger remedies

7. *The appropriate remedy for pharmaceuticals mergers creating a combined market share in excess of 40 per cent is to sell the products of one of the merging parties to a third party that is not currently competing in the relevant market*. On the surface, this restores market structure to what it was *ex ante* (that is, what we have termed 'prohibition within the market'). However, the restoration of market structure does not necessarily mean the restoration of competition.[32] While the Commission has taken care to ensure that buyers are suitably established firms, it has not taken account of the incentives to market and develop products when ownership is split across geographic markets. Since the merging parties inevitably choose to sell the older-generation, declining products from their combined portfolios, it is difficult to distinguish how much competition is lost by this.
8. *The appropriate form of sale for products as part of a remedy is to grant a licence for the brand name and all rights within the relevant market*. There appears to have been too little care in constraining the nature of the licences. Clean break licences have sometimes been imposed, but these cases seem to have followed the insistence of the US antitrust authorities. While we have not been able to tie down any explicit problems with shorter-term licences and royalty payments, we have not been able to observe the effects on marketing expenditures,

product development and other investments that are dependent on the incentives of unambiguous ownership. It remains a concern when licensing does not restore *ex ante* incentives, even when it restores *ex ante* market structure.

9. *Divestiture is a suitable remedy for significant overlaps that would be created by pipeline products in Phase III.* It is certainly important to remedy potential product overlaps when it is expected that the pipeline product would compete effectively in the market. Merging firms have a much-reduced incentive to develop products that would cannibalize the market share of their existing products. Also, given the low success rate of pipeline products, it is also probably appropriate to restrict attention to Phase III products. However, divestiture of a pipeline product will probably cause a delay in the time it takes to get it to market. There appears to be no appropriate remedy for this, and it is an impediment to competition that should be weighed in the overall context of the merger.
10. *The Commission can rely on trustees to ensure that businesses are not run down prior to sale, and that appropriate buyers are found.* While trustees have been effective in monitoring businesses pending sale, and the merging parties have been cooperative with buyers, trustees have shown little understanding or interest in the competition issues that lay behind the remedy. Their attitude is broadly that of an independent auditor paid by the firm to ensure a fair sale. They do not see themselves as being responsible to the Commission, other than to provide the required progress reports. This is typically their only 'contact' with the Commission. They are not even briefed on the competition issues!
11. *Divestiture (including licensing) is always better than a behavioural remedy.* While it is true that an appropriate form of divestiture is usually the best remedy, it is not universally true. In some cases, there is a tiny geographic market that, for idiosyncratic reasons, creates a competitive concern. The transaction costs of divestiture can then be high relative to any reasonable benefits, especially when the incentives for the buyer to compete may be limited. In such circumstances, simple, even Draconian, price controls combined with a commitment to continue supply is likely to be the superior outcome for customers. This is especially so when the customers are large (for example, a national health or insurance service) and can monitor such arrangements with ease. It may also be preferred by the merging parties if the relevant geographic market is tiny and so has no serious effect on revenues, and if the remedy maintains the integrity of unified global product ownership.

Overall, the analysis of competition in pharmaceuticals is much more subtle than could possibly be embodied in any simple rules or, indeed, a single simulation model. There is thus a significant trade-off between legal certainty (favouring simple rules) and economic efficiency (favouring the detailed analysis that would almost inevitably involve a Phase II inquiry). Remedies are needed to restore competition, not just market structure. At the very least, this requires a more active role for the Commission in setting out the exact terms of the sale and a strengthening of its interaction with divestment trustees. Finally, the large number of product and geographic markets that are inevitably created by mergers between large multinational pharmaceuticals companies suggests that the Commission should be extremely cautious before agreeing remedies in Phase I. It is simply impossible to conduct a convincing analysis of these complex markets in such a short time.

NOTES

1. Where applicable, the companies discussed in this chapter kindly consented to the inclusion of confidential data, but expressly on the understanding that they do not necessarily share the views of the authors of this study.
2. All such references refer to the published decision.
3. Highest where no problem found was the Netherlands (37.7 per cent); and lowest found to be dominant was Denmark (43.1 per cent).
4. More detailed (unreported) results also show that efficiencies mainly affect the prices of the brands affected, and have little effect on other products whether or not jointly owned.
5. Based on interview reports supplied by DG Competition as part of their study and our joint questionnaire responses.
6. In order to provide further support for this conclusion, we applied the first line elasticities for Austria to the market shares and efficiencies in Table 8.3 for Germany, and similarly the German elasticities to the Austrian market shares. Given the substantial assumed efficiencies, this reversed the results in Germany but only modestly, with BM/Roche prices rising by 0.9 per cent and market average prices rising by 0.6 per cent. This suggests that our conclusion that a 55 per cent combined market share with only 2.5 per cent increment is unlikely to do much harm in this case is fairly robust to reasonable elasticity assumptions. The application of German elasticities to Austria reduces merging firm and market average price rises to 5.3 per cent and 4.7 per cent respectively, suggesting similar robustness for the prediction of harm in Austria.
7. Compare betablockers in AstraZeneca, where ATC3 classes were combined; see Section 8.4 below.
8. For 'slow release', the parties' combined share was 30–40 per cent and decreasing, facing a market leader whose share was rising. Unusually for pharmaceuticals markets, the Commission states that it considered coordinated effects (no. 87), but dismissed fears of 'duopolistic dominance' due to likely entry (as evidenced by what was happening in Denmark) and the quality advantage revealed by the market leader (as evidenced by its increasing market share).
9. Precise market shares and price predictions have been excised for business confidentiality reasons. Following Commission practice, we report a range of 10 percentage points (or less for small percentages). The simulations use precise market shares.
10. For example, Ellison et al. (1997) and questionnaire answers from Roche/BM.

11. This is because the underlying economic model implies that, *ceteris paribus*, a more concentrated market structure is associated with higher prices. See Table 7.4 and the last paragraph of Section 7.6.
12. We had access to a detailed interview with the original buyers of the divested products, Recip and Bioglan.
13. No one appears to have told the Commission about this sale, and they only found out about it three months later when warning about the deadline for sale. Approval was given retrospectively.
14. Recip is one of two manufacturers of the morphine products for Bioglan.
15. There was no interview with the producer of Pethidin (APEX).
16. It is highly improbable that AstraZeneca would set a royalty low enough for parallel trade instigated by the Nordic licensees to undercut its other markets. This is a significant point given the low Nordic prices for Tenomin pre-merger.
17. If we did, we would take note of the Commission finding for Sweden and Norway 'that Zeneca has been actively promoting its plain betablockers (Tenormin) as a competitive alternative to Astra's largest selling betablocker in those countries' (no. 58).
18. Based on questionnaire answers.
19. Which was soon to be merged with Pharmacia Upjohn, which in turn was soon to be acquired by Pfizer (see introduction to Section 8.2).
20. This is made by Antigen (at least for the UK market).
21. Nevertheless, it is worth bearing in mind that, as already explained, if product 1 is too 'close' to either existing product, then price competition is expected to be fierce. The location of product 1 can be made endogenous, in which case it is likely to position such that δ is a little greater than ½. To see this, first note that $\delta(1-\delta)$ is maximized at $\delta = ½$. From equation (8.4), equilibrium price is also maximized at $\delta = ½$, or a little more to the extent that c_2 exceeds c_0. Thus there is no point in claiming much higher quality if it only reduces price. Furthermore, from (8.3) and (8.5), it is easily shown that as δ increases, the difference between equilibrium p_2 and p_0 rises, so q_1 is increasing in δ around $\delta = ½$. Inasmuch as the new drug can choose its position by the claims it makes during regulatory clearance, it will choose a δ greater than ½, but not too much greater.
22. Market shares are given in no. 83 of the Decision.
23. Market shares in no. 100, and trends in no. 104.
24. There is no reference in the merger Decision to work conducted on the US market for this particular group of drugs, and discussed in the previous chapter: Ellison et al. (1997). Ellison et al. use data for 1985–91. SKB's Anspor (cephradine, joint marketed by BMS as Velosef) is included as one of the first-generation cephalosporins, but even taking both firms together, they had only 4 per cent market share.
25. Further background can be found in nos 178–93.
26. A small overlap remains in the case of cephalosporins in Spain.
27. Basically, we assume that shares not accounted for by the leading five firms, for which data are given, are shared equally between the minimum number of possible firms subject to them not being bigger than those for which there is information.
28. No great significance should be placed on the predicted high price rises for Vectavir because its market share is so small and a price rise of this size would not in practice be implemented. It is more important to focus on the GWSB and market-weighted average price effects.
29. These were not quantified, and were not incorporated in the above simulations.
30. None of the reviewed pharmaceuticals mergers apparently raised concerns of coordinated effects, where balanced market shares would undoubtedly be an important issue.
31. This does not mean that bidding markets are automatically more competitive. See P. Klemperer (2005), 'Bidding Markets', UK Competition Commission occasional paper, available at: www.competition-commission.org.uk/our_role/analysis/bidding_markets.pdf.
32. This same problem arises with casual use of a simulation model that takes no account of efficiencies or incentive and ability to market a product effectively.

APPENDIX AN EXPERIMENTAL SIMULATION MODEL OF VERTICAL DIFFERENTIATION[1]

The purpose of this model is to examine whether the simple simulation methodology can be applied to the notoriously difficult situation of trying to predict the implications of the launch or suppression of a product still under development and yet to reach the market. More precisely, the model answers questions about how the entry of a new vertically differentiated product affects the pricing of existing products, and how this is affected by alternative ownership patterns. The starting point is a familiar two-product model that is summarized in Tirole (1989), but the three-product extension and other variants were developed for this project. To our knowledge, this sort of model has never before been calibrated or used for merger simulation.

The model implies fairly fierce price competition, and may in practice be moderated by more collusive pricing. However, there is no suggestion of any tacit collusion (or collective dominance) in the Commission Decision that motivated this model. As explained in Chapter 8, there are plenty of buyer interventions in pricing, which are often criticized as putting too much downward pressure on price, leaving too little reward for R&D. Although it is not possible to be confident of any pricing model in a market that is so heavily influenced by buyers, we suggest the following model as a way of understanding the type of pricing incentives in vertically differentiated markets. As such, it has applications in non-pharmaceuticals product markets. In other words, it is intended to illustrate another dimension of the range of simulation models that might eventually be built into a merger appraisal toolkit.

The Two-Product Market

We start with the assumptions for a two-product market, before introducing a third. Each product is under separate ownership. Initially, there are two products, labelled 0 and 2, with higher numbers representing higher inherent qualities, $u_2 > u_0$. These qualities relate to therapeutic properties as perceived by both physicians and payers (typically, private or public health insurers). No distinction is made between prescriber and payer in this model.

If all consumers had the same relative valuations, they would each select the same product. However, some customers are more willing to pay for quality than are others. This consumer specific preference for quality is θ, with $\theta \in [\underline{\theta}, \bar{\theta}]$, $\underline{\theta} > 0$.[2] Each consumer buys either one or no unit of one of the products. This is appropriate for most pharmaceuticals markets, where lower price may encourage more people to use a particular medication, but is unlikely to encourage a particular user to buy more. A consumer choosing one unit of product i gets net utility $\theta u_i - p_i$.

The consumer who is indifferent to choosing between products 0 and 2 is known as the marginal consumer, identified by $\theta = \hat{\theta}$ such that:

$$\hat{\theta} u_0 - p_0 = \hat{\theta} u_2 - p_2 \Rightarrow \hat{\theta} = \frac{p_2 - p_0}{\Delta}, \text{ where } \Delta = u_2 - u_0$$

Our first major simplifying assumption is that θ is uniformly distributed with unit density.[3] This is quite restrictive, especially as a new-generation product is often initially viewed as having a narrower range of uses than an existing product with widely understood therapeutic properties. The most parsimonious way to allow for this is to assume that product 0 has additional therapeutic uses with inelastic demand of quantity α, and that this market cannot be contested by product 2 (or, in a three-product market, by product 1).[4] Price discrimination between users is not feasible, so product 0 is sold at a single price p_0. For the following calculus to be relevant, it must be profitable for product 0 to contest the new-generation product, and not retreat into its additional market. This is the empirical case of interest to us here, and we assume this condition holds.

Focusing on the market that is contested, we further assume that the market is covered (that is, all consumers buy one of the products). This implies linear demand functions:

$$q_0 = \hat{\theta} - \underline{\theta} + \alpha = \frac{p_2 - p_1}{\Delta} \underline{\theta} + \alpha, \text{ and}$$

$$q_2 = \bar{\theta} - \hat{\theta} = \bar{\theta} - \frac{p_2 - p_0}{\Delta}.$$

If there are constant marginal costs, gross profits are:

$$\pi_0 = [p_0 - c_0] q_0, \text{ and}$$

$$\pi_2 = [p_2 - c_2] q_2.$$

The first-order conditions in the one-shot pricing game can be rearranged as the best reply curves:

$$p_0 = \tfrac{1}{2}[p_2 + c_0 - \Delta(\underline{\theta} - \alpha)], \text{ and}$$

$$p_2 = \tfrac{1}{2}[p_0 + c_2 + \Delta\bar{\theta}].$$

Solving for equilibrium prices:

$$p_0^* = \tfrac{1}{3}[(2c_0 + c_2) + \Delta(\overline{\theta} - 2(\underline{\theta} - \alpha))], \text{ and} \tag{8A.1}$$

$$p_2^* = \tfrac{1}{3}[(c_0 + 2c_2) + \Delta(2\overline{\theta} - (\underline{\theta} - \alpha)). \tag{8A.2}$$

Note that if costs are the same, then $\overline{\theta} > 2(\theta - \alpha)$ is necessary for the lower-quality product to survive. Also, with similar costs, the higher-quality product earns the higher gross profit margin:

$$p_0^* - c_0 = \tfrac{1}{3}[(c_2 - c_0) + \Delta(\overline{\theta} - 2(\underline{\theta} - \alpha))]$$

$$p_2^* - c_2 = \tfrac{1}{3}[(c_0 - c_2) + \Delta(2\overline{\theta} - (\underline{\theta} - \alpha))].$$

However, since $\alpha > 0$, it is not possible to identify which has the larger market share.

The Three-Product Market

Next, a third product under separate ownership enters the market. Consistent with industry expectations for the pipeline product motivating this model, this product has inherent quality u_1, where $u_0 < u_1 < u_2$. If the pricing equilibrium leaves each product with a positive market share, the marginal consumers for product 1 will be identified by preferences θ_0 in relation to product 0, and θ_1 in relation to product 2:

$$\theta_0 u_0 - p_0 = \theta_0 u_1 - p_1 \Rightarrow \theta_0 = \frac{p_1 - p_0}{\Delta_0}, \text{ where } \Delta_0 = u_1 - u_0, \text{ and}$$

$$\theta_1 u_1 - p_1 = \theta_1 u_2 - p_2 \Rightarrow \theta_1 = \frac{p_2 - p_1}{\Delta_1}, \text{ where } \Delta_1 = u_2 - u_1.$$

Writing $\delta = \frac{\Delta_0}{\Delta}$ and $(1 - \delta) = \frac{\Delta_1}{\Delta}$, this gives the demand curves:

$$q_0 = \theta_0 - \underline{\theta} + \alpha = \frac{p_1 - p_0}{\delta\Delta} - (\underline{\theta} - \alpha),$$

$$q_1 = \theta_1 - \theta_0 = \frac{p_2 - p_1}{\Delta_1} - \frac{p_1 - p_0}{\Delta_0} = \frac{(1 - \delta)p_0 - p_1 + \delta p_2}{\delta(1 - \delta)\Delta}, \text{ and}$$

$$q_2 = \overline{\theta} - \theta_1 = \overline{\theta} - \frac{p_2 - p_1}{(1 - \delta)\Delta}.$$

If the new product 1 has marginal cost c_1, and it continues to be profitable for product 0 to challenge products 1 and 2, optimal price relativities (best reply functions) are given by:

$$p_0 = \tfrac{1}{2}c_0 + \tfrac{1}{2}[p_1 - \delta\Delta(\underline{\theta} - \alpha)],$$

$$p_1 = \tfrac{1}{2}c_1 + \tfrac{1}{2}[\delta p_2 + (1 - \delta)p_0], \text{ and}$$

$$p_2 = \tfrac{1}{2}c_2 + \tfrac{1}{2}[p_1 + (1 - \delta)\Delta\overline{\theta}].$$

Solving for equilibrium prices:

$$p_0^{**} = \tfrac{1}{6}[(4 - \delta)c_0 + 2c_1 + \delta c_2] + \tfrac{1}{6}\delta\Delta[(1 - \delta)(\overline{\theta} - \underline{\theta} + \alpha) - 3(\underline{\theta} - \alpha)], \tag{8A.3}$$

$$p_1^{**} = \tfrac{1}{3}[(1 - \delta)c_0 + 2c_1 + \delta c_2] + \tfrac{1}{3}[\delta(1 - \delta)\Delta(\overline{\theta} - \underline{\theta} + \alpha)], \text{ and} \tag{8A.4}$$

$$p_2^{**} = \tfrac{1}{6}[(1 - \delta)c_0 + 2c_1 + (3 + \delta)c_2] + \tfrac{1}{6}(1 - \delta)\Delta[3\overline{\theta} + \delta(\overline{\theta} - \underline{\theta} + \alpha)]. \tag{8A.5}$$

Notice that if either $\delta = 0$ or $\delta = 1$ and if all costs are equal, then product 1 is in essentially Bertrand competition with product 0 or 1 respectively, and price equals marginal cost for that product quality.

In order to implement this as a simulation model, we can calibrate the $\Delta\theta$ parameters by using the pre-Chirocaine equilibrium prices, p_0^* and p_2^*, and the equilibrium price equations from the model. Given prices and costs, equations (8A.1) and (8A.2) have four unknowns: α, Δ, $\underline{\theta}$ and $\overline{\theta}$. Obviously, these cannot be solved in two equations, but all we need is the following two composite product differentiation parameters: $\Delta(\underline{\theta} - \alpha)$ and $\Delta\overline{\theta}$. These can be found by solving (8A.1) and (8A.2) for:

$$\Delta(\underline{\theta} - \alpha) = p_2^* + c_0 - 2p_0^*, \text{ and} \tag{8A.6}$$

$$\Delta\overline{\theta} = 2p_2^* - p_0^* + c_2. \tag{8A.7}$$

These are the key product differentiation parameters that can be estimated from information on pre-Chirocaine prices and marginal costs.

For the three-product market simulations, we also need an estimate of δ, which calibrates how near in apparent quality the intermediate product is to the top quality. Since the product is still in the pipeline, there is no alternative to the use of expert opinion to form an expectation of how its inherent quality will fall between the current high and low qualities. All that is needed is a proportion such as: 'we expect product 1 to have 80 per cent of the inherent quality advantage that product 2 has over product 0'. There are also certain technical limits to the value of α if all three products are to survive in equilibrium. The inevitable range of uncertainty in calibrating α

suggests that a sensitivity analysis should be undertaken to see how prices vary for a range of plausible values.

Similarly, but less speculatively, c_1 needs an expert estimate. This is likely to be closely related to c_0 and c_2. Finally, armed with this information on α, costs and quality parameters from (8A.6) and (8A.7), equations (8A.3), (8A.4) and (8A.5) can be used to predict post-entry prices for all three products.

For expositional convenience, since our assumption about product 0's additional uses is sufficient for α to enter the equilibrium pricing equations only when subtracted from $\underline{\theta}$ (and vice versa), we drop mention of α from our discussion in Section 8.4.4. Nevertheless, we must interpret whatever is said about $\underline{\theta}$ as being about $\underline{\theta} - \alpha$. This is important when considering quantities and market shares, but not when focusing on prices and margins.

NOTES

1. This model was presented at the 2004 EARIE Conference in Berlin.
2. Further imposing $\bar{\theta} = \underline{\theta} + 1$ might allow us formally to identify Δ (see below), but this would merely be an arbitrary standardisation.
3. If there were evidence for an alternative assumption, this could be incorporated. One alternative would be to have exactly two types of consumer (high θ and low θ) in some fixed proportion (for example, this might be appropriate in some markets where one type exhibited a preference for branded products and the other was content with generics). Another alternative would identify more people with intermediate tastes as compared with the extremes (for example, where only a few people were willing to pay for very expensive drugs of little extra therapeutic value above the intermediate product, and only a few considered a low inherent quality product of any value). Such modified assumptions would require at least one extra parameter to be calibrated (that is, the parameter or parameters of the distribution of θ between its maximum and minimum supports).
4. However, there must be some constraint in terms of buyer power or alternative therapies such that there is a limit on how high price can be raised in the inelastic market.

9. Conclusions and recommendations

9.0 INTRODUCTION

This book presents the results of our research into the competitive impact of merger remedies and how current practice can be improved. It provides a significant extension to the empirical literature by focusing on how basic simulation can be used as a practical methodology in this context. This is illustrated by detailed analysis of seven recent mergers in the paper and pharmaceuticals sectors. We also provide a substantial review of the emerging literature, which is currently very dispersed. This chapter summarizes our results and draws together our conclusions.

In Section 9.1, we set out the three main objectives of our research. First, we wanted to develop a practical methodology for assessing the effectiveness of remedies agreed by a competition authority as a condition for allowing a merger to proceed. Second, because it is not possible to consider remedies without first assessing expected competitive harm, we wanted to compare our basic simulation methodology with the Commission's starting point of market share analysis. Third, we wanted to take advantage of the parallel *ex post* study by DG Competition and modify our conclusions in the light of the practical problems of remedy implementation. Starting with the logically prior second of these, we set out our main finding on each in the following three sections. Section 9.4 then develops what we believe to be an appropriate and practical set of recommendations.

9.1 IDENTIFYING SIGNIFICANT IMPEDIMENT TO EFFECTIVE COMPETITION (SIEC): BASIC SIMULATION VERSUS THE COMMISSION'S MARKET SHARE PRACTICE

Before even considering remedies, it is necessary to identify whether the unremedied merger would result in a significant impediment to effective competition, and so be expected to harm consumers. Such an expectation may be formed on a range of evidence, including submissions from the merging parties, complaints from third parties (including customers and/or rivals), consultancy reports and the Commission's analysis of market shares and entry barriers. Our consideration of basic simulation is intended to take its place within that mix.

The essence of the basic simulation methodology is as follows. Faced with any merger, the first step is to form an opinion of the nature of competition in the market (or markets) concerned. This should be formalized into a relevant oligopoly model. The analytical implications of the merger are then derived within the model – both with and without remedies. This provides an appropriate 'theory of harm' as well as insight into the extent to which a well-implemented remedy might be expected to eliminate the problem. In order to quantify the expected harm, certain key variables and parameters need to be calibrated, notably: market shares; demand elasticities; and merger-specific efficiency savings. Thus simulation requires both formal theoretical analysis and a practical reading of market conditions. The process of constructing a simulation provides a disciplined framework for the case team to implement an effects-based policy.

Merger simulations are often associated with highly complex econometrics, particularly as a way to estimate elasticities. However, because such full-blown simulation methods can be expensive and time-intensive, we advocate simplified methods. For example, elasticities can be calibrated using expert opinions or surveys. This makes the methodology practicable and not excessively demanding in its data requirements. We have shown from our case study reworking of actual 'Decisions' that basic simulation can be applied even within the constraints of many Phase I cases, where the pressure on time can be intense.[1]

This does not mean that the simulation methodology is without its difficulties. As discussed in Chapter 4, Section 4.5, it is: more easily applied to horizontal mergers than vertical;[2] inappropriate if market shares are changing rapidly;[3] hard to model emerging markets and new products;[4] and unlikely to be robust for remedies that are not 'clean break'.[5] While acknowledging these and other limitations, the more pertinent question is whether it is an improvement on current practice.

The (implicit) practice of the Commission is based largely on the combined market shares of the merging parties, subject to a *de minimis* increment if one firm is trivially small in that market, and modified by the presence or absence of a 'strong' rival as defined by their market share. It would be a crude caricature to suggest that the *modus operandi* of the Commission, or any other antitrust body, is to base decisions purely on market shares, but they are discernibly the most important indicator of the Commission's Decisions in most cases.

One strand of our comparison of simulation and market shares was a general overview using one standard simulation model calibrated on a range of 'typical' market shares and elasticities.[6] This preliminary analysis showed two things. First, for a range of elasticities, a threshold market share of around 40 per cent provides a reasonable proxy for raising competitive concerns (that is, price-raising effects). But second, there are quite reasonable alternative values for which the same market share analysis will be quite misleading.

This concern was put to the test in our case studies, some key results of which are summarized in Table 9.1. The three columns headed '*ex ante* simulation' list the simulation models, combined markets shares and percentage price rise predicted by an unremedied merger. Combined market shares range from around 20 per cent to 90 per cent, yet the predicted price rises are only loosely correlated with market share. In fact, we predict a price rise for the merger with the smallest market share and a possible decline for the merger with the largest market share. Clearly, the different elasticity estimates make a very significant difference. It must be admitted that some of these substitutability effects can sometimes be picked up from the text of a Decision, but the beauty of a basic simulation is that it allows the analyst to combine issues of substitutability and market share in an appropriate way.

Overall, basic simulation methodology has a number of advantages over a broad reliance on market share analysis:

- It uses more of the available information.
- It provides a rough quantification of the price effects from any SIEC.
- It incorporates the roles of non-merging firms.
- It incorporates expected behaviour of the merging firms.[7]
- It disaggregates firms' aggregate market shares into brand portfolios.
- It can assess the efficiency gains which would be necessary to eliminate any SIEC.[8]
- It can explore the extent to which partial divestiture will eliminate the SIEC.
- It helps identify which brand divestments are critical.

But perhaps most importantly:

- The choice and calibration of a simulation model requires the analyst to ask the right questions.
- The additional information requirements are limited, and key parameters (for example, elasticities) can be estimated without requiring much extra time or resources.

To set against these advantages, simulation reduces (legal) certainty: if less weight were attached to market shares, firms would be far less able to 'read' the Commission's likely response to any particular merger in

Table 9.1 *Summary assessment of case study mergers and remedies*

Market		**Remedy type***	***Ex ante* simulation**			***Ex post* assessment**
Product and geographic			Model	Combined mkt share (%)	% price rise, absent remedy	
Kimberly-Clark/Scott						
Toilet tissues	UK/Eire	Divestment	PCAIDS	43	5.7–18.8	Success
Kitchen towels	UK/Eire	Divestment	PCAIDS	20	2.0–6.7	Success
Facial tissues	UK/Eire	Divestment	PCAIDS	34	1.7–17.6	Buyer later exited the market
SCA Packaging/Metsa Corrugated						
Cardboard boxes	Denmark	Divestment	Homog.	53	1.5–8.7	–
Hoffmann–La Roche/Boehringer Mannheim						
Clinical systems	Germany	Divest in 8	PCAIDS	55	−0.1–2.0	Divested business lost
	Austria	Eur. countries**	PCAIDS	78	3.8–9.2	market share
DNA probes	EEA	Worldwide non-exclusive tech. licences*	–		n.s.	Insufficient licences sold (due to licensing terms?)
Monsanto/Pharmacia & Upjohn						
Imm.-release analgesics	Sweden	Divest exclusive dist. in Sweden	PCAIDS	40–50	10–75.6	Stable sales but business twice sold on rapidly
Sanofi/ Synthélabo						
Stupefying substances	France	Divestiture	–		n.s. (n.d.)	High divestiture cost; some loss of sales
Astra/Zeneca						
Plain betablockers	Sweden Norway	10-yr excl. dist. in Sweden and Norway+	–		n.s.	Strong buyer; stable market share
Local anaesthetics	Germany	Reversal of	Vertical		17–45 for	Delay in product

Table 9.1 (continued)

Market		**Remedy type***	***Ex ante* simulation**			***Ex post* assessment**
Product and geographic			Model	Combined mkt share (%)	% price rise, absent remedy	
	UK	previous licensing agree.	diff., new product		base product; 11–18 for 'premium'++	development
Glaxo Wellcome/SmithKline Beecham						
Anti-virals	Germany UK Netherlands	Clean break divestiture for specific uses in EEA	PCAIDS PCAIDS	37 79	−2.7–0.4 13.3–20.6 n.s. (n.d.)	Strong buyer
Topical anti-virals	Germany UK Netherlands	Clean break divestiture for specific uses in EEA	PCAIDS PCAIDS –	48 88	−3.1–0.1 −1.4–2.8 n.s. (n.d.)	Strong buyer
Anti-migraine	Germany UK Netherlands	Licence for development for specific uses in EEA	–		n.s. (p.p.)	Too early to say
Chronic pulmonary	Germany UK Netherlands	Conditional divestiture of pipeline prod.	–		n.s. (p.p.)	Divestiture not triggered

Notes: n.s. = not simulated, (p.p.) = pipeline product; (n.d.) = no data. For more explanation, see Table 8.1.
* **All** remedies except the one marked * amount to 'prohibition in the market'.
** In practice, firms chose to divest the Europe-wide business.
\+ In practice, firms chose to include Finland and Denmark in the licence.
\+ \+ In this case, the merger would have prevented entry of a new product which would have caused the shown price falls in Astra's base and 'premium' products.

advance. Our view is that this is a price worth paying in return for an effective, effects-based analysis, and hence a more efficient merger policy.

The Table 9.1 summary cannot do justice to the detailed discussions in Chapters 6 and 8, but it serves to illustrate three important points about basic simulations in practice:

- *Robustness*: simulation is not an exact science, and the range of predictions for each market is generally large. This need not matter if the range is always positive (or negative).
- *Orders of magnitude*: despite this sometimes wide range, our simulations generally provide results that show either a clear market power problem (say, price rises of at least 2 per cent), or a relatively small range of expectations around a zero price effect.
- *Market share analysis*: perhaps most importantly, comparing the two columns, the simulations do not necessarily predict the same adverse consequences of a merger that would be implied by a simple market share analysis.

Taken together, we believe that these conclusions provide powerful support for the simple simulation approach.

9.2 PRACTICALITY OF BASIC SIMULATION FOR MERGER AND REMEDY APPRAISAL

What have our case studies demonstrated in terms of routine use of basic simulations?

Divestment and Prohibition within the Market

Divestment (including exclusive licences) is by far the most common remedy in the sample. This is unsurprising given that this is true for the population as a whole. However, what is perhaps more surprising is that, in nearly all of these cases, the divestments required that the merging firm divest itself entirely of the assets of one or the other of the two merging parties to a firm not previously present in the market in the country concerned. We refer to this as 'prohibition within the market'. This has particular significance in the present context because it means there is no need to simulate the remedy, which is merely the *status quo* (that is, the pre-merger market structure). Simulation of the original theory of harm, of course, remains valuable. In the majority of cases, then, our methodology raises no additional issues beyond those already present in merger simulation. One twist to this is that, if there is a concern that the buyer might be less efficient than the current owner of the assets, the consequences can be incorporated in the simulation (in much the same way as efficiencies for the merging parties can be incorporated).[9]

Types of Merger and Simulation Models

The types of simulation model we have employed were largely dictated by the nature of the specific mergers in our sample. This means that nearly all the emphasis has been on horizontal mergers and unilateral effects, and none on vertical mergers. This is not a strong bias given the apparent preponderance of such mergers as revealed by Commission Decisions.

We were able to explore the role of buyer power in a limited way. For example, in one paper case, the detail of the evidence suggested that it might be appropriate to impute all the bargaining power to manufacturers for branded products, but all the power to retailers for private labels. Simulation was easy to handle in that context, but more challenging cases would involve a potential shift in bargaining power as a consequence of the merger or remedy. In the pharmaceuticals cases, most of the markets operated in the shadow of some form of price regulation. Even in a regulated price market, large multinationals have a credible threat not to introduce a product in a particular country if an acceptable price cannot be negotiated. This source of bargaining power is enhanced if a merger removes independent therapeutic substitutes. Basic simulations, as currently developed, do not provide accurate predictions of the price-raising effects of such a merger in such cases, but they do provide insight into the incentive for merged firms to use their enhanced bargaining power to negotiate higher prices with the regulator.

Another major 'silence' in conventional simulation models concerns dynamic developments. In effect, most simulation models exhibit an element of change only in the conventional comparative static sense – comparing one equilibrium with another, in a timeless world of unchanged product quality. We touched on this difficult area by exploring the incentives to bring a pipeline pharmaceuticals product to market. We were able to confirm the Commission's Decision to require divestiture was necessary because there were strong economic incentives for the merged firm to 'kill' the pipeline product before it could be brought to market.

Data Requirements

We have argued throughout this book that simple simulation is very undemanding in terms of the number of key parameters that require calibration.

This has been confirmed by the specific cases considered. For example, in the homogeneous Cournot case, one needs estimates only of (1) the aggregate market demand elasticity, (2) the market share, or price cost margin of the acquired firm, and (3) estimates of the extent of spare capacity/short-run costs of 'outside' firms. In models of product differentiation the diversion ratio, in its simplest form, requires estimates of the pre-merger margins and market shares of the merging parties. Even the PCAIDS model requires information only on: (1) brand market shares, (2) the market elasticity, (3) the own-price elasticity of just one brand, (4) (optionally) sufficient information to impose nests, reflecting groups of more/less substitutable brands, and (5) (where appropriate) claimed efficiency gains.

In return for these minimal data requirements, PCAIDS in particular provides a rich portfolio of outputs:

- Brand-specific predicted price changes
- New equilibrium brand market shares
- Cross-price elasticities (which can be used as a 'reality check').

However, our experience in Chapters 6 and 8 is that even the simplest models of simulation require information that is not typically collected at the time of investigation. The most obvious examples are the market demand elasticity (in all cases), the extent of capacity constraints, and brand-level own-price and cross-price elasticities. We do not view this as a weakness of the simulation methodology *per se*, but more as a reflection of the fact that, when coming to decisions, the Commission may not always have asked the right questions.

In our own case studies, we have found it useful to collect and collate the relevant data within the structure of a stylized check-list. Had this, or something similar, been applied at the time of the investigation, our simulations would have been much facilitated. Arguably even more important, it would also have better informed the investigation itself.

Resource Costs of Simple Simulation

This raises the question of where the data would come from. Much (for example, market shares) is already collected routinely in the course of an investigation. The most important additional requirement is for elasticities of demand. Occasionally these will be available from academic studies. More frequently, independent economic experts may be able to provide estimates, but only if suitable data are readily available. More typically, neither of these would be available for Phase I. For such cases, we piloted questions in the DG Competition *ex post* questionnaire aimed at using knowledge and expertise from within the industry to provide estimates. For example, we asked what would be the effect on industry demand if all firms in the industry were to raise prices by 5 per cent; and what would happen if only the merging parties were to raise prices. The answers provide a readily available estimate from those whose job it is to set prices. Of course, there would be strong incentives for the merging parties to provide misleading answers during an investigation, so it would be important: (1) to ask also their main rivals and customers; and (2) to ask the merging parties for information (for example, on sales responses to price changes in recent years) that could corroborate their estimates. The various answers should be compared and put back to the respondents for comment and explanation if there were major differences. The remaining range of estimates could be used for a sensitivity analysis. There is no reason why this process could not become part of the routine request for information at effectively zero cost to the Commission. Either it would provide the relevant information, or it would bring to the surface, early in the investigation, difficulties that lie ahead in understanding competition in that industry.

Once the data have been collected, and the basic model of the way firms in the market compete has been chosen, the application of standard simulation models is very quick – typically less than an hour's work. However, where the model needs to be tailored to the market under investigation, the skills of an expert economist are necessary and there can be no guide as to how long it will take.

When Simulation Methods Might be of Limited Value

All markets have idiosyncrasies, but this does not mean that the simulation method is inappropriate. We have demonstrated how simple models can be adapted better to reflect the competitive conditions in hand, and we have argued that the advantages should be compared with the alternative benchmark of simple market share analysis. However, there were two sets of circumstances for which we found current simulation methods inadequate, or at least requiring very careful interpretation. First, any simulation has to be calibrated against the current market structure, and if that structure is changing very rapidly, then the method will be too static. This does not mean that no changes can be built in (for example, product introductions can be modelled), but great caution is necessary if market shares are obviously unstable. Second, current techniques are not well adapted for markets in which buyers or regulators have a strong influence. In principle, such influences can, and should, be built into a simulation model, but this requires both institutional understanding and, given the current state of the literature, high-level modelling skills. As an alternative, we have already addressed the issue of how to interpret current simple simulation models in the context of negotiated price regulation (see the above subsection 'Types of merger and simulation models').

9.3 PROBLEMS OF REMEDY DESIGN AND IMPLEMENTATION

Divestiture to Restore Market Structure or to Restore Competition?

Most of our cases involved the reinstatement of the *status quo* product market structure in selected member states by means of selective divestitures. Where this involved the entire overlap business of one of the merging parties, we have termed this 'prohibition within the market'. Generally, these were effective to the extent that there was a buyer, the divestiture was completed in reasonable time, and the business remained a going concern around five years on. On the other hand, the buyer was not always as vigorous a competitor as was the acquired party before the merger. In one case, the buyer resold the assets the following day, and in another, the buyer was interested only in acquiring capacity and failed to continue the brand (which was the key vehicle for competition in the relevant market).

The last column of Table 9.1 summarizes some further problems encountered in the transfer of assets. For example: several divested businesses lost temporary or permanent market share; and divestiture of pipeline products may have delayed product development. Sometimes it is difficult to tie problems to the divestiture itself,[10] but in many cases there is evidence that problems were at least exacerbated by the transfer of ownership.

Overall, it is important to recognize that the *restoration of market structure does not necessarily mean the restoration of competition*. While the Commission has taken care to ensure that buyers are suitably established firms, it has not necessarily taken other important issues into account; for example, the incentives to market and develop products when ownership is split across geographic markets.

Presumption that Structural Remedies are Better than Behavioural Remedies

While it is generally true that an appropriate form of divestiture is the best remedy, it is not universally true. Divestitures can have large transaction costs, particularly in the European context where there may be a competition concern in only one national market. While it is obviously necessary to address those genuine concerns, simple, even Draconian, price controls combined with a commitment to continue supply could be a superior outcome for customers.[11] This is especially so when the customers are large and can monitor such arrangements with ease. Alternatively, these might be enforced by a monitoring role for a long-term trustee. Behavioural remedies may also be preferred by the merging parties if this geographic market is tiny and so has no serious effect on revenues, and the remedy maintains the integrity of unified global product ownership. Very careful attention is required to the detail of any undertakings. For example, it is important that customers should have recourse to an arbitrator because court remedy is too expensive and unreliable. Such attention to detail has not always been evident in Commission remedies.

Licensing as a Clean Break Remedy

Once again, insufficient attention was also paid in several cases to licensing terms concerning royalties, arbitration and duration. While terms such as 'adequate compensation', 'supply the product at a price that will ensure that the third party distributor can compete effectively in the market', and 'normal and non-discriminatory commercial conditions' are referred to in Decisions, these are insufficient to ensure an effective remedy. In the absence of a genuinely clean break (including indefinite duration, no continuing royalty payments between the parties and no split of property rights across markets), licensing does not restore *ex ante* incentives, even when it restores *ex ante* market structure. Furthermore, it is important to recognize that even when the licensee is happy with the deal, this does not necessarily mean that it is good for customers, because the licensee may be compensated by the seller in some other way.

Design of Remedy Package

Much has been learnt from the pioneer FTC study (for example, it is appropriate to divest an existing, self-standing business, rather than a carve-out wherever possible). However, some typically European concerns were apparent in some of our cases. Residual barriers to the internal market mean that some geographic markets are often quite small national markets. Combined with narrow product markets, as is the case for pharmaceuticals, the relevant market for competition analysis can be very small. This means that a viable business within one relevant market can only attain that viability in the context of part of a product portfolio (for example, to support distribution economies of scope). This means that either or both geographic and product markets need bundling. On two occasions in our sample, the parties chose to bundle more than the Commission-required minimum in order to make a viable divestment. On the other hand, from the perspective of the capabilities of the buying firm, smaller buyers might become unbalanced if they were to absorb the full range of products in an existing business that ranged wider than the potential buyer's core competence; and larger buyers are often uninterested in niche products with low sales. Thus the design of the divestiture package might need to be flexible in response to the different needs of prospective buyers.

Furthermore, the successful design of remedies may take some time, and this time may not be available during a Phase I investigation. This raises some important trade-offs that we have been unable to quantify in this study. The apparent use of routine procedures by the Commission[12] to allow early clearance may, as we have found, superficially restore market structure, but not competition. This suggests the benefits of a more considered approach which might entail a Phase II inquiry. However, such investigations have substantial costs which must be weighed in formulating the most appropriate policy. The balance will depend *inter alia* on the availability of strong buyers for divested assets.

Use of Divestment Trustees

Firms typically have an incentive to run down assets before a divestiture in order to reduce their competitive success. Trustees (as currently used) appear to have been reasonably effective monitors until asset transfer, but were weak on their interest in, and understanding of, how to preserve long-run competition. Their attitude is broadly that of an independent auditor paid by the merging firms to ensure a fair sale. They do not see themselves as being responsible to the Commission, other than to provide the required progress reports. This was typically their only 'contact' with the Commission. They were not even briefed on the competition issues.

9.4 RECOMMENDATIONS FOR BETTER PRACTICE

We propose that the Commission should give full consideration to using basic simulation methods routinely in many of its merger and remedy appraisals. This should be a natural evolution of the use of market shares.

1. The Commission should develop its expertise on two fronts: (a) understanding the predominant forms of competition within the merger-intensive sectors, including an analysis of buyer power and its impact on upstream competition (such overviews should be facilitated by the recent reorganization of merger appraisal within DG Competition

along sectoral lines); and (b) developing a portfolio of simple simulation models that cover the main forms of competition and foreclosure, and which can be adapted to the details of the case in hand.
2. A data checklist should be developed that routinely asks the right questions whenever a merger comes to the Commission, and uses the answers with a view to suggesting an appropriate model of competition in the industry, in the context of which a potential SIEC might be identified. The checklist should also provide relevant estimates of elasticities.
3. Over time, as the first two steps become confidently balanced, the third step could be taken, to put together the appropriate model of competition with the data for calibration and simulation as a routine part of merger and remedy appraisal.

However, this is not a blanket proposal for the use of simulation. In particular, we recommend three broad types of exception:

- Simplified procedure cases, for which no market investigation is currently conducted on the grounds that there are unlikely to be competition concerns (the Commission informs us that, depending on the year, these account for between 35 per cent and 50 per cent of all cases).
- Markets for which market shares are changing rapidly.
- Those types of merger that have fallen outside our sample, and on which academic research has yet to provide any convincing precedents of successful simulation, notably vertical mergers, competition for the market, and coordinated effects.

These three exemptions are sensible. In the first, our methodology would needlessly increase the Commission's workload on cases where there is likely not to be any competition concern. The second refers to markets that may not be amenable to the equilibrium analysis implicit in the simulation methodology. In the third, current simulation techniques are undeveloped. The Commission might consider commissioning work on filling these gaps, but it would probably be better to wait for the academic literature to develop first. More usefully, further work might be commissioned on how best to incorporate buyer power into simple models.

Finally, our *ex post* analysis suggests a number of areas in which Commission practice should be tightened up, in particular in the detail of specifying and implementing remedies. Some of these are also obvious and have been made in the parallel study by DG Competition. In addition, our detailed reworking of our case study mergers, combined with the *ex post* interviews, lead us to recommend the following:

- For divestitures, the business plans of the buyers should be a routine requirement to ensure that they intend to continue with the business in a way that will at least maintain competition (and not, for example, immediately sell the business or discontinue a competitively significant brand). Also, divestiture trustees should be briefed by the Commission on the competition issues motivating the remedy – this should be a formal requirement.
- For licensing, the Commission should recognize the competitive importance of the detailed terms (for example, royalties, duration), and give more thought to specifying these in their Decisions, with a view to creating a clean break remedy.
- The Commission is in a unique position as a competition authority, in so regularly having to deal with products that compete in a large number of national markets. Where competitive conditions vary across national markets, the Commission should be concerned about the incentives to further develop products if the remedy results in divided ownership across geographic markets. Where a small national market is the only one creating a competitive concern, the Commission should be willing to consider a strong, simple set of behavioural remedies as an alternative to divestiture.

NOTES

1. This will not always be practicable. For example, in Chapter 8, we encountered a pharmaceuticals case with in excess of 100 relevant markets with potential competition concerns. It is not possible to provide an adequate analysis of competition, with or without simulation techniques, in so many markets within the strict time limits of a Phase I inquiry.
2. In this context, note that the Commission has told us that some 90 per cent of competition and remedy issues relate to horizontal mergers.
3. In such circumstances, of course, market share thresholds are also of limited use.
4. Though we show how pipeline products might be simulated (see Chapter 8 and its appendix).
5. That is, remedies that involve an ongoing relationship between the merging firms and either the buyer of a divested asset or a regulator (see Chapter 3, Section 3.3).
6. See Chapter 7, Section 7.9.
7. *Ex ante* market shares are a misleading indicator of what market shares might be post-merger. Oligopoly theory tells us that the merging firm will typically lose market share as a consequence of the price rises/output restriction which results from the merger. In fact, this must be the case if there are to be any unilateral effects.
8. This and the previous advantage apply to more sophisticated models like PCAIDS. More generally, not all these advantages apply to all simulation models.
9. See the text at the end of Chapter 8, Section 8.2.2 for an example.
10. For example, the merging parties inevitably choose to sell the older-generation, declining or less successful products from their combined portfolios, so it is not surprising that competition is sometimes reduced post-divestiture.

11. Price controls and some other behavioural remedies may raise particular problems for a supranational competition authority to enforce and monitor. These tasks would probably need to be delegated to a national authority, in particular when the relevant market is at the national level. The choice of national authority would then be an issue (for example, a national authority such as the OFT in the UK may have an existing competence, or certain industries such as pharmaceuticals may have existing national regulatory frameworks). In other cases, an independent auditor funded by the merging parties may be suitable.
12. At the time of the Decisions reviewed in this study.

References

Andrade, G., M. Mitchell and E. Stafford (2001), 'New evidence and perspectives on mergers', *Journal of Economic Perspectives*, **15** (2), 103–20.

Antitrust Source, The (2004), 'Whither merger simulation?', an ABA Section of Antitrust Law 'Brown Bag' program held 29 January, Moderator: M.S. Becker; participants: L. Froeb, D.T. Scheffman and G.J. Werden, accessed at www.antitrustsource.com.

Armstrong, M., S. Cowan and J. Vickers (1994), *Regulatory Reform: Economic Analysis and British Experience*, Cambridge, MA: MIT Press.

Baer, W.J. and R.C. Redcay (2003), 'Solving competition problems in merger control: the requirements for an effective divestiture remedy', in F. Lévêque and H. Shelanski (eds), *Merger Remedies in American and European Union Competition Law*, Cheltenham, UK and Northampton, MA, USA: Edward Elgar, chapter 3.

Balto, D.A. (2001), 'Lessons from the Clinton Administration: the evolving approach to merger remedies', *The George Washington Law Review*, **69** (5/6), 952–77.

Ben-Asher, D. (2000), 'In need of treatment? Merger control, pharmaceutical innovation and consumer welfare', *Journal of Legal Medicine*, **21**(3), 271–349.

Bergman, M., M. Jakobsson and C. Razo (2005), 'An econometric analysis of the European Commission's merger decisions', *International Journal of Industrial Organisation*, **23**, 717–37.

Berry, Steven (1994), 'Estimating discrete-choice models of product differentiation', *RAND Journal of Economics*, **25** (2), 242–62.

Besanko, D. and D. Spulber (1989), 'Antitrust enforcement under asymmetric information', *The Economic Journal*, **99**, 408–25.

Blumenthal, W. (2001), 'Reconciling the debate over merger remedies: a discussant's proposed decision rule', *The George Washington Law Review*, **69** (5/6), 978–95.

Boast, M.S. (2001), 'Federal Trade Commission merger remedies: shattering the myths', *The George Washington Law Review*, **69** (5/6), 996–1003.

Bougette, P. and S. Turolla (2006), 'Merger remedies at the European Commission: a multinomial logit analysis', paper presented at EARIE Conference, Amsterdam, September, 1996.

Bresnahan, T. (1981), 'Departures from marginal-cost pricing in the American automobile industry', *Journal of Econometrics*, **17**, 201–77.

Bresnahan, T. (1987), 'Competition and collusion in the American auto industry: the 1955 price war', *Journal of Industrial Economics*, **35**, 457–82.

Bresnahan, T. and P. Reiss (1990), 'Entry in monopoly markets', *Review of Economic Studies*, **57**(4) (October), 531–53.

Cabral, L.M.B. (2003), 'Horizontal mergers with free entry: why cost efficiencies may be a weak defence and asset sales a poor remedy', *International Journal of Industrial Organization*, **21** (5), 607–23.

Cary, G.S. and M.R. Bruno (1997), 'Merger remedies', *Administrative Law Review*, **49** (4), 875–87.

Caves, R., M. Whinston and M. Hurwitz (1991), 'Patent expiration, entry and competition in the US pharmaceutical industry', *Brookings Papers: Microeconomics*, 1–48, and following 'Comment' by P. Temin (57–62).

Christensen, R. and R.E. Caves (1997), 'Cheap talk and investment rivalry in the pulp and paper industry', *Journal of Industrial Economics*, **45** (1), 47–73.

Clarke, R., S. Davies, P. Dobson and M. Waterson (2002), *Buyer Power and Competition in European Retailing*, Cheltenham, UK and Northampton, MA, USA: Edward Elgar.

Clarke, R., S.W. Davies and N. Driffield (1998), *Monopoly Policy in the UK: Assessing the Evidence*, Cheltenham, UK and Northampton, MA, USA: Edward Elgar.

Cockburn, I. and R. Henderson (1994), 'Racing to invest? The dynamics of competition in the ethical drug industry', *Journal of Economics and Management Strategy*, **3**, 481–520.

Cohen, W. and R. Levin (1989), 'Empirical studies of innovation and market structure', in R. Schmalensee and R. Willig (eds), *Handbook of Industrial Organization*, vol. 2, North-Holland, pp. 1059–107.

Compte, O., F. Jenny and P. Rey (2002), 'Capacity constraints, mergers and collusion', *European Economic Review*, **46**, 1–29.

Cosnita, A. and J.-P. Tropeano (2006), 'Negotiating remedies: revealing the merger efficiency gains', Centre d'Economie de la Sorbonne, University of Paris 1, working paper.

Danzon, P. and L.-W. Chao (2000), 'Does regulation drive out competition in pharmaceuticals markets?', *Journal of Law and Economics*, **XLIII**, 311–57.

Davies, S.W. and A. Majumdar (2002), 'The development of targets for consumer savings arising from competition policy', Office of Fair Trading economic discussion paper 4.

de la Mano, M. (2002), 'For the customer's sake: the competitive effects of efficiencies in European merger control', Enterprise Directorate-General

European Commission enterprise papers no. 11, available at http://ec.europa.eu/enterprise/library/enterprise-papers/pdf/enterprise_paper_11_2002.pdf.

Dixit, Avinash K. and Joseph E. Stiglitz (1977), 'Monopolistic competition and optimal product diversity', *American Economic Review*, **67** (3) (June), 297–308.

Deneckere, R. and C. Davidson (1985), 'Incentives to form coalitions with Bertrand competition', *RAND Journal of Economics*, **16**, 473–86.

de Santi, S. (1996), 'Competition and efficiencies in merger analysis: proposal from the Federal Trade Commission Staff Report on Competition Policy in the New High-Tech, Global Marketplace', prepared remarks before the 1996 Annual Meeting Section of Antitrust Law, The American Bar Association, Orlando, FL, accessed at www.ftc.gov/speeches/other/ABASP.shtm.

DG Competition (2005), 'Merger remedies study', public version of in-house report: October, accessed at http://ec.europa.eu/comm/competition/mergers/studies_reports/remedies_study.pdf.

Drauz, G. (1997), 'Remedies under the merger regulation', *Annual Proceedings – Fordham Corporate Law Institute Conference*, **23**, 219–38.

ECMR (1989), European Commission Merger Regulation 4064/89, accessed at http://ec.europa.eu/comm/competition/mergers/legislation/regulations.html#merger_reg.

Ekelund, M. and B. Persson (2003), 'Pharmaceutical pricing in a regulated market', *Review of Economics & Statistics*, **85** (2), 298–306.

Elliott, G.P. (1999), 'The Gencor judgment: collective dominance, remedies and extraterritoriality under the merger regulation', *European Law Review*, **24** (6), 638–52.

Ellison S.F., I. Cockburn, Z. Griliches and J. Hausman (1997), 'Characteristics of demand for pharmaceutical products: an examination of four cephalosporins', *RAND Journal of Economics*, **28** (3), 426–46.

Epstein, R.J. and D.L. Rubinfeld (2002), 'Merger simulation: a simplified approach with new applications', *Antitrust Law Journal*, **69** (3), 883–919.

European Commission (2000), notice on remedies acceptable under Council Regulation (EEC) No. 4064/89 and under Commission Regulation (EC) No. 447/98.

Evans, D. and R. Schmalensee (1999), 'Some economics aspects of antitrust analysis in dynamically competitive industries', NBER working paper 8268.

Evans, D. and R. Schmalensee (2001), 'Some economics aspects of antitrust analysis in dynamically competitive industries', NBER working paper 8268.

Farrell, J. and M. Katz (2006), 'The economics of welfare standards in antitrust', *Competition Policy International*, **2** (2), 3–28.

Farrell, J. and C. Shapiro (1990), 'Horizontal mergers: an equilibrium analysis', *American Economic Review*, **80**, 107–26.

Farrell, J. (2003), 'Negotiation and merger remedies: some problems', in F. Lévêque and H. Shelanski (eds), *Merger Remedies in American and European Union Competition Law*, Cheltenham, UK and Northampton, MA, USA: Edward Elgar, ch. 6.

Federal Trade Commission (FTC) (1999), 'A study of the commission's divestiture process', accessed at www.ftc.gov/os/1999/08/divestiture.pdf.

Feenstra, R. and J. Levinsohn (1995), 'Estimating markups and market conduct with multidimensional product attributes', *Review of Economic Studies*, **62**, 19–52.

Feldman, R. (1994), 'The welfare economics of a health merger plan', *Journal of Regulatory Economics*, **6** (1) (February), 67–86.

Foer, A.A. (2001), 'Toward guidelines for merger remedies', *Case Western Reserve Law Review*, **52** (211), 211–30.

Frank, R. and D. Salkever (1997), 'Generic entry and the pricing of pharmaceuticals', NBER working paper W5306.

Frank, R. and D. Salkever (1992), 'Pricing, patent loss, and the market for pharmaceuticals', *Southern Economic Journal*, **59**, 165–79.

Fridolfsson, S.-O. and J. Stennek (2005), 'Hold-up of anticompetitive mergers', *International Journal of Industrial Organization*, **23**, 753–75.

FTC (1999), 'A study of the Commission's divestiture process', edited by W.J. Baer and the Staff of the Bureau of Competition.

Gabszewicz, J.J. and J.-F. Thisse (1979), 'Price competition, quality, and income disparities', *Journal of Economic Theory*, **20**, 340–59.

Gambardella, A., L. Orsenigo and F. Pammolli (2000), 'Global competitiveness in pharmaceuticals: a European perspective', report prepared for DGENTR, November.

Gans, J., D. Hsu and S. Stern (2002), 'When does start-up innovation spur the gale of creative destruction?', *RAND Journal of Economics*, **33** (4), 571–86.

Grabowski, H. and J. Vernon (1990), 'A new look at the returns and risk to pharmaceutical R&D', *Management Science*, **36** (7), 804–21.

Hannah, L. and J. Kay (1977), *Concentration in Modern Industry*, London: Macmillan.

Haskins, C. (Lord) (2000), 'The challenge to state regulation', in J. Blundell and C. Robinson (eds), *Regulation without the state . . . The Debate Continues*, reading 52, London: Institute of Economic Affairs.

Hausman, J. and G. Leonard (1997), 'Economic analysis of differentiated product mergers using real world data', *George Mason Law Review*, **5**, 321–46.

Hausman, J., G. Leonard and D. Zona (1994), 'Competitive analysis with differentiated products', *Annales d'Economie et de Statistique*, **34**, 159–80.

Hellerstein, J.K. (1998), 'The importance of the physician in the generic versus trade-name prescription decision', *RAND Journal of Economics*, **29** (1), 108–36.

Hotelling, H. (1929), 'Stability in competition', *Economic Journal*, **39**, 41–57.

Ivaldi, M. and F. Verboven (2005), 'Quantifying the effects from horizontal mergers in European competition policy', *International Journal of Industrial Organisation*, **23** (9–10) (December), 669–91.

Jacobzone, S. (2000), *Pharmaceutical Policies in OECD Countries: Reconciling Social and Industrial Goals*, OECD Directorate for Education, Employment, Labour and Social Affairs, labour market and social policy occasional paper no. 40, Paris: OECD.

Jayaratne, J. and C. Shapiro (2000), 'Simulating partial asset divestitures to "fix" mergers', *International Journal of the Economics of Business*, **7** (2), 179–200.

Jenny, F. (2003), 'Design and implementation of merger remedies in high-technology industries', in F. Lévêque and H. Shelanski (eds), *Merger Remedies in American and European Union Competition Law*, Cheltenham, UK and Northampton, MA, USA: Edward Elgar, ch. 10.

Joskow, P. (1991), 'The role of transaction cost economics in antitrust and public utility regulatory policies', *Journal of Law, Economics and Organization*, **7**, 53–83.

Joskow, P. (2002), 'Transaction cost economics, antitrust rules and remedies', *Journal of Law, Economics and Organization*, **18** (1), 95–116.

Kemp, J. and T. Pitkänen (1999), 'Mergers: recent developments and important decisions', *Commission Competition Newsletter*, **3**, 43–9.

Kreps, D. and J. Scheinkman (1983), 'Quantity precommitment and Bertrand competition yield Cournot outcomes', *Bell Journal of Economics*, **14**, 326–37.

Lancaster, K. (1991), *Modern Consumer Theory*, Aldershot, UK and Brookfield, USA: Edward Elgar.

Le Blanc, G. and H. Shelanski (2003), 'Telecommunications mergers in the EU and US: a comparative institutional analysis', in F. Lévêque and H. Shelanski (eds), *Merger Remedies in American and European Union Competition Law*, Cheltenham, UK and Northampton, MA, USA: Edward Elgar, ch.11.

Lévêque, F. (2001), 'A preliminary assessment of merger remedies in the EU electricity sector', paper presented at symposium held at Ecole des Mines de Paris, 4 October.

Lévêque, F. and H. Shelanski (eds) (2003), *Merger Remedies in American and European Union Competition Law*, Cheltenham, UK and Northampton, MA, USA: Edward Elgar.

Levy, R. (1999), 'The pharmaceutical industry: a discussion of competitive and antitrust issues in an environment of change', Federal Trade Commission Bureau of Economics Staff Report.

Lindsay, A., E. Lecchi and G. Williams (2003), 'Econometrics study into European Commission merger decisions since 2000', *European Competition Law Review*, **24** (12), 673–82.

Lu, Z.J. and W. Comanor (1998), 'Strategic pricing of new pharmaceuticals', *The Review of Economics and Statistics*, **80** (1) (February), 108–18.

Lyons, B.R. (2001), 'What do we conclude from the success and failure of mergers?', *Journal of Industry, Competition and Trade*, **1** (4), 411–22.

Lyons, B.R. (2002), 'Could politicians be more right than economists? A theory of merger policy', University of East Anglia, CCR discussion paper 02/01.

Lyons, B.R. (2004), 'Reform of European Merger Policy', *Review of International Economics*, **12** (2), 246–61.

Lyons, B.R., C. Matraves and P. Moffatt (2001), 'Industrial concentration and market integration in the EU', *Economica*, **68**, 1–26.

Lyons, B. and A. Medvedev (2007), 'Bargaining over remedies in merger regulation' Centre for Competition Policy working paper 07-3.

Medvedev, A. (2004), 'Structural remedies in merger regulation in a Cournot framework', TILEC discussion paper DP 2004-006.

Monti, M. (2003), 'The Commission's notice on merger remedies', in F. Lévêque and H. Shelanski (eds), *Merger Remedies in American and European Union Competition Law*, Cheltenham, UK and Northampton, MA, USA: Edward Elgar, ch. 1.

Morgan, E. (2001), 'Innovation and merger decisions in the pharmaceutical industry', *Review of Industrial Organization*, **19**, 181–97.

Morgan, E. (2002), 'Steering mergers through the EU's regulatory rocks: remedies under the EU merger control regulation', *European Management Journal*, **20** (5), 549–61.

Motta, M., M. Polo and H. Vasconcelos (2003), 'Merger remedies in the European union: an overview', in F. Lévêque and H. Shelanski (eds), *Merger Remedies in American and European Union Competition Law*, Cheltenham, UK and Northampton, MA, USA: Edward Elgar, ch. 7.

Motta, M., M. Polo and H. Vasconcelos (forthcoming), 'Merger remedies in the EU: an overview', *Antitrust Bulletin*.

Neale, A.D. (1970), *The Antitrust Laws of the USA: A Study Of Competition Enforced by Law*, Cambridge: Cambridge University Press.

Neven, D., R. Nuttall and P. Seabright (1993), 'Merger in daylight: the economics and politics of European merger control', CEPR, London.

Nevo, A. (2000), 'Mergers with differentiated products: the case of the ready-to-eat cereal industry', *RAND Journal of Economics*, **31**, 395–421.

Nightingale, P. (2003), 'Pharmaceuticals', in P. Johnson (ed.), *Industries in Europe: Competitions, Trends and Policy Issues*, Northampton, MA, USA and Cheltenham, UK: Edward Elgar, ch. 6.

OECD (2001), 'Competition and regulation issues in the pharmaceutical industry', Paris: OECD, February.

OECD (2004), 'Merger remedies', round table series, DAF/COMP (2004) 21, accessed at www.oecd.org/dataoecd/61/45/34305995.pdf.

Office of Fair Trading (1999) 'Quantitative techniques in competition analysis', research paper no. 17, prepared for the OFT by the LECG, October,

Oldale, A. (2002), 'Fixing remedies in European merger control', *NERA Competition Policy Insights*, July/August, 1–5.

Pammolli, F., M. Riccaboni and L. Magazzini (2004), 'European competitiveness in pharmaceuticals', document prepared for DG Enterprise.

Parker, R.G. and D.A. Balto (2000), 'The evolving approach to merger remedies', FTC antitrust report.

Pavcnik, N. (2002), 'Do pharmaceutical prices respond to potential patient out-of-pocket expenses?', *RAND Journal of Economics*, **33** (3), 469–87.

Perry, M.K. and R.H. Porter (1985), 'Oligopoly and the incentive for horizontal merger', *American Economic Review*, **75**, 219–27.

Pesendorfer, M. (2003), 'Horizontal mergers in the paper industry', *RAND Journal of Economics*, **34** (3), 495–515.

Peters, C. (2006), 'Evaluating the performance of merger simulation: evidence from the U.S. airline industry', *Journal of Law and Economics*, **XLIX**, 627–49.

Posner, R.A. (1976), *Antitrust Law: An Economic Perspective*, Chicago, IL: Chicago University Press.

Prais, S. (1976), *The Evolution of Giant Firms in Britain*, Cambridge: Cambridge University Press.

Rakovsky, C. (2000), 'Remedies: a few lessons from recent experience', in IBA conference volume *EC Merger Control: Ten Years On*.

Rey, P. (2001), 'Towards a theory of competition policy', in M. Dewatripont, L. Hansen and S. Turnovsky (eds), *Advances in Economics and Econometrics: Theory and Applications, Eighth World Congress of the Econometric Society*, Cambridge: Cambridge University Press, ch. 3.

Rey, P. (2003), 'Economic analysis and the choice of remedies', in F. Lévêque and H. Shelanski (eds), *Merger Remedies in American and*

European Union Competition Law, Cheltenham, UK and Northampton, MA, USA: Edward Elgar, ch. 8.

Rubinfeld, D.L. (2003), 'Access remedies in high-technology antitrust cases', in F. Lévêque and H. Shelanski (eds), *Merger Remedies in American and European Union Competition Law*, Cheltenham, UK and Northampton, MA, USA: Edward Elgar, ch. 9.

Salant, S., S. Switzer and R. Reynolds (1983), 'Losses from horizontal merger: the effects of an exogenous change in industry structure on Cournot–Nash equilibrium', *Quarterly Journal of Economics*, **98**, 185–99.

Salop, S. (1979), 'Monopolistic competition with outside goods', *Bell Journal of Economics*, **10**, 141–56.

Scherer, F.M. (1993), 'Pricing, profits, and technology progress in the pharmaceutical industry', *The Journal of Economic Perspectives*, **7** (3), 97–115.

Shapiro, K. (1995), 'Mergers with differentiated products', address to the American Bar Association, Washington, 9 November.

Shaw, R. and P. Simpson (1986), 'The persistence of monopoly: an investigation of the effectiveness of the UK Monopolies Commission', *The Journal of Industrial Economics*, **34**, 355–72.

Shaw, R. and P. Simpson (1989), *The Monopolies Commission and the Market Process*, London: Institute of Fiscal Studies.

Sims, J. and M. McFalls (2001), 'Negotiated merger remedies: how well do they solve competition problems?', *The George Washington Law Review*, **69** (5/6), 932–51.

Sutton, J. (1991), *Sunk Costs and Market Structure: Price Competition, Advertising, and the Evolution of Concentration*, Cambridge, MA: MIT Press.

Sutton, J. (1998), *Technology and Market Structure: Theory and History*, Cambridge, MA: MIT Press.

Tirole, J. (1989), *The Theory of Industrial Organization*, MIT Press.

US Department of Justice and Federal Trade Commission (DoJ/FTC) (1995), 'Antitrust guidelines for the licensing of intellectual property', accessed at www.usdoj.gov/atr/public/guidelines/0558.htm.

US Department of Justice Antitrust Division (2004), *Antitrust Division Policy Guide to Merger Remedies*, accessed at www.usdoj.gov/atr/public/guidelines/205108.pdf.

UK Competition Commission (2004), 'Application of divestiture remedies in merger inquiries', *Competition Commission Guidelines: CC8*.

UK Competition Commission (2007), 'Understanding past merger remedies: report on case study research', internal report published on the commission's, website at: www.competition-commission.org.uk/our_role/analysis/evaluation_reports.htm.

Vasconcelos, H. (2007) 'Efficiency gains and structural remedies in merger control', CEPR discussion paper 6093.

Werden, G. (1996), 'A robust test for consumer welfare enhancing mergers among sellers of differentiated products', *Journal of Industrial Economics*, **44**, 409–13.

Werden, G.J. and L.M. Froeb (1994), 'The effects of mergers in differentiated products industries: logit demand and merger policy', *Journal of Law, Economics, and Organization*, **10**, 407–26.

Werden, G.J., L. Froeb and S. Tschantz (2005), 'Incentive contracts as merger remedies', Vanderbilt law and economics research paper no. 05-27.

Whish, R. (1989), *Competition Law*, London: Butterworths.

Willcox, T.C. (1995), 'Behavioral remedies in a post-Chicago world: it's time to revise the vertical merger guidelines', *Antitrust Bulletin*, **40** (1), 227–56.

Williamson, O.E. (1968), 'Economies as an antitrust defense: the welfare tradeoffs', *The American Economic Review*, **58** (1), 18–36.

Williamson, O.E. (1993), 'Transaction cost economics meets Posnerian law and economics, *Journal of Institutional and Theoretical Economics*, **149** (1), 99–118.

Williamson, O.E. (1996), *The Mechanisms of Governance*, Oxford: Oxford University Press.

Willig, R. (1976), 'Consumer's surplus without apology', *American Economic Review*, **66** (4), 589–97.

Winckler, A. (2003), 'Some comments on procedure and remedies under EC merger control rules: something rotten in the kingdom of the EC merger control?', in F. Lévêque and H. Shelanski (eds), *Merger Remedies in American and European Union Competition Law*, Cheltenham, UK and Northampton, MA, USA: Edward Elgar, ch. 5.

Wood, D.P. (2003), 'A comparison of merger review and remedy procedures in the United States and the European Union', in F. Lévêque and H. Shelanski (2003) (eds), *Merger Remedies in American and European Union Competition Law*, Cheltenham, UK and Northampton, MA, USA: Edward Elgar, ch. 4.

Index